the

Rottweiler Experience

The dog makes no distinction between the great and the humble, between the rich and powerful and those who have nothing to offer him except their company.

He walks with Kings and Queens, he protects the lonely and leads the blind, he shares our pleasures, our labors, our sports, our follies, our triumphs and disasters, our homes and our families. Through the dog we enrich our lives and in return he asks only that we give him what he gives us—friendship."

(From a speech delivered by Wilson Stephens at the Centenary Banquet of the Kennel Club, England, in May 1973.)

" . . . a dog with unfailing good humor and with a willingness to forget unpleasant events . . . "

(From *Der Rottweiler* by Hans Korn, on Rottweiler temperament.)

the

Rottweiler Experience

From the Golden Age to Predictions for the 21st Century

Joan R. Klem
and
Susan C. Rademacher

HOWELL
BOOK
HOUSE

Howell Book House
A Simon and Schuster Macmillan Company
1633 Broadway
New York, NY 10019

Library of Congress Cataloging-in-Publication Data
Klem, Joan R.
    The Rottweiler experience : from the golden age to predictions for
the 21st century / Joan R. Klem and Susan C. Rademacher.
        p.   cm.
    ISBN: 0-87605-296-0
    1. Rottweiler dog.   I. Rademacher, Susan C.   II. Title.
SF429.R7K54   1996
636.7'3—dc20   96-46188
                                                                          CIP

Manufactured in the United States of America
98   9 8 7 6 5 4 3 2

Book Design: Michelle Laseau
Cover Design: George Berriam

Dedication

Perrin G. "Pat" Rademacher
June 13, 1918–May 19, 1991

Pat Rademacher's interest in the Rottweiler launched Rodsden. It was his genuine love for our dogs, and for all animals, that sustained Rodsden. His legacy has been passed to his son Peter and daughter Susan, co-author of this book.

Pat Rademacher with Harras.

Richard F. Klem
March 7, 1922–July 8, 1978

Dick's support and devotion to Joan's Rottweiler interests, tempered with a sense of humor granted to very few, made what might have been simply a family hobby into a splendid avocation with a long-term "ripple effect" that has been felt the world over.

Richard and Joan Klem with
Kluge as a puppy.

Contents

Foreword

There was a time, not too long ago, that when Rottweilers did appear at an American dog show, their numbers were usually small in keeping with their status as an infrequently shown breed. Today, the breed's status has done a complete 180-degree turn. In 1995, with 93,656 dogs registered, the Rottweiler stood second in popularity among all breeds currently recognized by the American Kennel Club.

Whenever a breed grows to such a large number of registrations there are serious concerns among sincere fanciers for its current and future stability. Under these circumstances, initiatives must be taken to assure that breed's continued integrity. One of the most effective tools is enhanced communication among all levels of those who call the breed their own. Fortunately, communication among Rottweiler people is free-flowing and continuous.

In *The Rottweiler Experience*, Joan R. Klem and Susan C. Rademacher present a potent vehicle to further enhance the vital link of communication so basic to the Rottweiler's well-being. As the publishers of this extraordinary new book, we at Howell Book House are gratified that we can assist the ongoing dialogue in the education of the Rottweiler fancy. We are also pleased to present a book that all who make the Rottweiler an important part of their world can enjoy, learn from and use as they immerse themselves in *The Rottweiler Experience*.

The Publishers

Acknowledgments

Our journey through the Rottweiler experience was made so very memorable, educational and entertaining by the many interesting and remarkable people we had the good fortune to meet along the way. There have been so many that to mention them all would take another book! But we must mention Friedrich Berger, without whose help we would have never gotten Harras, and Elizabeth Eken, without whose help we would never have gotten Dux. And, we would never have gotten *The Rottweiler Experience* to the publisher without the tremendous interest and support of all those interesting, remarkable people we cannot specifically name here because page space does not permit us to do so.

There are, however, a few who deserve "honorable mention" for their part in this production. Marthajo Rademacher, Mike Rowan and Larry Klem, who endured through the reading and editing of the first drafts, and Duane Pickel, Carol Krickeberg, Wally O'Brien, Susan Traynor, Mary Lou Stott, Wayne Budwick, Tony Stockanes and Robert Cole, whose contributions have added so much to *The . . . Experience.*

The Authors

What is truly remarkable about the authors of this book is that their own Rottweiler experience is a family affair spanning almost a half-century. Since the late 1940s, the Klems and Rademachers have had a tremendous impact on the Rottweiler, and their activity continues with great vigor, even into the third generation of devoted fanciers.

Joan Rademacher Klem bred her first litter of Rottweilers in 1949, and has been active in every phase of the breed ever since. She co-owned the highly successful AKC-registered prefix "Rodsden" with her brother, the late P.G. Rademacher, and now with her niece and co-author, Susan C. Rademacher. Rodsden Rottweilers have accounted for the first two Bests in Show for the breed among the sixteen they have won, as well as nineteen Specialty Bests of Breed and/or Bests of Opposite Sex throughout the United States.

Co-author Joan Klem with puppies by
Ch. Dasso v. Eichterdingen ex Astrid of
Rodsden in 1949.

She is a prodigious force in the Rottweiler Fancy in the United States and around the world, having served in numerous administrative and instructional capacities in the clubs and associations to which she belongs.

One of the breed's most highly esteemed judges, Mrs. Klem has fulfilled numerous Specialty and all-breed assignments. Some of her credits are as familiar as the Medallion, Colonial and ARC events and others are from exotic places like Taiwan, Trinidad and the Transvaal among a tremendously varied host of others.

A complete listing of Joan Klem's accomplishments is far too long to include here. Dedicated fancier, gifted breeder, judge, author and ambassador for the Rottweiler, Mrs. Klem is an inexhaustible champion of her chosen breed, and a constant advocate for the Rottweiler's many assets.

Susan Cady Rademacher literally grew up with Rottweilers. Her "nanny" and protector was Alaric of Rodsden! With such a family background, it is no surprise that Susan Rademacher grew up in junior showmanship, conformation and obedience competitions. All through school she has been active in the Rottweiler Fancy, finishing no fewer than twenty-three champions and putting titles from CD to TD on many of her dogs. She owned the first champion/CDX in the MRC. Under the Rodsden prefix, she has bred and/or co-bred twenty-six Rottweiler litters since 1969.

Like her aunt and co-author, she has been actively involved in the ARC and the MRC, serving in many offices during the long tenure of her membership. She is also a member of the German Parent Club, the ADRK. A judge of the breed since 1992, her credits include judging the National Specialty in 1996, as well as judging for the Colonial, Medallion and Golden State Rottweiler Clubs and numerous others.

Susan Rademacher awarding BIS at the 1996 American Rottweiler Club National Specialty to Am. and Can. Ch. Serrant's Bannor (Ch. Tobant's Grant ex Ch. Tobant's Honey Bun v. Whelan), owned by B.J. Thompson and Scott Russell. *Mitchell*

The authors on a visit to Rottweil in 1993.

Chapter 1

Lore of the Rottweiler

We surmise that the Rottweiler descends from one of the "work horses" of antiquity. When the Romans spread into Europe around 74 AD, they brought along the Molosser dogs—those formidable proto-Mastiffs which fought in the coliseums and then accompanied their masters over the Alps, herding and guarding the livestock. As sites of civilization arose along the legions' roads, so did various types of dogs. One road led to an army encampment on the Neckar River in what was to become the state of Swabia in southern Germany. This camp flourished as a trading center and was eventually called Rottweil (*Rote Wil* after its red-tiled roofs). Here, a remarkable breed of dog developed which eventually became known as the Rottweiler.

An often-repeated story in "Rottweiler lore" holds that the butchers of medieval Rottweil depended on their dogs to assist with business. These butchers' dogs, or *Metzgerhunds,* were first used to help the butchers herd cattle to market; then, after the cattle were slaughtered, the dogs pulled the butchers' carts. Finally, when the meat was sold, the purses were tied around the dogs' necks to keep the money from bandits or perhaps from any butchers who might spend too much time in the beer hall!

This favorite yarn illustrates that the Rottweiler developed as a drover, draft dog, and guard dog and that with these purposes came the necessary traits of endurance, strength, loyalty, and above all, intelligence. Such a versatile dog kept busy in the manner described until about the mid-19th century, when railroads replaced droving for getting livestock to market. And using dogs as draft animals was ultimately outlawed (due in part to abuses).

Our helpmate, the Rottweiler, then fell on hard times as his customary jobs were being eliminated thanks to industrial progress. If instincts, or shall we say talents, are not used, will they be lost? Apparently not, at least in the case of the Rottweiler. More than a century after herding ceased to be a part of the Rottweiler's professional repertoire, American Rottweiler fanciers petitioned the American Kennel Club to allow the Rottweiler to compete in

AKC herding events based not only on the breed's herding heritage, but primarliy on documented proof in modern herding trials that the instinct remains strong in the breed. In 1994, the American Kennel Club made the Rottweiler one of the rare exceptions to its rules, and allowed a designated breed in the Working Group, the Rottweiler, to compete in herding trials usually restricted to the designated breeds in the Herding Group.

But here we are ahead of our story. Herding ability didn't save the breed in the late 1800s. Those traits mentioned previously—endurance, strength, loyalty and intelligence—were found to fit the requirements needed for guard dogs, and the Rottweiler's talents were put to new uses with the police and military. It was toward suitability for those tasks that the modern Rottweiler was developed.

ORGANIZING THE ROTTWEILER FANCY

The Rottweiler we recognize today really began with the formation of the first Rottweiler Club in Germany. We need to remember that the early Rottweiler clubs were organized by practical, hard-working tradesmen whose

They even pose for postcards.

goal was to develop a similarly practical, hard-working dog that would be fit to serve them in their livelihoods. Initially, function was stressed above everything else.

The first Standard for the breed was written by the first club—a combined club for the Rottweiler and the Leonberger in 1901. The Leonberger is a large, long-coated breed developed in Leonberg, Germany. The characteristic heavy mane in male Leonbergers is supposed to give the dog a lion-like appearance and reflect the city's name. The Leonberger is also probably descended from Roman dogs, making them Swabian cousins of the Rottweiler.

The first Rottweiler Standard gave as a general description, "Medium to large, strong-boned, robust figure, square build, seeming short rather than too long. Bitches always smaller and longer in back." This description is not too different from our present-day Standard. Where the original Standard radically departs from its current counterpart is that colors other than black were allowed as a base. The 1901 Standard states regarding color: "Preferably and most commonly black with russet or yellowish markings over the eyes, at the lips, and on the inner and under side of the legs as well as on the bottom. Alternatively, black stripes on an ash-gray background with yellow markings, plain red with black nose, or dark wolf-gray with black head and saddle, but always with yellow markings. White markings on the chest and legs occur very frequently and are admissible if they are not too extensive."

The Rottweiler would have been a truly colorful breed had the early fanciers not decided that while allowing the registrations of Rottweilers-of-many-colors, they would primarily breed only from those with our present-day black and mahogany pattern. (One wonders if this chosen pattern has anything to do with black and brown being the state colors of Swabia.) So ingrained is this popular color scheme that in the fifty years we have been involved with Rottweilers, we have never seen any purebred Rottweiler in any other color. In fact, our current Standard states that any base color other than black is a disqualification. Regrettably, today's Rottweiler has fallen into the hands of a few breeders without the conviction to hold the color pattern, so we now see advertisements of "rare red Rottweilers." In discussing this problem with fellow fanciers in Germany, we were told that there have been no colors other than the black with mahogany appearing in over 100 generations in the German stud books.

While the success in eliminating strange base colors is recognized, the mention of white markings in the 1901 Standard is interesting because we still see white hairs in dogs being bred today. This venerable genetic marker is a reminder that the Rottweiler is related to other descendants of Roman cattle dogs, the Swiss Sennenhunds. The most popular member of this family in the United States is the Bernese Mountain Dog, but the Greater Swiss Mountain Dog is probably more closely related to the Rottweiler.

With a name and a Standard, the Rottweiler could compete in dog shows, and an interesting story is told of a particularly fine specimen that was

The old gate of Rottweil in a 1993 photo by Joan Klem.

exhibited at the Heidelberg Kennel Club in 1905. So admired was this dog that fanciers determined to establish a systematic approach to reproducing this dog's exceptional qualities. Because our modern lines descend from the breedings following the Heidelberg show, one could say, we suppose, that Heidelberg is the true birthplace of our modern Rottweiler. However, the name Heidelberger doesn't roll off the tongue nearly as well as Rottweiler!

The Rottweiler-Leonberger Club, founded in 1899, was of short duration. It was followed by the German Rottweiler Club in 1907, and then by a South German Rottweiler Club in the same year. These two clubs were followed by an International Rottweiler Club, which absorbed the South German Rottweiler Club at about the time that another South German Rottweiler Club was formed in 1919. All these clubs kept stud books, which, as one can imagine, caused a great deal of confusion within the Fancy. However, the goal of all the clubs was similar—to locate dogs that were of "Rottweiler type," and concentrate on them to establish a Standard of perfection to be aimed for in selective breeding based on ideals for appearance and performance. For the Rottweiler breed there remained only the necessity of establishing one strong club that could be entrusted with the responsibilty of progressing and improving the breed. This one club had to be invested with a discipline that gave it control over breeding and registration and the establishment of breeding rules for the protection and preservation of the breed.

THE ESSENTIAL CLUB EMERGES

Enter the *Allgemeiner Deutscher Rottweiler Klub* (ADRK) in 1921, whose motto became "The Breeding of Rottweilers is the Breeding of Working Dogs."

Following negotiations in 1920, the Rottweiler clubs that existed in Germany all united into the ADRK with registrations of about 3,000 Rottweilers. This was an incredible accomplishment, especially when one considers that the various stud books were kept through a World War and that the ADRK began its life at a time when Germany was suffering horrible inflation and the after-effects of losing a long and devastating conflict.

The early stud books are full of amusing entries, not the least of which are the dogs' names. Imagine having to write Laskar v.d. Politzeidirektion on every dog show entry! There apparently were no limits to the number of letters that could be used in a dog's name. A short name that appeared quite frequently was "Stumper" (pronounced *Schtoomper*), which no doubt refers to the dog's short, or stumpy tail. The first Standard mentions that dogs can be born with naturally short tails, although most are not. Today we rarely hear of a litter with "stumpers," but our experience has been that the short tail is still long enough to require docking to meet the current Standard.

This 19th Century painting by George D. Rowlandson, titled "Patience," depicts two Rottweiler babies preparing to break up a card game.

In 1924, the ADRK published its breed Standard along with its first stud book. In introducing the Standard, the ADRK said

The Rottweiler is an excellent police, protection, companion, and guard dog. We try to achieve a powerful dog [literally: bursting with energy!] of square build, with beautiful red and yellow markings, who is noble as well as powerful in appearance.

And the general description says

. . . the dog shows high intelligence, excellent faithfulness, willingness to work, obedience, and incorruptibility, as well as great power and stamina. The first look at him reveals naturalness and courage. His quiet gaze expresses good nature and unchangeable faithfulness. The gaze does not show any restlessness, hastiness or foolishness. Meanness or falseness are never among his properties.

Here then was the "basic" Rottweiler; not all that different seventy years ago from the Rottweiler as he is today.

Best Team in the Working Group, International KC 1962, consisted of Ch. Baron of Rodsden, CD, Ch. Bruin v. Hohenzollern, CDX, Ch. Quelle v.d. Solitude, CD and Ch. Deidre of Rodsden, CD. They were handled by Pat Rademacher and Stuart Schroeder to this good win under the legendary authority, Percy Roberts. The authors recall, "It was like the sea opening up for Moses when they entered the ring." *Frasie.*

Erwin, whelped in 1940, tied together many of early pioneers.

Chapter 2

The Rottweiler Comes to America

In the late 1920s, the ADRK was busy refining the Rottweiler while keeping the policy of performance first, beauty second well in mind. Membership in the club had increased to 312 members by 1930. Little did these dedicated fanciers realize that when three of their members emigrated to the United States in 1928, the history and fortunes of the Rottweiler breed would be forever changed—and the future, today's Rottweiler, would be taken out of their caring hands.

THE TRAILBLAZERS

Otto Denny, Fred Kolb, and August Knecht all settled on the East Coast of the United States. Denny's bitch, Zilly v.d. Steinlach, whelped a litter in 1930, but because the breed was not yet recognized by the American Kennel Club, the litter was registered in Germany with the ADRK. It is interesting that an American-born litter was allowed to be registered by the ADRK as you will realize when you read about the ADRK's registration requirements later in this book. It is good to remember that throughout the breed's infancy in the United States and, in fact, through what we feel was the "Golden Age of Rottweilers," the ADRK and its fellow European fanciers were a source of invaluable guidance for American enthusiasts.

The first Rottweiler registered by the AKC was Stina vom Felsenmeer, owned by August Knecht, in 1931. The AKC apparently had confidence in the ADRK as it allowed Stina and her contemporaries to be registered four years before adopting a breed Standard in 1935. On January 26th, 1931, Stina whelped the first litter of Rottweilers registered by the AKC. This was Mr. Knecht's "A" of Wellwood litter, which was also registered with the ADRK. Jon v.d. Steinlach and Irma v.d. Steinlach, littermates whelped in 1929, were the second and third AKC-registered Rottweilers and were the offspring of Zilly. In fact, of the first fifty Rottweilers registered between 1931 and 1937, twenty-five were either children or grandchildren of Zilly v.d. Steinlach.

The first Rottweiler to be published as having earned an Obedience degree was Gero v. Rabenhorst, owned and trained by Arthur Alfred Eichler of Wisconsin. Gero earned his Companion Dog (CD) degree in 1939, his Companion Dog Excellent (CDX) degree in 1940, and his Utility Dog (UD) title in 1941. Gero holds a special place in the history of the breed for his achievements in Obedience. It was another twenty-seven years before Ch. Don Juan, UD, owned and trained by Margareta McIntyre, became the second UD Rottweiler. He also holds a special place in the hearts of our family, for we were privileged to see that great old dog compete in Obedience for the last time when he was eleven years old!

It is especially appropriate that the first titles awarded to a Rottweiler were working titles because, even today, more Rottweilers earn working titles each year than earn championships. Ours is still a breed of function! In 1948, Ch. Zero, owned by Noel Paul Jones of California, was awarded the first AKC championship, followed in 1949 by Zero's littermate Ch. Zola, owned by Erna Pinkerton, also of California.

Rottweilers may have first stepped on American soil on the East Coast, but by the mid- and late 1940s, they were found across the country. Our family, of course, is most familiar with the early dogs of the Midwest. In 1945, Perrin G. (Pat) Rademacher acquired his first Rottweiler, August der Grosse, a son of Tropf v. Hohenreissach and out of Alva of Crestwood, who was from a first-generation breeding by Mr. Eichler. At the time of purchase, Pat met Eugene Schoelkopf of Palos Park, Illinois, an expatriate of the ADRK. His family's kennel name in Germany had been Zuffenhausen (the first ADRK stud book lists Flora von Zuffenhausen as the 11th dog registered), but here he took the kennel name "of Palos Park." Early Schoelkopf imports were Dasso v. Echterdingen and Seffe vom Gaisburg, which became the seventh and eighth AKC champions. Schoelkopf's breeding, Asta of Palos Park, made her way east where she produced Ch. Asta of Roberts Park who was bred to Krieger v. Hohenreissach, owned by Mrs. Geraldine R. Dodge. Mrs. Dodge owned Giralda Farms and was the major supporter of the legendary Morris & Essex Kennel Club show. Mrs. Dodge was probably the first of a long line of noteworthy dog enthusiasts to own and breed Rottweilers.

In looking for a bitch to be bred to August der Grosse, Pat Rademacher found two females and a male for sale. The owner was unwilling to part with the more attractive of the two bitches, Alva of Crestwood, without also selling the other two dogs. Alva was bred by Martin E. and Henrietta Herrmann, of Wisconsin, whose kennel name "Crestwood" appeared in many early pedigrees. So, for $100, Pat Rademacher brought home Alva, another bitch later sold, and Alva's sire, Erwin, whelped on August 5, 1940. Erwin was a grandson of Alma of Wellwood from that first AKC-registered litter, and grandfather of the first two AKC champions, Zero and Zola, and the fifth AKC champion, Ch. Kurt. Erwin was a splendid example of the breed at that time and he had an indomitable character. A favorite family story tells how Erwin and some members of the Rademacher family were visiting a stable when a stallion broke out of his stall and came charging down the aisle of the barn straight for the family. Erwin stood his ground, and the horse veered off into a stall just yards before reaching the startled people. You could say that, but for Erwin, you wouldn't be reading this book, for one of the authors was a startled, small child in that horse's path. If we hadn't understood what indomitable spirit meant before this incident, we did afterward. In 1948, August der Grosse was bred to Alva of Crestwood and the first Rodsden litter was whelped in the basement of "Rod's den," as Pat's father, Henry S. (Roddy) Rademacher's home was called.

Erwin was not only representative of the time, he was a dog that tied together many of these early Rottweiler pioneers. He was from a litter out of Fried of Wellwood by Prinz v. Hoheneck, bred by William Huppert of New York. Sold to Noel Jones in California, Erwin was bred to the Eichler bitch, Herlind v.d. Schwarzen Eiche, CD. This mating produced Delga, owned by Noel Jones, who in turn was the mother of those three early AKC Rottweiler champions, Zero, Zola, and Kurt. When Ami of Crestwood was bred to

Herman Heid with Weltsieger (world champion) Hektor v. Burgtobel, SchH I.

Erwin, Alva, the mother of the first Rodsden litter, and Bonnie of Crestwood, who found a home with Mr. and Mrs. Hermann Heid, of Canton, Ohio, resulted. The Heids, in subsequent decades, imported and produced some of the best dogs in the Midwest. Erwin died at the ripe old age of eleven in the home of Rademacher in-laws, the Emil Klems.

How many of our present Rottweilers trace lineage back to these early dogs is anyone's guess, although we once traced a stud dog we owned in the 1970s, Ch. Northwind's Donar of Rodsden, and found that his lineage did go back to those first AKC Rottweilers. As Donar appears in many of the more recent Rodsden pedigrees, one can be assured that the old guard is still there if one is willing to go back far enough. Of course, these early dogs have no influence on contemporary Rottweilers except as historical entities. For the historian, we recommend Muriel Freeman's book, *The Complete Rottweiler*, (New York, Howell Book House, 1983), as she presents a very thorough history of those early breeders.

THE ROTTWEILER CATCHES ON

In the 1950s, the Rottweiler started gaining notice outside the small circle of those early fanciers. In 1958, fifty-eight Rottweilers were registered with the AKC and we felt we were on our way! (NO ONE ever dreamed that we would see a registration of over 100,000 a year in 1994! Nor, in 1945, did we know that Erwin was really a Model T to a breed on the brink of explosion.)

To provide an idea of this explosion, consider the accelerating American Kennel Club registration figures since 1940:

YEAR	# REGISTRATIONS
1940	11
1950	67
1960	77
1970	428
1980	4,701
1994	102,596
1995	93,656

Understandably, throughout World War II little if any importing was done, but by the late 1950s, several prominent sires living in the Midwest were of German birth. One was the 1956 Weltsieger Hektor vom Burgtobel,

SchH I, owned by the Heids of Ohio, and another was Ch. Arras v. Stadthaus, owned by William Devore, also of Ohio. Mr. Devore's kennel, "Follow Me's," shone brightly during the 1950s, producing many good dogs, including Ch. Follow Me's Jahn. Jahn, in turn, sired Ch. Baron of Rodsden, CD (out of Ch. Diedre of Rodsden, CD) who sired many of the early Rodsden champions, such as Ch. Dirndl of Rodsden, CDX, TD, owned and trained by James Woodard. "Heidi" earned her TD at over nine years of age in an era when few bitches completed more than a CD degree; her accomplishments were companion to the long participation in Rottweiler affairs by Jim and Erna Woodard. One should remember that a dog's contributions to the breed may not be just the dog itself, but the person on the other end of the leash!

In Chicago, Ludwig Gessner had imported Ch. Alf v.d. Kugellagerstadt as well as Ch. Cora aus dem Lenbachtstadt, two dogs which did much to impress the general public when exhibited at shows. Because the males are generally larger and thus more imposing, they are also more easily remembered. Cora was, however, an unusually lovely bitch, as was Herman Heid's import, Diana vom Remstahl, a daughter of Hektor. They had what it takes to get noticed in a ring full of males.

Sometimes a bitch can be extremely memorable, and we were fortunate to have owned such a one. She was Ch. Quelle von der Solitude, CD, Rodsden's first import and foundation bitch. She was purchased as a puppy from the revered head breed warden of the ADRK, the late Jacob Kopf. Quelle was a stud fee puppy from Mr. Kopf's stud dog, Droll v.d. Brotzingergasse, SchH II, who was considered an outstanding progenitor of the breed. Quelle was hard and athletic, yet feminine, with tremendous drive and unshakable temperament. Those qualities should make a good show dog—and she was, having gotten Best of Breed at the International Kennel Club in Chicago at a time when bitches were simply "the other sex," and was also Best of Opposite Sex at the Colonial Rottweiler Club Specialty in 1961.

On the East Coast, an import, Ch. Jaro von Schleidenplatz, burst upon the scene and, in 1958, became the first Rottweiler to win a Working Group 1st. He was joined in the show world by Ch. Dervis von Weyershof, imported and owned by Swen and Gladys Swenson, whose kennel name, Townview, was very active in the early 1960s. The third of the "big Eastern three" was Ch. Arno vom Kafluzu, owned and successfully handled to a Colonial Rottweiler Club Best of Breed in 1962 by Felice Luburich of Srigo Kennel fame.

In the far West, another import, Ch. Emir von Kohlenhof, was used in the breeding program of Barbara Roloff, who is known today as AKC breeder-judge Barbara Hoard Dillon, founder of Panamint Kennel.

These were impressive imports, and their contribution to the American Rottweiler gene pool illustrated how close we still were to the bosom of the ADRK. But the 1950s were a transitional period, as American dogs with American kennel names were beginning to gain notice. Along with Townview, Panamint, Srigo, and Rodsden, we include "von Stahl," the kennel of Mr.

and Mrs. William F. Stahl. The von Stahl list of champions includes Ch. Rex von Stahl, Ch. Baron von Stahl, Ch. Missy von Stahl, and Ch. Gerhardt von Stahl. Gerhardt, the twentieth AKC champion, would have been famous if for no other reason than he was the first Rottweiler champion owned by Mr. and Mrs. Bernard Freeman and was the beginning of Freeger Rottweilers. Muriel Freeman, our senior AKC breeder-judge (now retired) and our first American Rottweiler Club delegate to the AKC, has been a vital force in the breed since the early sixties. She has tried, perhaps harder than anyone, to educate American fanciers on the responsibilities of owning and breeding a dog that the Germans had so carefully developed. Unfortunately, "dedicated breeding" is not something easily learned.

THE GOLDEN AGE OF ROTTWEILERS

We feel that the years between 1960–1980 were the Golden Age of Rottweilers. So what defines a Golden Age? To begin with, it was a period in which outstanding dogs made their appearance, a time of many "firsts" for the breed, and an era of tremendous optimism about the future of the breed. All this against the backdrop of the establishment and growth of American Rottweiler clubs.

Without the American clubs, the "firsts" would not have been possible. The first American club, organized under the AKC, was the Rottweiler Club of America—an ambitious name for a club mostly on the West Coast that lasted from 1948 to the late 1960s and which really predates the Golden Age. One notable accomplishment was that using the name made it impossible for any later National club to use the same name! More importantly, it held the first AKC-sanctioned matches in 1948–49 and the first Rottweiler Specialty in conjunction with the Oakland Kennel Club in 1950.

The Colonial Rottweiler Club

The first Golden Age American Rottweiler club was the Colonial Rottweiler Club (CRC), formed in 1956 with a membership on the East Coast, primarily centered in the Philadelphia area. Arthur Ritch, a local exhibitor, was a guiding light in its formation and William C. Stahl was the first president. Two names prominent in CRC history are the aforementioned Mrs. Freeman and Charles Tuttle. Besides being a past CRC president, Mrs. Freeman's prominence in the breed propelled the CRC into the limelight. Charles Tuttle, also a past CRC officer, was instrumental in promoting the club through various projects. One project was a full-figure Rottweiler statue which became the model for many Specialty trophies to follow. Another was the publication of *Studies In The Breed History of The Rottweiler*, by Manfred Schanzle of Stuttgart, translated by John Macphail of England and published jointly by the Colonial Rottweiler Club and the Medallion Rottweiler Club in 1969.

The "Schanzle Thesis," as it is popularly called, was a dissertation submitted for the degree of Doctor of Veterinary Medicine at the University of Munich by Manfred Schanzle in 1967. This was the second milestone in American Rottweiler literature, the first being the translation of Hans Korn's *Der Rottweiler*, written in the late 1930s, but published in the United States in 1968. American fanciers were hungry for whatever written material about the breed they could get their hands on. Unfortunately, with Rottweiler registrations low at the time, the market for such books was so small that profits were negligible. So it was a real service to the breed that the CRC contributed the actual printing task and made it possible to sell the Schanzle Thesis at cost. Our own worn and tattered copy still serves as a reference source today. (The Schanzle Thesis is now available from Mrs. Clara Hurley at Powderhorn Press.)

In 1959, the CRC held its first Rottweiler Specialty in conjunction with the beautiful Trenton Kennel Club show in New Jersey. From the 1960s until 1988, the first weekend in May was marked by our annual pilgrimage to Trenton, and later to the Bucks County show for the CRC Specialty. Rhododendrons in bloom, dogwood, quaint stone fences, more than the occasional spring showers, and a gathering of good Rottweilers marked the end of what was usually a long, gray winter. The CRC Specialty was the beginning of the year's Rottweiler activities. In 1989, the CRC held its first independent Specialty, and, perhaps because of those famous "Trenton showers," moved the show to an indoor venue in a motel ballroom. Having judged for the CRC at Trenton, Bucks County, and in the motel, we must say that our favorite image of the CRC Specialty will always be those brightly colored tents rising on the meadow of the Trenton show grounds at Washington Crossing State Park back in the 1960s.

Through the 1960s and 1970s, several dogs dominated the CRC show scene. Ch. Ferdinand v. Dachsweil, owned by Ed Berreta, was a consummate show dog who bridged the gap in breed type between the 1950s and 1960s. He was sired by Ch. Jaro v. Schleidenplatz and was a grandson of Ch. Arras v. Stadthaus. In winning Best of Breed at the CRC Specialty in 1968, Ferdinand retired the Arthur Ritch memorial trophy donated by the Stahls.

Special mention should be made of the bitches who won the CRC Specialties because the Rottweiler breed has always shown a bit of male chauvinism. The difference in size and demeanor between dogs and bitches favors the dogs, so for a bitch to win, especially during the 1960s, meant she had to be "some bitch." The first to win BOB at the CRC was a bitch bred by the authors, Ch. Rodsden's Felicia, owned by Meyer and Maryjane Sachs. "Molly," as she was affectionately called, was a daughter of Ch. Baron of Rodsden, CD, and our import, Ch. Quelle v.d. Solitude, CD. Molly had followed her dam's lead in winning Best of Breed at the International Kennel Club in Chicago in 1965. A bitch who impressed us all was Ch. Srigo's Madchen v. Kurtz, owned by Lucille and Donald Kurtz and shown

Ch. Rodsden's Felicia, the breed's first Specialty-winning bitch, made her place in history at the 1965 Colonial Specialty. *William Gilbert*

impeccably by her breeder, Felice Luburich. Madchen was a daughter of Ch. Erno v. Wellesweiler, SchH I, which we will discuss later, and Ch. Srigo's Econnie v. Lorac. The third bitch was a striking German import, Hella v. Marchenwald, owned by Ida and Meyer Marcus. Hella was a daughter of Int. Ch. Elko v. Kastanienbaum, SchH I, and Cora v. Reichenbachle. Hella's win was all that more exciting because she had not yet completed her championship requirements and won from the classes. All three bitches showed great ring presence, which made them appear heads above the competition— even if they weren't bigger by physical size!

Throughout this book the reader will note that, more than likely, notable dogs were produced from noteworthy parents. Depth in pedigree is one factor that separates good breeding from good luck.

The interests of the CRC were by no means limited to beauty of conformation. Since 1969, the CRC has sponsored Obedience at its Specialties.

Year	Best of Breed/ Best In Show	Best Of Opposite Sex to Best of Breed	High In Trial
1959	Ch. Riedstadit Rudigar	Unknown	——
1961	Ch. Jaro v. Schiedenplatz	Unknown	——
1962	Arno v. Kafluzu	Romona's Heidi of Townview	——
1963	Ch. Dervis v. Weyershof	Ch. Quelle v.d. Solitude	——
1964	Ch. Schon of Townview	Ch. Isolde v. Rau of Wunderkinder	——
1965	Ch. Rodsden's Felicia	Ch. Ferdinand v. Dachsweil	——
1966	Ch. Ferdinand v. Dachsweil	Srigo's Econnie v. Lorac, CD	——
1967	Ch. Ferdinand v. Dachsweil	Srigo's Econnie v. Lorac, CD	——

Year	Best of Breed/ Best In Show	Best Of Opposite Sex to Best of Breed	High In Trial
1968	Ch. Ferdinand v. Dachsweil	Ch. Priska v. Kursaal	——
1969	Rodsden's Panzer v.d. Harf	Northwind's Brikka	Landau's Bruno v. Wyncraft
1970	Dago v.d. Ammerquelle	Srigo's Madchen v. Kurtz	none qualified
1971	Ch. Rodsden's Duke du Trier	Ch. Srigo's Madchen v. Kurtz	Ch. Rodsden's Kato v. Donnaj, CDX
1972	Ch. Srigo's Garret v. Zahn	Ch. Srigo's Madchen v. Kurtz	Rodsden's General Max
1973	Ch. Srigo's Madchen v. Kurtz	Ch. Falco v.h. Brabantpark	Rodsden's Alexander The Great
1974	Ch. Titon Sujon	Ch. Shearwater Indian Sunrise	Rodsden's Helsa v. Eberle
1975	Ch. Srigo's Viking Spirit	Ch. Srigo's Madchen v. Kurtz	none qualified
1976	Ch. Titon Sujon	Ch. Riegele's Agreta Maid	Rodsden's Windsong Drava
1977	Ch. Donnaj VT Yankee of Paulus, CD	Ch. Andan Indy Pendence of Paulus	Ch. Donnaj VT Yankee of Paulus, CD
1978	Ch. Hella v. Marchenwald	Ch. Donnaj VT Yankee of Paulus, CD	Ch. Rodsden's Bruin v. Hungerbuhl
1979	Ch. Donnaj VT Yankee of Paulus, CDX	Ch Andan Indy Pendence of Paulus	Candlemas Sunflower
1980	Ch. Donnaj VT Yankee of Paulus, CDX	Ch. Reza Birs v. Haus-Schum	Candlemas Sunflower
1981	Ch. Rodsden's Kane v. Forstwald, CD	Ch. Radio Ranch's Christmas Spirit	Edition Farm's Duke
1982	Ch. Northwind's Kaiser	Ch. Birch Hill's Juno, TD	Ch. von Bruka Brutus, CDX
1983	Bronco v. Raubefeld	Ch. Dorroh's Just Grand, TD	Radio Ranch's Vixen v. Ebony, CD
1984	Ch. Donnaj Green Mountain Boy	Ch. Sunnyside's Royal v. Meadow, CD	Radio Ranch's Vixen v. Ebony, CDX

Year	Best of Breed/ Best In Show	Best Of Opposite Sex to Best of Breed	High In Trial
1985	Ch. Mirko v. Steinkopf	Ch. von Bruka's Fiona, CD	Astrid of Jordan Hollow Farm
1986	Ch. Mirko v. Steinkopf, CD	Ch. von Bruka's Fiona, CD	Magnum v. Meadow III, UD
1987	Ch. Goldeiche Ara v. Brader, CD	Ch. von Bruka's Fiona, CD	Magnum v. Meadow III, UD
1988	Ch. von Brader's Eiger	Ch. Reza v. Ross	OTCH Magnum v. Meadow III
1989	Goldeiche Ara v. Brader, CD	Ch. Epic's Devine Intervention	OTCH Magnum v. Meadow III
1990	Ch. Cannon River Oil Tanker	Ch. von Bruka's Fiona, CD	OTCH Magnum v. Meadow III
1991	Pioneer's DJ Star Stuben, CD	Ch. Golt's Heidi von Kriegerhof	Exsel's Trouble Every Day
1992	Ch. Noblehaus Klark Kent	Ch. Kennrich's Keepsake	Von der Brin's Flying Frisbee
1993	Oakbrook's Caliber v. Doroh	Ch. Woodmere's Unfug Hersteller, CD	Srigo's Good Luck Charm
1994	Ch. Corinthian's Heart Breaker	Ch. Helkirk Weissenburg's Chance	Nordike Gotcha Goin Lebi, CD
1995	Ch. Adler Rock's Diamond Jack	Ch. Von Hottenstein's Up and Atem	Nordike's Igor v. Aluger
1996	Ch. Gamegard's Moonraker	Ch. Vom Viraus Sweet Sox	Heidihaus Hollywood Idol, CDX

In addition to CRC Obedience support, two pioneers of Rottweiler tracking, CRC members Arthur Twiss and his late wife Ruth, were instrumental in presenting tracking to the Fancy.

Although there is no doubt that the Colonial Rottweiler Club supported those interested in working their dogs, it was the next club to be discussed that promoted the Rottweiler in all areas of working ability.

These happy people at the 1966 Medallion Rottweiler Club match are Joan Klem, chairperson, with ADRK Head Breed Warden Friedrich Berger, judge (standing), Tilla Berger and Brigetta Mecherman, translator (seated).

Ch. Rodsden's Duke du Trier (Ch. Rodsden's Kluge v.d. Harque CD ex Ch. Franzi v. Kursaal), owned by Dr. and Mrs. Nelse Olson, was a celebrated BIS and multiple specialty winner. *Booth*

The Medallion Rottweiler Club

The Medallion Rottweiler Club (MRC) was founded in 1959 in the Chicago area and, like Chicago's motto "a city that works," the MRC is indeed a club that works. The name derives from an imported German Rottweiler medallion that was adopted as the club logo. Names for clubs in those days reflected the AKC's preference that local breed clubs use names not associated with a

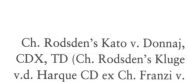

Ch. Rodsden's Kato v. Donnaj, CDX, TD (Ch. Rodsden's Kluge v.d. Harque CD ex Ch. Franzi v. Kursaal), owned, trained and handled by Jan Marshall, was the first Rottweiler to become an all-breed BIS winner.

specific geographic area. Hence the Colonial Rottweiler Club instead of the Philadelphia Rottweiler Club, and the Medallion Rottweiler Club instead of the Chicago Rottweiler Club. Today, the AKC has reversed itself and we have The Rottweiler Club of Kansas City, The Houston Area Rottweiler Fanciers Club and The Dallas/Ft. Worth Rottweiler Club—just to name a few.

From a charter membership of twenty-three local fanciers, the MRC has grown into a club that rivals the parent club in membership size and scope, and that routinely presents the largest Rottweiler Specialty show in the world.

In 1969 the MRC celebrated its tenth anniversary by holding its first Rottweiler Specialty in conjunction with the Wheaton (Illinois) Kennel Club Show. In 1973 the MRC held the first independent Rottweiler Specialty show in the United States. At this show, ADRK judge Heinz Eberz officiated, thereby continuing the MRC policy of inviting foreign experts to judge, beginning in 1964 with Mrs. Gerd Hyden of Sweden judging an MRC match. Over the years the MRC has invited German, Dutch, Swedish, Finnish, Danish, and English authorities to participate in Specialty shows, breed seminars and character tests, giving the MRC a broad look at the total Rottweiler.

To balance a successful conformation endeavor with working interests, the MRC held the first all-Rottweiler Obedience trial in the United States in 1979, the first all-Rottweiler tracking (TD) test in 1981, the first all-Rottweiler tracking dog excellent (TDX) test in 1982, the first all-Rottweiler combined TD/TDX test in 1984, and the first all-Rottweiler Variable Surface Tracking Test in 1996. These are all AKC events; however, the MRC certainly did not limit itself to promoting only working activities sanctioned by the American Kennel Club. In 1984 the MRC sponsored an all-Rottweiler schutzhund trial under the auspices of the *Deutscher Verband der Gebrauchshundsportvereine* (DVG), which is the German Alliance of Utility

Dog Sports Club. The MRC continued holding yearly trials until 1990, when they stopped due to restrictions imposed by the AKC, which will be discussed in a later chapter. The MRC has also taken an active lead in promoting herding and carting—two of the breed's legacies from the 19th century.

The MRC held Sweepstakes in 1977, 1978 and 1981. Celebrating twenty-five years in 1984, the MRC initiated a Puppy Futurity, conceived by Carol Krickeberg, which requires litters to be nominated by their breeders and then individual puppies to be enrolled by their owners prior to the show date. All the litters nominated also must be from parents bred under the MRC's code of ethics. The Futurity rewards the foundation of our breed—the breeders. Jackpotted cash prizes are awarded to the breeders, owners of the sires and owners of the winning Futurity puppies. At this writing, the MRC is the only Rottweiler club that holds a Futurity, and because of the limitations, one would suspect that a Futurity would be considerably smaller than a Puppy Sweepstakes. To the contrary, the Futurity has grown each year. In 1994 the entry was 215 compared to an entry of 209 for the Puppy Sweepstakes at the National Specialty. Perhaps the concept has not caught on with the other clubs because of the paperwork involved in conducting a Futurity.

Throughout the 1960s and 1970s, a name prominent in the winners circle at MRC Specialties was Rodsden. From 1969–1980, 24 MRC winners out of fifty-two either carried the Rodsden prefix or were imported by Rodsden. The Golden Age was a time in which one active kennel could greatly influence a club just as a great dog could influence an entire breed. The MRC was fortunate to have at its core people whose dedication to the breed has continued over the decades—Jane Wiedel (Birch Hill Rottweilers, MRC board member, and present treasurer of the National club), Jeffrey Kittner (president of the MRC), and Geraldine Kittner (Kertzenlicht Rottweilers), George Chamberlin (Ironwood Rottweilers, past president of both the ARC and the CRC), Carol Krickeberg (MRC board member and vice-president of the ARC at this writing), Kerry Krickeberg (Brentwood Rottweilers), and Sandra Gilbert (Dra-Tar Rottweilers, Dog Writers Association of America award nominee) are just a few who have belonged to the Medallion Rottweiler Club for more than twenty years.

One of the MRC's charter members and early presidents was to greatly influence the third of "the big three" local Specialty clubs to arise during the Golden Age.

MEDALLION ROTTWEILER CLUB WINNERS

Best Of Breed/ Best In Show	Best Of Opposite Sex to Best Of Breed	High In Trial
1969 Ch. Dago v. Kallenberg	Ch. Nodette v. Hampleman	(not held)

Best Of Breed/ Best In Show	Best Of Opposite Sex to Best Of Breed	High In Trial
1970 Ch. Axel v. d. Taverne, UDT	Starkrest's Freya-R	(not held)
1971 Ch. Rodsden's Duke du Trier	Ch. Rodsden's Tessa v. Romoser	(not held)
1972 Ch. Rodsden's Duke Du Trier	Hella v. d. Grurmannsheide	(not held)
1973 Ch. Dux v. Hungerbuhl, SchH I	Rodsden's Ingar	(not held)
1974 Ch. Panamint Banner v. Hohenwald, CD	Rodsden's Tally v. Hungerbuhl	(not held)
1975 Ch. Panamint Banner v. Hohenwald, CD	Asta v. Forstwald	(not held)
1976 Ch. Alck v.d. Spechte	Ch. Dina v. Schloss Rietheim, CD	(not held)
1977 Ch. Centurion's Che v.d. Barr	Ch. Andee vom Haus Kalbas	(not held)
1979 Ch. Rodsden's Kane v. Forstwald, CD	Ch. Czarina v. Stolzenfels, CD	Ch. Northwind's Kriemheld
1980 A/C Ch. Erno v.d. Gaarn, CD	Ch. Minden F v. Hawthorne	(not held)
1981 Ch. Birch Hill's Hasso Manteuffel, CDX, TD	Weissenburg's Don't-U-Dare	Rodsden's Wendy Kastanienbaum
1982 Am. & Can. Ch. Birch Hill's Governor, Am. & Can. CD	Ch. Rodsden's Toni v. Forstwald, A/C CD	Ch. Birch Hill's Hasso Manteufel, CDX, TD
1983 Am. & Can. Ch. Birch Hill's Governor, CD	Ch. Birch Hill's Nanna v. Brader, TD	Outlook Knite Stalker v. Jedi
1984 Ch. Rodsden's Tristan Forstwald, CD, TD	Ch. Sunnyside's Royal v. Meadow, CD	Heidi v. h. Kertzenlicht
1985 Am. & Can. Ch. Rodsden's Berte v. Zederwald, Am. & Can. CD	Ch. Gemstone's Aura of Brilliance	Brinx v. Forstwald der Hoffen, CD
1986 Ch. Beaverbrook Eisen v. Bruin	Ch. Vroni v. Hohenhameln	Ch. Heidi v.h. Kertzenlicht, CDX

Best Of Breed/ Best In Show	Best Of Opposite Sex to Best Of Breed	High In Trial
1987 Ch. Santo v. Schwaiger Wappen, SchH III	Ch. Tanmar Beaverbrook Bess	Arko v. Pickel, UD
1988 Ch. Rodsden's Tristan v. Forstwald, CD, TD	Ch. Tanmar Beaverbrook Bess	Tealaska Aurora Beau
1989 Ch. Cannon River Oil Tanker, CD	Ch. Aryan's U.S.S. Ursula, CDX, TDX	Haserway's Challenger, UDT
1990 Ch. Nelson v.h. Brabantpark	Ch. Lyvngwerth's Devotion v. Ponca	Rottidox Limerick
1991 Ch. Haakon Moby v. Reishoff, CD	Ch. Windrock's Sophi v. Richter	Tealaska Aurora Beau, UD
1992 Am. & Can. Ch. Nordike's Aluger v. Lindenwood	Am. & Can. Ch. Tri-Lee's Down The Road, TD	Tealaska Aurora Beau, UD
1993 Ch. Tobant's Grant	Am. & Can. Ch. Tri-Lee's Down The Road, TD	OTCH Carla vom Kasseler-Hof
1994 Ch. Roborott's Arco v. Ilko, TD	Ch. Helkirk Weissenburg's Chance	Stefen Imazadie's Hannelore, TDX, CDX
1995 Ch. Andreca's Aramis v.d. Mond, CD	Ch. Von Baker's Sweetest Taboo	Nordike's Itara Aluger

MRC High in Schutzhund Trials

1984	Janek's Falk v.k. Buck, SchH III
1985	Ch. Dux v.d. Blume, CDX, TDX
1986	William's Bronson v. Grant, CDX, VB, Can. CD
1987	Barry vom Lohlein, SchH III, FH
1988	Ch. Rodsden's Quito of Wylan, CDX, TDX, SchH I
1989	Ch. Liberty's A Chip Off the ARK, CDX
1990	Rodsden's Phaedra v. Eppo, CD, SchH II, BH

The Golden State Rottweiler Club

The Golden State Rottweiler Club, based in southern California, began with a nucleus of five interested fanciers, one of whom was Gerry Fitterer who had moved from Illinois and the MRC to California. The other members were

Margareta McIntyre (previously mentioned as the owner and trainer of Ch. Don Juan, UD), Hubertus von Rettberg, Leanne Camarillo and Anita McCullough. Following a series of get-togethers at shows and dinners, the group organized to form a club temporarily called the Southern California Rottweiler Club, which by 1962 was officially the Golden State Rottweiler Club (GSRC).

From 1962 through 1968, the GSRC supported various area shows with entries and trophies until 1969, when the GSRC held its first Specialty in conjunction with the Santa Barbara Kennel Club.

Charter members Margareta McIntyre and Gerry Fitterer, who became an AKC Obedience judge and whose kennel name "Gertase" shows up on so many fine obedience dogs, were naturally involved in performance events. It is not surprising that the GSRC honored top Obedience dogs from the very beginning.

GOLDEN STATE ROTTWEILER CLUB WINNERS

Year	Best Of Breed Best In Show	Best Of Opposite Sex to Best Of Breed	High In Trial
1969	Ch. Rodsden's Kurt v.d. Hargue		Charlemagne Bulloides
1970	Ch. Blitz v. Lucas	Ch. Rodsden's Kirsten du Trier	B Eine Kline Glockenspiel
1971	Ch. Rodsden's Kirsten du Trier	Ch. Rodsden's Canon	Kleinste Bettina of Fair Lane
1972	Ch. Rodsden's Duke du Trier	Ch. Freeger's Ingela, CD	Gertase Tarnation O'Westwind, CD
1973	Ch. Dux v. Hungerbuhl, SchH I	Jaheriss' Baaca	Garm of Gertase
1974	Am. & Can. Ch. Panamint Banner v. Hohenwald, CD	Ch. Rodsen's Rally	Freeger's Lotta Gatstuberget
1975	Sussis Jens	Ch. Bea Mathilda v. Haus Kalbas, CD	E-Z Dodger of Gertase
1976	Edelhund Aga	Ch. Trollegen's Aparri, CD	Ebonstern Corso v. Klanherhof
1977	Ch. Rodsden's Rough Diamond	Ch. Trollegen's Aparri, CD	Honey Bear de Germaine

Year	Best Of Breed Best In Show	Best Of Opposite Sex to Best Of Breed	High In Trial
1978	Ch. Arlo Jens v. Golden West	Ch. Brandywein v. Kleinholz	Fraulien of Gertase-R, CDX
1979	Ch. Oscar v.h. Brabantpark	Siskiyou Erda Sue	Walor's Krug Spatlese
1980*	Ch. Quanto v.h. Brabantpark	Ch. Trollegen's Fantasy	Tegelhagen's Cassandra
1981	Ch. Donar v.d. Hoeve Cor Unum	Ch. Powderhorn's Gwen of Wencrest	Gertase Sio Calako Koshari, CD
1982	Ch. Birch Hill's Hasso Manteuffel, CDX, TD	Am. & Can. Ch. Trollegen's Kyra v. Sonnenhaus	Ch. Trollegen's Bear
1983	Ch. Rexford von Gorog, CD	Windrift's Atari v. Printz	Margaret Cardenas
1984	Ch. Argus Maximus du Camelot	Ch. Windrift's Atari v. Printz	Rodsden's Streber v. Forstwald
1985	Ch. Piece of the Rock	Ch. Jessie v. Odenwald	Jazz v. Odenwald
1986	Ch. Rodsden's Danzig v. Gasto, CD, TD	Bandera's Kira v. Brando	Olga A v. Golden West, TD
1987	Ch. Bandera's Kira v. Brando	Ch. Hans v.h. Brabantpark	Way-Mar's Rocky Raccoon, UD
1988	Ch. Donar v. Reishoff	Ch. Ironwood's Citizen Canid	Way-Mar's Rocky Raccoon, UD
1989	Ch. Von Der Hess Braxx v. Ryatti	Von Der Lors Anastashia Cade	Way-Mar's Rocky Raccoon, UD
1990	Ch. Donar v. Reishoff	Ch. Duchess Peace of Axel	Way-Mar's Rocky Raccoon, UD
1991	Ch. Von Der Lors Anastashia Cade	Ch. Imaygo's Midnight Cruiser	Lucy
1992	Ch. Blackwood Dante v. Lyvngewerth, CD	Windcastle's Shaka	Rubicon's Mad Max
1993	Ch. Von Der Lors Braxx Nelson	Ch. Von Der Lors Anastashia Cade	Von Marc's Keisha

Year	Best Of Breed Best In Show	Best Of Opposite Sex to Best Of Breed	High In Trial
1994	Ch. Powderhorn's Mile of Wencrest	Ch. Bandera's Lili Marlene v. Lore	
1995	Ch. Degrasso's Jacob v. Waxel	Jacaranda's Rariah v. Braxx	Nighthawk's Hugs And Kisses For You
1996	Ch. Degrasso's Jacob v. Waxel	Ch. Von Pavel's Canyon Lake Kate	Jan-nel's Dream Katcher

* Not a specialty; paperwork not filed with AKC

After reading the names of all the Specialty winners, the name of the 1972 GSRC Specialty Best of Breed should be familiar by now. Ch. Rodsden's Duke du Trier won Specialties of all three clubs. Owned by Dr. and Mrs. Nelse Olson and handled by Richard Orseno, Duke was the second Rottweiler to win an American all-breed Best in Show. His younger brother, Ch. Rodsden's Kato v. Donnaj, CDX, TD, won a Best in Show just the day before, on May 29, 1971, owner-handled by Jan Marshall who is now an AKC breeder-judge. Duke and Kato were the products of one of the most successful of the Golden Age breeding combinations—the pairing of Ch. Rodsden's Kluge v.d. Harque, CD and Ch. Franzi vom Kursaal. From this combination came littermates Ch. Rodsden's Kahlua du Trier, Winners Bitch at the 1971 CRC Specialty, Ch. Rodsden's Kari du Trier, Winners Bitch at the 1969 MRC Specialty, and Ch. Rodsden's Kristin du Trier, Best of Opposite Sex at the 1969 and 1970 GSRC Specialties and Best of Breed at the 1971 GSRC Specialty.

Through the 1960s and 1970s, Rottweiler exhibitors were still a fairly small community, so it was no surprise to see the same outstanding dogs show up at the various Specialties from year to year, although it was more common, because of the distance involved, to see the same dogs at the CRC and MRC Specialties. Somewhat in isolation, the GSRC faced, with forthright determination, a problem Rottweiler fanciers all over the country saw.

Hip dysplasia in dogs is an inherited disease usually associated with the larger, heavier breeds and implies a faulty conformation of the head of the femur and the acetabulum (the ball and socket of the hip joint). Rottweiler owners had been aware of the disease even before they knew its name. There were those dogs that limped, or were stiff when rising, or just "moved funny." Although singularly members of the three clubs were actively searching for ways to prevent this crippling disease, the GSRC was the first club to actively support a program aimed at eradicating hip dysplasia with a mandatory code

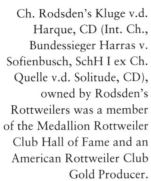
Ch. Rodsden's Kluge v.d. Harque, CD (Int. Ch., Bundessieger Harras v. Sofienbusch, SchH I ex Ch. Quelle v.d. Solitude, CD), owned by Rodsden's Rottweilers was a member of the Medallion Rottweiler Club Hall of Fame and an American Rottweiler Club Gold Producer.

of ethics, adopted in 1969, for its club members to follow. At this time the Orthopedic Foundation for Animals (OFA) had come into prominence and had begun issuing OFA numbers (RO-numbers) to Rottweilers who had been found free of hip dysplasia as determined by its reading of X-rays submitted to the OFA. One of the provisions of the GSRC code was that only those dogs free of hip dysplasia, as determined by the OFA, were permitted to be bred.

GSRC member Clara Hurley not only supported the club's OFA policy, but began a Rottweiler Registry, a Biodex, that not only lists the dogs that have passed the OFA, but includes hip dysplasia information on its parents and siblings. To date, it is the only source of information this complete for the American Rottweiler. It does, however, depend on breeders and owners sending the information to Mrs. Hurley.

The MRC followed with its own mandatory code of ethics in 1975, and the CRC in 1979. (The MRC's Code of Ethics is reproduced in the appendix.)

Throughout the 1960s and 1970s, the "big three" shared many common features in addition to a mandatory code of ethics and specialty shows—all had monthly or bi-monthly newsletters, supported area shows with trophies, held seminars and clinics to educate their members, shared judges with each other, and contributed to funds for projects to help the breed. And they all operated with an AKC breed Standard that had been approved by the AKC in 1935. A breed Standard guides both breeders and judges, so it is very important that the Standard clearly define breed type. This antiquated 1935 Standard certainly did not reflect the Rottweiler of the day. Something had to be done, but under the AKC's rules, only a National club or "parent" club could do it.

The impetus to form a National club had been provided in the East by CRC members Muriel Freeman and Charles Tuttle, in the Midwest by MRCers Klem-Rademacher family and Jim and Erna Woodard, and from the GSRC Clara Hurley and Margareta McIntyre. The three clubs decided to send two delegates each to a meeting to be held in the Chicago area following the 1971 MRC Specialty. Thus you could say, the children gave birth to the "parent," because at this meeting the American Rottweiler Club (ARC) was born.

Formation of the American Rottweiler Club

Because the formation of the ARC was so significant, we are reprinting the official minutes from that first meeting in Illinois:

MINUTES OF MEETING OF ROTTWEILER PARENT CLUB DELEGATES.

The first meeting of Rottweiler Parent Club Delegates was held on Sunday, June 13, 1971, at the home of Mr. and Mrs. Franz Lipp, 27 W. 720 Robin Lane, West Chicago, Illinois 60185, with the following persons present:

Mr. Bert Daikeler—Colonial Rottweiler Club

Mr. William C. Stahl—Colonial Rottweiler Club

Mrs. Joan Klem—Medallion Rottweiler Club

Mrs. Erna Woodard—Medallion Rottweiler Club

Mrs. Clara Hurley—Golden State Rottweiler Club

Mrs. Margareta McIntyre—Golden State Rottweiler Club

The meeting was opened informally at 11:30 AM. Mrs. Erna Woodard was asked to record the minutes of the meeting.

Purpose of the Meeting: To begin formation of a Rottweiler Parent Club by drawing up a Constitution and set of by-laws acceptable to the American Kennel Club, and to the membership of the Colonial Rottweiler Club, Medallion Rottweiler Club, and the Golden State Rottweiler Club. To this end, the Delegates studied in detail a proposed Constitution for Rottweiler Parent Club in America originally worked up by Mr. Charles Tuttle in January 1970. This proposed Constitution was based upon the American Kennel Club's sample constitution and by-laws for a Specialty Club with nationwide membership. Delegates discussed the following subject matter in the proposed Constitution:

Constitution

Article I—Name and Objective

By-Laws

Article I—Membership

Article II—Meetings

Article III—Directors and Officers

Article IV—The Club Year, Voting, Nominations, Elections

Article V—Committees

Article VI—Discipline

Article VII—Amendments

Article VIII—Dissolution

Article IX—Order of Business

Under each Article were listed Sections that were carefully studied by the Delegates, who inserted, deleted, or changed words, phrases, clauses, and sentences to make them pertinent to a Rottweiler Parent Club. All suggested changes made in the proposed Constitution were noted by Mr. Bert Daikeler on his copy of the Constitution. Mr. Daikeler will retype the Constitution, making the suggested changes, and will send the revised copy to each Delegate. Mr. William Stahl will take his revised copy of the Constitution to the American Kennel Club, discuss with them the changes proposed by the Delegates, and will try to get American Kennel Club approval of these changes. Each delegate will take his/her revised copy of the Constitution back to his/her local Rottweiler Club for discussion.

It was decided that the present delegates, plus the alternates, would serve as officers and directors until the next annual meeting (approximately one year). Officers and directors for this period of time would be:

President	Mr. William Stahl (Delegate)
Vice-President	Mrs. Clara Hurley (Delegate)
Recording Secretary	Mrs. Margareta McIntyre (Delegate)
Corresponding Secretary	Mr. Bert Daikeler (Alternate)
Treasurer	Mrs. Joan Klem (Delegate)
Director	Mrs. Erna Woodard (Delegate)
Director	Mr. Robert Schauer (Delegate)
Director	Mrs. Ann Alexander (Alternate)
Director	Mrs. Gerry Fitterer (Alternate)

It was agreed that because of the detail involved in forming a Parent Club, a Rottweiler Parent Club would not come into existence for at least three years.

Meeting was adjourned at 3:00 PM.

Respectfully submitted,

Erna Woodard

Secretary pro tem.

It was a slow and deliberate process to go from this meeting and eventually emerge as the National club we know today. In fact, it was not until 1990 (nineteen years later) that the AKC recognized the American Rottweiler Club as a member club and thus gave it the responsibility for approving all AKC-sanctioned Rottweiler events in the country. However, although not yet a member club, the ARC accomplished a great deal during the 1970s and 1980s. The AKC breed Standard was updated in 1979, accomplishing the original goal of the club. Although falling short of the German breed Standard, this updated 1979 AKC version was far superior to the 1935 Standard.

In 1981 the ARC held its first Specialty. As with the other clubs, the ARC also supports both Obedience and Tracking.

AMERICAN ROTTWEILER CLUB WINNERS

Year	Best Of Breed Best In Show	Best Of Opposite Sex to Best Of Breed	High In Trial
1981	Ch. Donnaj vt Yankee of Paulus, CDX	Ch. Radio Ranch's Christmas Spirit	Finnberg's Bulli
1982	Ch. Birch Hill's Hasso Manteuffel, CDX, TD	Froni v. Sachsen	Honch of JR
1983	Ch. Doroh's Just Grand, TD	Ch. Birch Hill's Governor, CD	Fairhaven's Heidi v. Ort, CD
1984	Ch. Birch Hill's Governor, CD	Ch. Sunnyside's Royal v. Meadow, CD	Ch. Von Gailingen's Dark Delight, CDX, TD
1985	Ch. Von Bruka Fiona	Arri v.d. Hembachbrucke	Nobile's Honnig Kind, CD
1986	Ch. Don Ari's Harras	Gipfel's Cloud Nine Ebony	Ch. Marlo's Sohn v. Axel
1987	Ch. Cannon River Oil Tanker, CD	Cendy v. Siedlerpfad	OTCH Dolly v. Odenwald, TD
1988	Ch. Cannon River Oil Tanker, CD	Ch. Sophie v. Bergenhof, CD	Summers Glory Da Bratiana, CD
1989	Ch. Vom Sonnenhaus Krugerrand, CD	Ch. Tri-Lee's Champagne	Summers Glory Da Bratiana, CD

Year	Best Of Breed Best In Show	Best Of Opposite Sex to Best Of Breed	High In Trial
1990	Ch. Cannon River Oil Tanker, CD	Ch. Jessnics Marvelous Mamie Cade	Welkerhaus' Gutherzig Bear, CD
1991	Ch.Von Der Lors Anastashia Cade	Ch. Beaverbrook Phantom v. Rika	OTCH Carla v. Kassler-Hof
1992	Ch. Gamegard's Image De Femme	Ch. Akemos Apache von Goodhart	Starshine's Astra
1993	Black Oak Chance v. Coldar, CD	Ch. Tri-Lee's Gypsy Arabesque	Rubicon's Mad Max
1994	Ch. Oakbrook's Caliber	Ch.Rivera's Anka	Summers Glory Da Bratiana, UD
1995	Ch. Dillon v. Wacissa, CD	Ch. Noblehaus High C V Gruppstark, CD	Eichenberg's Black Diamond
1996	Ch. Serrant's Bannor	Ch. Von Boylan's Boldly Bridgette, CD, BH	Valley View's Election Day

In addition to the National Specialty, the ARC sponsors regional Specialties held throughout the United States. This sponsorship enables local breeders and Rottweiler clubs to present Specialties in areas where no Specialty shows are usually held. The ARC also briefly held schutzhund trials during the National Specialty activities in 1987, 1988 and 1989. ARC members such as Peter Piusz, Bill and Linda Michels, Sue Suwinski and Peter Rademacher worked to promote the sport within the club during that period and continue to individually appreciate and participate in the sport today.

An ARC project well received by the Fancy has been the publishing of the Rottweiler Pictorials. These Pictorials, begun by Dorothea Gruenerwald and Ann Mauer, list the conformation and Obedience records, photos and pedigrees of current dogs. An invaluable addition to one's library, the first Pictorial of 1975–1976 recorded 225 Rottweiler titleholders. The latest, and fifth, Pictorial chronicles more than 700 Rottweilers. This is one more measure of the growth of the Rottweiler breed!

One area of leadership where the ARC has lagged behind the big three is in adopting a mandatory code of ethics. This was rectified in 1996 when the club approved an ARC Mandatory Practices.

There were, of course, many local Rottweiler clubs that came into being during the Golden Age which did not seek AKC sanction and remained, essentially, social clubs. The most notable is the Western Rottweiler Owners, which supports shows and Performance Events in its area of northern California and has a strong membership.

The Great Dogs

Within the framework of the Specialty clubs and their members, the Golden Age saw the importation of dogs whose influence on the breed during that era was undeniable. We will begin with a dog who was as famous to the Rottweiler breed as Man O' War was to the thoroughbred horse.

The ADRK has had only two dogs who ever won the *Bundessieger* title three times (the *bundessieger* show is an all-breed show that had, prior to 1971, been the ADRK's "Specialty" show for Rottweilers). The first dog was Dieter vom Kohlrwald, Bundessieger for 1950–1952, and the second was Int. Ch. Harras vom Sofienbusch, SchH I, Bundessieger for 1960–1962. Although we never met Dieter, his pictures depict a large, elegant dog whose type was clearly beyond what we saw in the American show ring during the same period. In the early 1960s, Harras was just as exceptional and much more memorable!

INT. CH. HARRAS VOM SOFIENBUSCH, SCHH I

In 1963 Rodsden Kennels, through the help of the head breed warden for the ADRK Friedrich Berger, imported Harras. The "great dog," as he was being called with some fondness by the Germans, was almost seven years old, beyond his prime, but was still being trotted around to German shows on exhibition. Harras arrived after a long flight (via a stop in Canada) and emerged from his crate as the most magnificent Rottweiler we had ever seen—and one of the dirtiest! His first American experience was a trip to a kennel for a bath—the first and last indignity that Harras let us impose on him.

Harras should be remembered as one of the truly great Rottweiler phenotypes. It isn't surprising that almost thirty years after his death, he is still used in current literature as the example of the ultimate male Rottweiler. And we should all be grateful for his quality because he appears in practically every American Rottweiler's pedigree—if you look far enough back. The following is a translation of Harras' official critique given at his *Korung* (breeding evaluation in Germany):

Large (very substantial), strong, balanced male, well-muscled with strong bones. 66 cm tall, 31 cm depth of chest, 89 cm chest circumference, 76 cm body length. Head is dry, strong male, skull strong, generally straight line to the stop, strong close-fitting lips on muzzle. Eyes medium sized, almond shaped, dark. Ears set correctly. Good strong scissors bite. Body outline

Int. Ch. 1960, 1961, 1962 Bundessieger Harras v. Sofienbusch, SchH I, imported and owned by Rodsden's Rottweilers, was the first inductee into the MRC Hall of Fame.

deep and broad—good forechest, ribs well-sprung, good top and bottom line, well-developed testicles, good angulation, deep front, well-placed shoulders, tight close-set elbows, straight correct legs, good pasterns, feet well-arched, pads hard, toes tight, well angulated deep rear with broad, somewhat sloping croup. Strong muscular broad upper thighs, straight forward stifle joint, straight hocks. Floating, ground covering reaching movement; a natural trotter. Full of temperament, steady nerved, natural and controlled with high courage and fighting instincts.

Harras had been allowed to become dog aggressive, perhaps tolerated because of his great beauty or because the Germans were much more indifferent to that trait than we were at the time. But as those who fed, cleaned up after, and handled Harras, we must say that he had great affection (and tolerance) for his friends—even if there were just a few of us! Harras was the second dog we owned to have floating, ground covering, reaching movement—the first being his son, Ch. Bengo vom Westfalenpark, CD. But Harras was more impressive because what was floating along was so much more dog! What Harras had in abundance was presence. He entered the show ring with as much command as we would guess George Washington commanded in front of his troops.

Harras was also the first dog inducted into the Medallion Rottweiler Club's Hall of Fame. Beginning with the MRC, the various Rottweiler clubs sought to establish systems for honoring outstanding Rottweilers of the day. The MRC's Hall of Fame is based on a point system that includes titles earned, titles earned by offspring, and outstanding accomplishments for Rottweilers owned by MRC members. The American Rottweiler Club set up production awards—gold, silver and bronze—based on the accomplishments of the progeny. This labor of love by Arcite Catherine Thompson is monumental work because of the sheer number of Rottweilers we have today. The Colonial Rottweiler Club has a system based on accomplishments of dogs that are owner-handled.

Harras finished his American championship in short order; consequently, only a limited number of people saw him in the flesh. That is a shame because, for fanciers to develop an expert eye for the breed, it helps if they see great dogs. Harras's legacy to the Fancy, other than as a breed type to try to emulate, were his children. In very limited breedings, Harras sired fifteen American champions. In the 1960s breeders were not so quick to ship bitches; in fact, only two individuals sent bitches to Harras, perhaps partly because of his age.

One of Harras's champion sons, the aforementioned Bengo, sired the first American-bred international champion. Int. & Am. Ch. Rodsden's Goro v. Sofienbusch, UDT, Can. UDTX., Mex. UDT, SchH I (out of Frolich v. Rau of Wunderkinder) was just half of a remarkable team—the other half being his owner/trainer/handler Jim Fowler. Goro and Jim lived in a high-rise apartment in Chicago, and before getting Goro, Jim had never trained a dog. It was not what one would consider the ideal situation in which to place a young male Rottweiler—and is still not—but few dog/human partnerships have been as exceptional. We used to joke with Jim that he would read a book on training, then tell it to Goro, and the next day Goro would master the routine. Obviously it was not as simple as that! But through the years we marveled at what extraordinary communication existed between Jim and Goro.

Although not many American bitches found their way to Harras, fortunately for the breed, many did in Europe. One of Harras' American champion offspring arrived in the United States first as a German Bundessieger.

The 1965 Bundessieger and Weltsieger, Int. Ch. Erno vom Wellesweiler, SchH I (out of Alke von Gomaringen, SchH II) was imported by Freeger Kennels. Of Erno, Muriel Freeman wrote in *The Complete Rottweiler*, "while he was not quite the phenotype of his sire, Harras vom Sofienbusch, he was nevertheless a showstopper." As a sire, he was also impressive. Two imported daughters from the same litter came to the United States and earned championships. Ch. Priska vom Kursaal (out of 1963 Bundessiegerin, 1964 Swiss Siegerin Assy von Zipfelbach, SchH II) became one of the foundation dams for Freeger Kennels, while her sister, Ch. Pia vom Kursaal, joined Quelle v.d. Solitude as a brood bitch at Rodsden.

Two of Erno's sons to have profound influence on the breed were littermates bred by Ms. Tony Huyskens of The Netherlands—Farro van het Brabantpark (out of Rona v.d. Brantsberg) at stud in Germany, and Ch. Falco van het Brabantpark, imported by Rodsden. More on Falco will appear later.

An imported Dutch Harras son on the West Coast was Ch. Bullino v.d. Neckarstroom (out of Recora v.d. Brantsberg), who was an important sire for the Panamint Kennels.

One of those far-thinking individuals to send a bitch to Harras was Mrs. William (Dorothea) Gruenerwald. Abington Aphrodite (a daughter of Ch. Arras von Stadthaus) whelped one puppy, which grew up to become Ch. Lorelei, the foundation bitch for the Gruenerwald Kennels. Dorothea

Gruenerwald continues her interest in Rottweilers today as one of our AKC breeder-judges of Rottweilers.

The Harras breeding to have the most influence on the American Rottweiler was surely the combination of Harras and Quelle v.d. Solitude. The first litter they produced consisted of one puppy who became Ch. Georg of Rodsden, CD. Georg, in turn, was the foundation sire for Mrs. Shelley Moore's Merrymoore Kennels. The second breeding produced a larger litter (to our relief), two of which made history in their day. Ch. Rodsden's Kurt v.d. Harque, owned by Marilyn Putnam in California and handled by Frank Housky, swept the West Coast competition in the show ring, whereas brother Ch. Rodsden's Kluge v. Harque, CD became an ARC Gold Producer, siring thirty-three champions. Incidentally, a question often asked is why wasn't Harras, the father of them all, also an ARC Gold Producer. One of the requirements is that the producer must have sired one offspring that earned an advanced working title in the United States, and while Harras had many schutzhund-titled offspring in Europe, none achieved CDX titles here.

Harras's impact on the American Rottweiler is almost impossible to fully outline. Consider the following example: Harras sired Kluge who sired thirty-three champions, one of which was Ch. Northwind's Donar of Rodsden, a Bronze ARC Producer who sired seven champions, one of which was Best in Show Winner, Ch. Rodsden's Kane v. Forstwald, CD, an ARC Gold Producer who sired twenty-two champions, one of which was Best in Show Winner Ch. Rodsden's Tristan v. Forstwald, CD, TD, an ARC Bronze Producer who has sired nine champions so far. Now imagine tracing the producing records of other Harras offspring.

The second individual who sent a bitch to be bred to Harras was Patricia Clark, then Lecuyer, of the Northwind Kennel in Canada. Her bitch, Can. Ch. Northwind's Tina (Ch. Dervis vom Weyershof ex Katherina's Adorn of Townview) could be traced back to the first American Rottweilers and old Erwin. Harras proved too old by this time, and so Tina was bred to Ch.

Ch. Rodsden's Kurt v.d. Harque (Harras ex Quelle), owned by Marilyn Putnam.

Rodsden's Kluge v.d. Harque, CD. From this combination came Am. & Can Chs. Northwind's Barras, Brikka, Danka, CD, Darras, Della, Dagmar, Dina, CD, Dolf and Donar of Rodsden. Thus the baton was passed from Harras to his son. Harras suffered a few small strokes and then died quietly in his sleep. We knew we would never see his like again.

With more Rottweilers and owners being more mobile, Kluge had the opportunity to be bred to a wider variety of bitches than Harras. Bred to Rodsden's Gypsy (a Bengo v. Westfalenpark daughter and herself an ARC Gold Producing dam), the Rodsden's "W" v.d. Harque litter included Ch. Rodsden's Willa v.d. Harque, UDT. Willa was the foundation bitch for Birch Hill Kennels and brought to the breed her owner, Jane F. Wiedel—again demonstrating that milestones in the breed aren't necessarily measured by the dog alone. In addition to breeding some of the most successful show and Obedience dogs of their day, Jane is also an AKC TD and TDX judge, and an AKC breeder-judge in conformation.

Another Kluge ex Gypsy offspring, Ch. Rodsden's Nomad v.d. Harque, became the foundation sire of the Radio Ranch Kennel. A Kluge daughter, Ch. Rodsden's Quelle v.d. Harque, UD, SchH II (out of Ch. Rodsden's Lady Luck, CD), owned and trained by Charles Goodman, became the first American-bred Rottweiler to earn a SchH II title.

During this time a number of outstanding German dogs were imported by Paul Harris, who was very active in Rottweilers, especially in the MRC, for a short time. The imports included Fetz vom Oelberg, SchH II, Bodo v. Stuffelkopf, Assi vom Dahl, a Fetz daughter and Axel v.d. Schwanenschlag. Fetz, an elegant dog, was unfortunately too sharp for the American show ring, so few were fortunate to see him. He was considered prepotent for good hips. Bodo, Assi, and Axel, however were shown and finished their championships. Assi was a sister to the "divine" Adda v. Dahl that many considered the most beautiful bitch of her day. She retired also to the USA and the home of Meyer and Ida Marcus where, unfortunately, she never produced a litter.

Through the late 1960s, the Harras grandchildren were proving themselves. In the East, an imported bitch, Ch. Cara v.d. Chausee, was bred to Kluge, producing among others Ch. Erika v. Schauer for the von Schauer Kennels of Robert and Meryl Schauer. Ch. Ferdinand v. Dachsweil, bred to a Kluge daughter, produced the Lyn-Mar Acre's "A" v. Kinta litter for veteran multiple Group judge Mrs. M. Lynwood Walton.

CH. DUX VOM HUNGERBUHL, SCHH I

If the 1960s were dominated by Harras and his descendants, the 1970s was a decade reflecting one terrific, little import from Germany.

This author remembers calling home from Germany. "I found a dog to import but be aware he's not real big." Back came a question from the other author, "Well Sue, if he isn't real big, is he real good?" He was *spectacular*, and out of his crate bounced Ch. Dux vom Hungerbuhl, SchH I.

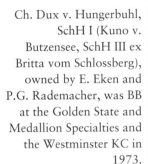

Ch. Dux v. Hungerbuhl, SchH I (Kuno v. Butzensee, SchH III ex Britta vom Schlossberg), owned by E. Eken and P.G. Rademacher, was BB at the Golden State and Medallion Specialties and the Westminster KC in 1973.

In 1971 the ADRK held its first "Specialty" show, the Klubsieger show in, of all appropriate places, Rottweil, Germany. Festooned with banners and attended by local bands and costumed natives, Rottweil, which at this time actually had no resident Rottweilers, welcomed with open arms its most illustrious (and successful) export. Dogs and owners came from all over Germany and spectators came from all over the world. Two brothers arriving for this show were destined to have tremendous impact on the breed on two continents.

International Ch. Bulli vom Hungerbuhl, SchH II (Kuno v. Butzensee ex Britta vom Schlossberg), the older brother, won a permanent place in history as the first ADRK Klubsieger. He repeated the title in 1972. The author had the opportunity to meet Bulli as he put on a charming and good-natured exhibition of ball playing prior to the Klubsieger show. Already a popular stud dog, Bulli would go on to be THE German stud dog of his era. One was struck by what a really "pretty" dog he was. And could there be another dog with as beautiful color? Perhaps a brother? Prior to the Hungerbuhls, we Americans tended to think of Rottweilers in terms of black with brown markings, or worse yet, black with tan markings. The words "mahogany" and "rust" came into fashion after the importation of Bulli's younger brother.

Dux vom Hungerbuhl, SchH I, arrived at the show with much less fanfare. He was slightly smaller than Bulli and much less known. Having a famous brother is perhaps the only reason that through "persistence, patience and damn good luck," Elizabeth Eken and Rodsden were finally able to import Dux. The good luck is that because the dog was imported at three years of age, the Germans, perhaps, were unaware of what they were losing in a stud dog. One Dux son active in Germany was Int. Ch. Benno vom Allgauer Tor, SchH III, FH (out of Evi vom Oberen Argental, SchH I) who succeeded Bulli as the stud dog of his era. One would be hard-pressed to decide whose influence was greater in Europe—Bulli's or Benno's. There is no doubt in the United States—it was MRC Hall of Famer Dux.

Perhaps the best way to describe Dux is to read an official critique of him written by a German breed warden at his breed approval test:

> Beautiful, middle-sized, strong, noble male, excellent in type; very good head, dark brown eyes, small well-carried ears, scissors bite; first-rate chest, straight strong back, excellent front and rear angulation, beautiful tight feet; rich rust coloring; gait is free and far-reaching; temperament is self-confident, lively, attentive, nerves firm with good courage and protection desire; superlative—without fault."

While a description like the preceding is one that an owner or breeder would love to plaster on a billboard outside the Westminster Kennel Club show, there is, in fact, no dog without fault. However, perhaps when evaluating a dog described by experts as, "exemplifying true greatness in phenotype and genotype . . . and as good movement as has ever been seen in the Rottweiler ring," one may be a bit blinded to any faults. For the record, Dux could have used more neck, and some felt he needed more forechest, while others thought him a bit straight in front.

His show career was successful enough to have pleased any owner—he is the first Rottweiler to whom the title BISS (Best in Specialty Show) was awarded when he won the first independent Rottweiler Specialty show in the United States—the Medallion Rottweiler Club Specialty in 1973, handled by Richard McKenney. That win had been preceded by his winning the Golden State Rottweiler Club Specialty earlier in the year. Dux also won Best of Breed at Westminster in 1973, handled by D. Roy Holloway.

It was as a producer, however, that his extraordinary phenotype shone through in his children and grandchildren. A sire of thirty-nine champion offspring, Dux inherited a title that we had amusingly given to Harras—"kennelmaker." A Harras granddaughter bred to Dux produced Ch. Rodsden's Windsong Phaedra, who was an early addition to Marcia Tucker's Sunnyside Kennel. (Mrs. Tucker is now an AKC Rottweiler judge.) Catherine Thompson, an ARC president and AKC breeder-judge, brought her Ch. Natasia v. Hohenreissach, CDX to Dux and produced her "A" von Gailingen litter—the first in a long line of Gailingen Rottweilers specializing in excellent conformation coupled with an aptitude for Obedience. In California, Margareta McIntyre bred her bitch, Ch. Freeger's Ingela, CDX, to Dux, establishing her own kennel name with the Gatstuberget's "E" litter. One of those puppies became Ch. Gatstuberget's Eskil Jarl, CD, who not only

Ch. Rodsden's Bruin v. Hungerbuhl, CDX (Dux ex Ch. Rodsden's Frolich Burga, CD, TD), owned, bred and trained by Jeff Kittner, was a multiple BIS winner, MRC Hall of Fame member and ARC Gold Producer. *Kullander*

"This picture worth a thousand words" of Ch. Eppo v.d. Keizerslanden, CDX, Can. CD, BH, imported and owned by Rodsden's Rottweilers was taken by his owners.

trotted into the winner's circle frequently in California, but trotted in with his owner Michael Grossman (Wencrest). Mike's association with Clara Hurley has produced the Powderhorn-Wencrest Kennel under whose banner some of the most outstanding examples of Rottweilers have been shown.

A breeding on the West Coast to Can. Ch. Jaheriss Baaca resulted in Maureen and Howard Wilkinson's Trollegen's "F" litter of dogs that were so very much like their sire in type.

It is to one dog, however, that Dux's legacy owes a great deal. When Ch. Rodsden's Frolich v. Burga, CD, TD, a granddaughter of Harras, was bred to Dux, the result was Ch. Rodsden's Bruin v. Hungerbuhl, CDX, bred, owned, and trained by Jeffrey Kittner and the foundation sire for Jeff and Geraldine Kittner's vh Kertzenlicht Rottweilers. Bruin was the unparalleled show dog of his day. It was a perfect pairing of Bruin and his handler, Brian Meyer, who brought the breed its first seven-time all-breed BIS winner. This

Am. & Can. Ch. Weissenberg's Don't-U-Dare, CD (Bruin ex Ch. Marlee Bear v. Gruenerwald, CD) owned by Beverlee and Marvin Smith. *Stephen Klein*

Belgian, Luxemburg Sieger Ch. Falco v.h. Brabantpark, MRC Hall of Fame, ARC Gold Producer, imported and owned by Rodsden's Rottweilers. *Booth*

was a remarkable record at the time because the Working Group had not yet been split into the Working Group and Herding Groups. Working was the largest variety Group at the time, and few judges had the opportunity to see many Rottweilers and develop an appreciation for the breed. Therefore, seeing a Rottweiler make it to the Best in Show ring was very unexpected. Winning so many Bests in Show implies that Bruin had to be campaigned vigorously, and he was. But it will always be to Jeff Kittner's credit that at the height of Bruin's conformation career, Jeff pulled Bruin to train for and

Ch. Rodsden's Ansel v. Brabant (Falco ex Ch. Rodsden's Gay Lady, TD), MRC Hall of Fame, ARC Gold Producer, owned by Ruth O'Brien.

earn his CDX title. That so many of the Kertzenlicht dogs carry advanced Obedience titles at the ends of their names reflects the Kittners' long dedication to the working aspects of the Rottweiler.

As a sire, Bruin produced fifty-one champion offspring, including Ch. Birch Hill's Hasso Manteuffel, CDX, TD, bred by Jane Wiedel and owned by Vicki Wassenhove. Hasso won the ARC, GSRC and MRC Specialties, as well as earning High in Trial honors, before an untimely death. A particularly lovely Bruin daughter was Ch. Weissenburg's Don't-U-Dare, CD, beloved by her breeder-owners Beverlee and Marvin Smith. Don't-U-Dare's successes in the show ring were matched by her record as a brood bitch.

Retired with Elizabeth Eken at the base of majestic Mt. Spokane in Washington state, Dux died at ten years of age with his beautiful color intact and nary a gray hair.

We will end the Golden Age by discussing two more European dogs— one by birth and the other by conception—and an American-bred dog to be proud of.

CH. FALCO V.H. BRABANTPARK

Ch. Falco v.h. Brabantpark was one of the first great dogs to be imported from Holland. A son of Erno v. Wellesweiler out of Dutch Ch. Burga v.h. Brabantpark, Falco arrived at Rodsden in 1972. Already carrying with him the title of Belgium and Luxembourg Sieger, Falco debuted in the American show ring at the 1972 MRC Specialty by going Best of Winners. He later won Best of Opposite Sex at the 1973 CRC Specialty.

Falco was the second in a line of American champions bred by a remarkable lady in Holland, Tony Huyskens. There are few, if any, American breeders who can match her successes in the American show ring, starting with Ch. Oda v.h. Brabantpark, TD, Falco, Ch. Jack v.h. Brabantpark, Ch. Dutch Daxter v.h. Brabantpark, Ch. Hans v.h. Brabantpark, Ch. Wasatch

Am. & Can. Ch. Zarras v. Brabant, Am. & Can. CD (Ch. Rodsden's Axel v. Brabant ex Ch. Oda v.h. Brabantpark, TD), MRC Hall of Fame, was also BB at the 1978 MRC Specialty, owned by Gwen Chaney and P.G. Rademacher.   *Joe C.*

Rock v.h. Brabantpark, CDX, Ch. Quinto v.h. Brabantpark, CD, Ch. Disco v.h. Brabantpark, through BIS winners Ch. Oscar v.h. Brabantpark, Ch. Quanto v.h. Brabantpark, right down to the top-winning Rottweiler (ARC system) for 1990 and 1991, the BISS and BIS winner, Ch. Nelson v.h. Brabantpark. Both Falco and Nelson are ARC Gold Producers. Tony also bred one of the very few ARC Gold Producing dams and an MRC Hall of Famer, Can. Ch. Wyvonie v.h. Brabantpark, CD, TD.

Falco sired twenty-five champions, one of which was Ch. Rodsden's Ansel v. Brabant (out of Ch. Rodsden's Gay Lady, TD). Owned by the late Ruth O'Brien, Ansel produced forty-nine champion offspring. Two particularly beautiful Falco sons were Ch. Rodsden's Axel v. Brabant (out of Ch. Rodsden's Lady Luck, CD) owned by Jayne Harstad and littermate Ch. Rodsden's Ander v. Brabant, a foundation sire for ToBant Rottweilers and Sheri Page. Axel sired Ch. Rodsden's Zarras v. Brabant, CD (out of Ch. Oda v.h. Brabantpark, TD), winner of the 1978 MRC Specialty and foundation sire for Earl "Chip" and Gwen Chaney's Ebenhaus Rottweilers. Zarras, in turn, sired Am. & Can. Ch. Birch Hill's Governor, CD (out of Rodsden's Birch Hill Bess, CD, TD) bred by Jane Wiedel. "Guv" and his owner Michael Conradt were an inspiration to owner-handlers everywhere as the team won numerous Specialties and all-breed Bests in Show. Governor produced 39 champion offspring.

Falco, ever a gentleman and one of the nicest housedogs one could hope for, outlived many of his children and died at age twelve at the Klem household.

In 1976 Gundi v. Reichenbachle (Berno v. Albtal, SchH III, FH ex Anje v.d. Wegscheide) was imported from Germany in whelp to Int. Ch. Elko vom Kastanienbaum, SchH I (Elko v. Kaiserberg, SchH I ex Gitta vom Bucheneck). From the resulting litter, a male puppy was kept to replace Falco. This puppy

Am. & Can. Ch. Birch Hill's Governor, Am. & Can. CD (Zarras ex Ch. Rodsden's Birch Hill Bess, CD, TD), owned and handled by Mike Conradt, is also an MRC Hall of Fame dog and ARC Gold Producer. *Martin Booth*

Am. & Can. Ch. Rodsden's Elko Kastanienbaum, CDX, TD, Can. CD (Int. Ch. Elko v. Kastanienbaum, SchH I ex Ch. Gundi v. Reichenbachle) MRC Hall of Fame, ARC Gold Producer, owned by Gary Klem.

Ch. Doroh's Just Grand, TD (Elko ex Ch. Doroh's Grand Escapade), a Specialty winner and MRC Hall of Fame member, owned by Dorothy Wade. *Bruce Harkins*

Am. & Can Ch. Birch Hill's Juno, CD, TD (Elko ex Ch. Rodsden's Birch Hill Bess, CD), MRC Hall of Fame, owned by Jane Wiedel.   *William Gilbert*

Am. & Can. Ch. Rodsden's Berte v. Zederwald, CDX, Can. CD (Elko ex Ch. Rodsden's Yana v. Nordwald), owned by Lew Olson, is a BIS and Specialty winner, MRC Hall of Fame member and ARC Gold Producer. *Kim Booth*

turned out to be Am. & Can. Ch. Rodsden's Elko Kastanienbaum, CDX, Can. CD. Named after his sire, our Elko was to bridge the gap from the Golden Age to modern times.

Best in Sweepstakes at the CRC in 1978, Elko went on to Winners Dog at the 1978 MRC Specialty. He finished with four majors, handled by a variety of handlers including one of the authors. He was the sire of 31 champions, one of whom, Ch. Doroh's Just Grand, TD (out of Ch. Doroh's Grand Escapade), was the first bitch to win BIS at the ARC National Specialty. This historically significant event took place in 1983. Just Grand was

Ch. Rodsden's Kane v. Forstwald, CD (Ch. Northwind's Donar of Rodsden ex Ch. Asta v. Forstwald, CD), owned by J. Klem and E. Thompson, is a multiple Specialty winner, an MRC Hall of Fame member and ARC Gold Producer. *Chuck Goodman*

bred and shown by Dorothy Wade, Doroh Rottweilers. Dorothy and her daughters, Ronnie and Monika, brought real professionalism to the owner-handler ranks as Dorothy watched and supported her daughters growing up in junior showmanship. It was rare back then, and continues to be unusual today, to see Rottweilers shown in Junior Showmanship.

Two Elko daughters bred by Jane F. Wiedel were Jane's own Ch. Birch Hill's Juno, CD, TD (out of Ch. Birch Hill's Bess, CD, TD) and her full sister, Frank Brader's Ch. Birch Hill's Nanna, TD. Juno not only won Winners Bitch at the 1980 MRC Specialty and Best of Opposite Sex at the 1982 CRC Specialty, but proved to be a great brood bitch and a loving companion. One of her sons was Ch. Birch Hill's Quincy, CD, TD, a dog found in many pedigrees today and cited as an example of a truly elegant Rottweiler. Nanna won Best of Opposite Sex at the 1983 MRC Specialty, and her son, Ch. Von Brader's Eiger (by Ch. Eiko vom Schwaiger Wappen, CDX, SchH III) was a BIS winner as well as a top producer for Frank Brader.

An Elko son, Ch. Rodsden's Berte v. Zederwald, CDX, Can. CD (out of Ch. Rodsden's Yana v. Nordwald), owned by Lew Olson, was BIS at the 1985 MRC Specialty. Of the thirty-nine champions sired by Berte, one of special note was Ch. Cannon River's Oil Tanker, CD (out of Panda's Tugboat Annie), bred and owned by Elfi and George Rice. Oil Tanker inherited Bruin's crown for the most BIS wins. He ended his show career by winning BIS at the MRC Specialty in 1989. Another Elko son, Ch. Donnarschlag v.h. Kertzenlicht, CDX (out of Phara vom haus Kertzenlicht, CD) became famous as the sire of Ch. Ironwood's Cade, CD (out of Ch. Disco v.h. Brabantpark). Many believe Cade to be the top producing Rottweiler of modern times.

Unfortunately, we were not able to enjoy Elko's retirement years as he died from bone cancer before becoming a veteran.

Ch. Rodsden's Tristan v. Forstwald, CD, TD, (Kane ex Ch. Rodsden's Roma v. Brabant), owned by Yvonne Fine, won the MRC Specialty in 1984 and 1988. *Kim Booth*

Ch. Goldeiche Ara von Brader, CD (Ch. Eiko v. Schwaiger Wappen, SchH III, CDX ex Ch. Rodsden's Hella v. Forstwald, TD), bred by Frank Brader, owned and handled by Dale Innocenti, is in the MRC Hall of Fame, is an ARC Gold Producer and won the Colonial Specialty in 1987 and 1989. *Bernard Kernan*

The Golden Age produced "golden crosses" in breeding. Two already mentioned were Harras with Quelle v.d. Solitude, and Kluge and Franzi vom Kursaal. A third for Rodsden was the pairing of Ch. Rodsden's Kane v. Forstwald, CD and Ch. Rodsden's Roma v. Brabant (a daughter of Falco). Kane, a son of Ch. Northwind's Donar of Rodsden and the import Ch. Asta vom Forstwald, CD, started his show career auspiciously with an MRC BIS in 1979 under ADRK judge Heinz Eberz. Two years later he won BIS at the CRC Specialty under the esteemed breeder-judge Muriel Freeman.

An MRC Hall of Famer and ARC Gold Producing sire of twenty-two champions, eleven of Kane's champion children were from the combination of Kane and Roma. One, Ch. Rodsden's Tristan v. Forstwald, CD, TD, went BIS at the 1984 MRC Specialty, repeated that win as a veteran in 1988, and in the intervening years won Bests in all-breed shows. Another, Ch. Rodsden's Hella v. Forstwald, TD, was the dam of another hugely successful show dog. Ch. Goldeiche Ara v. Brader, CD (Ch. Eiko v. Schwaiger Wappen, SchH III, CDX ex Hella) and Ara's owner-handler Dale Innocenti followed in the wake of "Guv" and Mike Conradt as dog and owner-handler team supreme.

Kane, Tristan and Kane's mother Asta, lived long and happy lives with Yvonne Fine, who today continues to enjoy the children, grandchildren, and great-grandchildren of the Kane ex Roma pairing.

There are many, many notable dogs that are by necessity not named in this chapter—but not unappreciated. Harras, Dux, Falco, Elko and Kane's, achievements, descendants and owners defined our particular experience during the Golden Age. What is apparent is that it was an age where individual dogs could influence the breed, and individual people could guide the Fancy. We look back with yearning to that time when we saw real improvement in the breed, knowing that today "saving the breed" may be beyond our reach.

Am. & Can. Ch. Donnaj VT Yankee of Paulus, CDX (Ch. Axel v. Schwanenschlag ex Ch. Amsel v. Andan), owned by Jan Marshall, was an all-breed BIS winner, a four-time Specialty winner and an ARC Gold Producer.

Chapter 3

Today's Rottweiler

If we were to give a title to the period from the ending of the "Golden Age," say 1980, to the present, we would be tempted to call it the "age of commercialization" or the "age of exploitation." Neither paints a very pretty picture of the breed for the last fifteen or so years.

What permeates the Fancy today is the sheer number of Rottweilers being bred—and never mind those dogs that are claimed as purebred but are not actually AKC-registered. From an annual AKC registration total in 1980 of 4,701 Rottweilers, in less than fifteen years the AKC now annually registers over 100,000 Rottweilers! With such an explosion in numbers, the breed was bound to face myriad problems; those dedicated to the breed have been forced to change how the breed is presented to the public.

Of course, not all changes have been for the worse. With a tremendous increase in the number of breeders and owners, there has been a considerable increase in the number of Rottweiler clubs. We have already discussed the big four—Colonial, Medallion, Golden State and American. To these can be added the following Rottweiler clubs which have been or probably will be working for AKC Specialty-giving status: Aloha State Rottweiler Club, Inc., Dallas/Ft. Worth Rottweiler Club Inc., Dogwood Rottweiler Club of Metropolitan Atlanta, Emerald Valley Rottweiler Club of Greater Cleveland, Greater Cincinnati Rottweiler Club, Great Lakes Rottweiler Club of Southeast Michigan, Greater New York Rottweiler Club, Gulfstream Rottweiler Club of Greater Miami, Inc., Mile-High Rottweiler Club of Greater Denver, Colorado, Northstar Rottweiler Club, Seminole Rottweiler Club of Greater Tallahassee, Rottweiler Club of Kansas City, Rottweiler Club of Knoxville, Wasatch Rottweiler Assoc. and Western Pennsylvania Rottweiler Club. There are many local clubs seeking AKC recognition that we have not named but which in the future will attract members and hopefully offer guidance in living with our wonderful breed.

CAMPEONATO MUNDIAL CANINO

Int. Ch. Dominican, Puerto Rican, Mexican, South American, Champion of the Americas, 1988 World Siegerin, Ch. Green Mtns. Flora, Am., Puerto Rican, Dominican CD, Mex. TD (Am., Can. Ch. Donnaj Green Mtn. Boy ex Rasmussen's Nasty Mounster), owned by Frank Fiorella, a MRC Hall of Fame member.

Most of these newly formed clubs have benefitted from the older clubs. Whereas the members of the CRC, GSRC and MRC went through painful metamorphoses in adopting codes of ethics, members of the new clubs joined organizations formed with codes already in place and modeled after those of the older clubs. The experiences the older clubs had in running shows, arranging matches, holding clinics and educating members served to guide the new clubs. And benefits flowed in both directions as fresh ideas and new approaches originating with the younger clubs were welcomed by the original four.

The relationship between the clubs changed somewhat with the AKC admission of the American Rottweiler Club as a member club. With a few exceptions, each breed has one member club, the national club or parent club, which represents the breed within the AKC. The member club sends a delegate who, as directed by that club, votes on all the issues brought before the AKC delegates. This includes changes to AKC rules and regulations, AKC policies, internal organization, and many other matters. On September 11, 1990 the ARC became a member club of the AKC.

For fifty-nine years the Rottweiler had been virtually "voiceless" within the AKC except for a cry for new breed standards (in 1979 and 1990) which the AKC heard. The CRC, MRC and GSRC had been, more or less, on equal footing with the national club. Each club separately requested permission from the AKC to hold sanctioned events. Organizations outside the AKC, such as the International Federation of Rottweiler Freunde (IFR, which will be discussed later), treated each club in much the same manner. The price for a voice was that the "big three" be relegated to a position below that of the ARC, even though, in the case of the MRC, the club was actually bigger than

The city of Rottweil takes its name from the red tiles of its roofs. Many of those red-tiled roofs are intact to this day.

Ch. Birch Hill's Nanna von Brader, TD, is as comfortable around the trappings of the breed's work as were her ancestors that actually did draw carts and tend herds. Nanna was owned and trained by Frank Brader.

Bundesseiger and Worldsieger for 1965 was Int. Ch. Erno vom
Wellesweiler, SchH I (Ch. Harras vom Sofienbusch ex Alke von
Gomarinegen, SchH II), imported and owned by Mrs. Bernard
Freeman.

Ch. Wasatch Rock v.h.
Brabantpark, CDX,
TD (Bundessieger, Int.
Ch. Benno v. Allgauer
Tor SchH III, FH ex
Dutch Ch. Odessa v.h.
Brabantpark), owned
by Sue Rademacher.

Ch. Ironwood's Cade, CD (Ch. Donnarschlag v.h. Kertzenlicht, CDX ex Ch. Disco v.h. Brabantpark), owned by George Chamberlin, has distinguished himself as a BIS winner, a member of the Medallion Rottweiler Club Hall of Fame and an American Rottweiler Club Top Producer. *John Ashbey*

Am. & Can. Ch. Cannon River Oil Tanker, CD (Rodsden's Berte v. Zederwald, CDX ex Panda's Tugboat Annie), owned by Elfi and George Rice, is one of the breed's greatest winners. A multiple Specialty and all-breed BIS winner, MRC Hall of Fame and ARC Gold Producer, he is shown in a Westminster Group third under the esteemed breed authority Muriel Freeman. *John Ashbey*

Ch. Mirko v. Steinkopf, SchH III, IPOIII, FH, CDX (Klubsieger, Bundessieger, Europasieger Dingo v. Schwaiger Wappen, SchH III ex Esta v. Steinkopf), owned by Dr. and Mrs. Richard Wayburn, claims an impressive list of international distinctions. The 1983 Klubsieger, he was also an all-breed and Specialty BIS winner, an international champion with numerous titles, an MRC Hall of Fame member and ARC Gold Producer. *John Ashbey*

Ch. Tobant's Grant (Ch. Nelson v.h. Brabantpark ex Tobant's Texas Tootsie), owned by Joseph W. Thompson, II and B. J. Thompson, a Specialty and all-breed BIS winner as well as an MRC Hall of Fame member.

Int. Dutch, Luxembourg, Belgian, Am., Can. Ch. Barto v't. Straotje, IPO III, Am. & Can. TD (Dingo v.d. Marorie, SchH I ex Int. Ch. Dutch Ch. Quinty v't. Straotje, IPO I), owned by Frank Fiorella, an MRC Hall of Fame member.

the ARC, and in the case of the CRC, MRC and GSRC, the clubs were much older. Although there were club members who resented having to ask permission of the ARC to hold AKC events that these clubs had, in many cases, been holding before the ARC existed, most members felt that having a voice at the AKC was worth the price.

The Rottweiler needed representation as its popularity approached present levels—that of being number two in AKC registrations in 1994 for all breeds. How did this large German utility breed bump out the popular little Cocker Spaniel for this august position? With a great deal of breeding and "a little help from our friends," that's how.

As you have read, we owed a great deal to the German fanciers who made imports available that improved the breed here in the United States. Those early imports were, for the most part, dogs of superior type. They were famous stud dogs past their prime, semi-retired show winners or dogs with impeccable pedigrees. We have no doubt that the goal of those German breeders was to help the fledgling Fancy in the United States. And, surely motivated in part by real pride in what Germany was producing, the breeders tried to send us some of their best. Sometime after the Golden Age, the Germans stopped taking us under their wing. The age of commercialization reached Germany, and we began calling it the "Age of the Imports."

Dog magazines now featured pages upon pages of listings of imported Rottweilers. The Americans created the demand, the Germans were filling it and both countries suffered for it.

"If it is German, it must be better" is a hard philosophy to shake when speaking about a breed that the Germans have so carefully developed and nurtured for a century. But even the Germans couldn't possibly be producing as many good dogs as were being advertised here, "just off the boat with schutzhund title in tow." Filling the demand has cost the German breeders

Ch. Nelson v.h. Brabantpark, (Simba v.h. Brabantpark ex Golda v.h. Brabantpark), owned by Clara Hurley and Mike Grossman, was a Specialty and all-breed BIS winner, a Systems top winner, MRC Hall of Fame member and ARC Gold Producer.

Am., Can. Ch. Pico v. Hegestrauch, BH (Arri v. Hertener Wappen, SchH III ex Gamba v. Giesenend, SchH I, owned by Diana and Robert Lane.

as well. How many great stud dogs have left Germany before the Germans realized they were gone?

That a large guard dog replaced a lap-sized companion dog in popularity says volumes about our current society. The fact that Rottweilers are so intelligent, so trainable, so protective and now so plentiful has made the breed the primary choice in some circles for a "thinking gun with four legs and a (docked) tail."

In 1995 there were 30, 950 litters of Rottweilers registered with the AKC. How many of those were bred by those who had invested enough in the breed

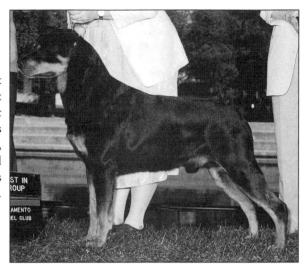

Ch. von der Lors Braxx Nelson (Nelson ex Friendships Midnight Sadie), owned by James and Gloria Kepler, a Specialty and all-breed BIS winner and a Systems top winner.

Ch. Powderhorn's Mile of Wencrest (Nelson ex Ch. Babsy v. Reinaartshof), owned by Clara Hurley, Michael Grossman and Missy Taylor, a Specialty and All-Breed BIS winner, and Systems top winner.

to join a breed club—let alone join a breed club with a mandatory code of ethics—is anyone's guess. We would suggest less than 10 percent. Breeding from poor-quality stock and lack of training and socializing for both adults and puppies has put our noble breed in jeopardy.

It is through education that conscientious breeders and Rottweiler clubs everywhere are trying to save the breed. We have a tremendous breed, but the ownership of a Rottweiler carries with it greater than average moral and legal responsibilities. AKC judge and columnist Deborah Lawson wrote, "In the wrong hands, the Rottweiler can be a disaster in the making, but for the

right person with the right attitude, the Rottweiler can be a dream dog."
Forewarned, let's now talk about the right people with their dream dogs.

WHO IS RIGHT FOR A ROTTWEILER?

Increased Rottweiler numbers means that we see more Rottweilers competing not only in the traditional AKC events such as Tracking, Obedience, and recently, Herding and Agility, but also in activities sanctioned by other organizations such as schutzhund, draft dog competitions, weight pulling, and therapy work. Therapy work is especially rewarding for those involved, who visit nursing homes, care centers and hospitals with their well-behaved Rottweilers. A dog that did a great deal to promote Rottweilers in therapy work was the exceptional 1983 German Klubsieger, Int. & Am. Ch. Mirko v. Steinkopf, SchH III, IPO III, FH, CDX (Klubsieger, Bundessieger, Europasieger Dingo vom Schwaiger Wappen, SchH III ex Esta vom Steinkopf), owned by Dr. Richard and Revera Wayburn. Although he was a top producer, two-time CRC BISS winner, as well as a multiple all-breed BIS winner, Mirko's greatest legacy to the breed may be that his outstanding service in therapy work inspired countless owners to have their dogs follow in his wake. The value to the breed from a public relations perspective is incalculable. Mirko was also the #1 Rottweiler "all systems" for 1985.

SYSTEMS, SYSTEMS, SYSTEMS

It was inevitable (because of human nature) that as the sport of purebred dogs grew, so did the interest in keeping track of which dogs were the big winners and producers. So various systems were developed to record such achievements. We have already mentioned in passing those production award systems for the CRC, MRC and GSRC. The first system, outside a specific breed club, was the Phillips System. This system was developed and first published in 1956 by the late Irene Castle Phillips (later Schlintz). The Phillips System became the *Kennel Review* System, and the first Rottweiler to make an appearance as a top producer was none other than Harras, followed in later years by son Kluge. Receiving a letter back in the 1960s from Mrs. Phillips notifying us of the award was a great surprise. With so many systems now in effect and profusely advertised, much of the "surprise" may have been lost for the owners of the winners, but certainly not the delight in having one's dog so distinguished.

Current systems, such as the Phillips System, which now is carried on by Mrs. Schlintz's daughter, are tabulated by individuals, by dog food companies such as the Pedigree System from Pedigree dog food, and dog magazines such as *ShowSight*, *Canine Chronicle*, *Dog News*, and *The Rottweiler Quarterly*. The latter magazine is yet another indicator of the Rottweiler's popularity. A national magazine owned and edited by Robin Stark and Tomi

Ch. Ironwood's Galahad, CDX (Ch. Donnerschlag v. Kertzenlicht, CDX, TD ex Ch. Disco v.h. Brabantpark), an MRC Hall of Fame member owned by Maureen Bourgeois.

Edmiston, this quarterly publication usually runs well over 400 pages of breed-specific articles, show reports and display ads in each issue.

Some systems are based on numbers of dogs defeated, some on Group placements and Best in Show wins, obedience and schutzhund systems on scores, and producer awards on number of champion offspring during a year's time. The systems Rottweiler owners can call their own are those of the breed clubs, and surely the two most respected are the MRC Hall of Fame and the ARC Gold Producers.

MRC HALL OF FAME (AS OF 1995, TITLES REFLECT THOSE EARNED AT TIME OF INDUCTION)

Int. Ch. 1960, '61, '62 Bundessieger, Am. Ch. Harras vom Sofienbusch, SchH I

Ch. Quelle von der Solitude, CD

Ch. Afra vom Hasenacker, CD, SchH I

Ch. Dirndl of Rodsden, CDX, TD

Ch. Rodsden's Felicia

Ch. Axel von der Taverne, UDT, Can. CD

Cicero vom Rich, CDX, SchH I

Ch. Rodsden's Kluge von der Harque, CD

Ch. Rodsden's Lady Luck, CD

Am., Can. Ch. Rodsden's Kato v. Donnaj, CDX, TD

Int. Ch., Am., Can. Ch. Rodsden's Goro v. Sofienbusch, Am., Can., Mex. UDT, Can. TDX, SchH I

Belgium, Luxembourg Sieger, Ch. Falco van het Brabantpark

Ch. Dux vom Hungerbuhl, SchH I Am., Can. Ch. Panamint Banner v. Hohenwald, Am., Can. CD, TD

Ch. Rodsden's Quelle von der Harque, UD, SchH II

Ch. Rodsden's Willa von der Harque, UDT, Can. CDX

Ch. Trollegen's Aparri, CD

Ch. Gatstuberget's Elegant Essi, UDT

Am. & Can. Ch. Birch Hill's Governor, Am. & Can. CD

Ch. Birch Hill's Hasso Manteuffel, CDX, TD

Ch. Dachmar Adah v.d. Barenhof, CDX, TD, SchH II

OTCH, Ch. Way-Mar's Disco Dawg, UD

Ch. Doroh's Fantastic Serenade, Am. & Can. CDX

Ch. Doroh's Just Grand, TD

Ch. Esmerald's Punch, UDT, SchH III

Am. & Can. Ch. Fraulein Anka Von Ascothaus, CDX, Can. UD

Am. & Can. Ch. Gamecard's Ninette

Can. Ch. Northwind's Juno, Can. CDX, SchH I

Ch. Rodsden's Anna Feeka Brabant, CDX, TDX

Ch. Rodsden's Ansel v. Brabant

Ch. Rodsden's Birch Hill Bess, CD, TD

Ch. Rodsden's Birch Hill Hanna, CDX, TD

Ch. Rodsden's Bruin v. Hungerbuhl, CDX

Am. & Can. Ch. Rodsden's Elko Kastanienbaum, CDX, TD, Can. CD

Ch. Rodsden's Frolich Burga, CD, TD

Ch. Rodsden's Frugl v. Brabant, UD, TDX, SchH III

Ch. Rodsden's Kane v. Forstwald, CD

Ch. Rodsden's Roma v. Brabant

Ch. Rodsden's Ussi vom Forstwald, UD

Am. & Can. Ch. Rodsden's Zarras v. Brabant, Am. & Can. CD

Am. & Can. Ch. Rodsden's Ander v. Brabant

Trollegen's Berg, Can. CD, Can. TDX, SchH III

Int. Ch., 1983 Klubsieger, Amer. Ch. Mirko von Steinkopf, CDX, SchH III, IPO III, FH

Arenenberg Albert Little, CD, TD, SchH III

Can. Ch. Winterland's Bubba, Can. CDX, TD, SchH III

Barsoom's Dejah Thoris, CDX, TDX

Ch. Gundi von Reichenbachle

Ch. Rodsden's Gay Lady, TD

Dutch, Belg. Ch., Amer. Ch. Oscar van het Brabantpark

Ch. Weissenburg's Blau Max

Ch. Asta von Forstwald, CD

Rodsden's Tara v. Ludwig, CD

Ch. Duke's Own Lady Bianca, CDX

Ch. Amsel von Andan, CD

Ch. Freeger's Ingela, CDX

Ch. Don Juan, UD

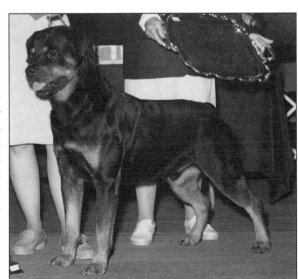

Ch. Beaverbrook's Eisen v. Bruin (Ch. Rodsden's Bruin v. Hungerbuhl, CDX ex Ch. Beaverbrook Alexa v. Iolkos), owned by Jerry Gomer and bred by Laura (Brewton) Catron.

Ch. von Der Lors Anastashia Cade (Ch. Ironwood's Cade, CD ex Friendships Midnight Sadie), owned and handled by Laura Worsham, was the seventh bitch to win a Specialty Best of Breed.

Ch. Alma Axa v. Aragoss, UD

Arrakis Brinka of Ebonstern, UD

Am. & Can. Ch. Birch Hill's Juno, CD, TD

Ch. Birch Hill's Minuteman, CD

Am. & Can. Ch. Birch Hill's Nanna v. Brader, TD

Birch Hill's Ouijt v. Hungerbuhl, UDTX, SchH II, FH, VB

Am. & Can. Ch. Birch Hill's Ringmaster, UDTX

Brimstone's Baron von Otto, SchH III, VB

Am. & Can. Ch. Cannon River Oil Tanker, CD

Diamond's Aim To Please, UDT

Ch. Dora v.h. Kertzenlicht, CD

Ch. Dux von der Blume, CDX, TDX, SchH III

Ch. Eppo v.d. Keizerslanden, CDX, Can. CD, BH

Ch. Gasto vom Liebersbacherhof, CDX, TD, SchH I

Gipfel's Calypso, CD, SchH III, VB

Ch. Graudstark's Luger, CD

Int. Ch., World Siegerin, Champion of the Americas, Am. & Can. Ch. Green Mtns. Flora, Amer./Puerto Rican/Dominican Republic CD, Mex. TD

Can. OTCH Haserway's Challenger, UDT

Haus Kalbas Leesha, Am. & Can. CDX, Amer. TDX

Ch. Heidi v.h. Kertzenlicht, Am. & Can. CDX, BH

Ch. Koskemo Furst Hasso, SchH III, FH

Kuno vom Dorfbrunnen, TD, SchH III, IPO III

Ch. Kyna vom Odenwald, CD

U-CD Lolita von Feldshausen, UDTX, Can. CD

Ch. Nancy von Tengen, SchH III, IPO III, FH

Ch. Pioneer's Beguiled

Ch. Rodsden's Axel v.h. Brabant

Am. & Can. Ch. Rodsden's Berte v. Zederwald, CDX

Rodsden's Happi v. Forstwald, CD, TDX, SchH I, VB

Ch. Rodsden's Heika v. Forstwald, CD, VB

Ch. Rodsden's Omar v. Wyko, UDT, SchH III

Ch. Roja's A Gumbo File, UD

Am. & Can. Ch. Weissenburg's Don't-U-Dare

William's Bronson von Grant, CDX, Can. CD, Am. & Can. TD, SchH III, IPO III, VB

Am. & Can. Ch., Can. OTCH Winterhawk's Chief Justice, UDT, Can. TD, VB

Can. Ch. Wyvonie van het Brabantpark, CD, TD

Ch. Von Brader's Eiger

Am. & Can. Ch. Goldeiche Ara v. Brader, Am. & Can. CD

Camas Valley Anna vom Ali, UDT

Int. Ch., Am. & Can. Ch. Barto v't. Straotje, TD, IPO III

Kuno vom Dorfbrunnen, TD, SchH III, IPO III, FH

Rodsden's Patton von Eppo, UD, TDX

Am. & Mex. Ch. Birch Hill's Magnum Opus, CD, Mex. CD

Welkerhaus In Diamonds, CDX, TD

Ch. Rodsden's Quito of Wylan, CDX, TDX, SchH III, IPO III, FH, BH

Ch. Donnerschlag v. Kertzenlicht, CDX, Can. CD, TD

Bron vom Frasertal, SchH III, FH

Ch. Trinity's Danke v. Dachmar, CDX

Bushwak's Ernie of Chutzpah, CDX, TD, SchH II

Ch. Birch Hill's Warwick, CDX, TDX, SchH I

Tealaska Aurora Beau, UD, Can. CD

Ch. Von Brader's Breena Medellin, CDX, Can. CD

Am., Can. & Mex. Ch. Quick von Siegerhaus, Am. & Can. CD, SchH I

Ch. Sara Die Kleine, CD

Ch. Inka v.d. Flugschneise, TD, SchH III

Klubsieger, Int. Ch. Bronco vom Rauberfeld, SchH III, FH (Int. Ch., Bundessieger Benno v. Allgauer Tor, SchH III, FH ex Centra v. Durschtal, SchH III), owned and handled by Felice Luburich, Best of Breed at the Colonial Rottweiler Club Specialty under judge Joan R. Klem.

Ch. von Bruka's Indra v. Yden (Ch. Eiko v. Schwaiger Wappen, SchH III ex Gundy v. Luckshof), owned by Liz Wertz.

Ch. Gasto v. Liebersbacherhof, CDX, TD, SchH I (Benno v. Amselhof, SchH III ex Dolli v. Liebersbacherhof), an MRC Hall of Fame member and ARC Gold Producer owned by Peter M. Rademacher and Sue Rademacher.

Am. & Can. Ch. Birch Hill's Quincy, CD, TD

Am. & Can. Ch. Mad River's Magnum von Worley

Ch. Tri-Lee's Champagne, CD

Ch. Seren's Atomahawk of Neshobe, CD, TD, SchH III

Am. & Can. Ch. Windrock's Flora von Richter, CDX, Can. CD, TD

Gypsy Rose von Holm, UD

Ch. Rodsden's Sun-Burst Truffa, CDX, TDX

Can. Ch. Rodsden's Lindenwood Lamia, Am. & Can. CDX, VB

Ch. Nelson van het Brabantpark

Birchhill Arno v. Blackforest, UDTX, Can. CDX

Ch. Twin Pine's Amber Again, CDX

Iayla vom Hausmiles, TD, SchH I, FH, BH

Rodsden's Iranda v. Foxbrier, UD, Can. CD, Mex. CDX

Ch. Nordike's Brinka v. Gruppstark, Am. & Can. CDX, BH

Von Gailingen's Mike Hammer, UD, TDX, Can. CDX

Triple Oak Woodland Liesel

Am. & Can. Gemstone's Aura of Brilliance, CD

Am. & Can. Ch. Goldeiche Brick v. Mikon, Am. & Can. CDX

Am. & Can. Ch. Rottidox Hurricane Hanna, Am. & Can. CDX

Ariel v. Haus Flusternder Wind, Am. & Can. CD, Can. CDX, Am. & Can. TD

Rodsden's Phaedra von Eppo, CD, TD, SchH III, BH

Ch. Boss v.d. Biestse Hoeve, CD, TD, SchH III, IPO III

Ch. Brinka von Ross, CD

Ch. Ironwood's Ella of Birch Hill, TD

Ch. Disco van het Brabantpark

Ch. Von Brader's Jem of Phantom Wood, CDX, Can. CD, TDX

Ch. Aryan's U.S.S. Ursula, CDX, TDX, SchH II

Am. & Can. Ch. Marksman von Turick, CD

Reba Richard v.h. Miacis, UD, Can. CDX

Am. & Can. Ch. Vanlare's Celebration, UD, Can. CDX

Ironwood's Guenevere, UDT

Am. & Can. Ch. Tri-Lee's Down the Road, TD

Arnie vom Bruhlhof, TDX, Can. TD, FH, BH

Dar-Don's Tasha von Quincy, Am. & Can. UD

Ch. Roxer's Rhiannon, CDX

Am. & Can. Ch. True Lee Chelsea v. Gunner, Am. & Can. CDX

Am. & Can. Ch. Whispering Winds Allura

Ch. Merrymoore's Imp von Dorow

Ch. Sophe von Bergenhof, CD

Langhoffen's Eick, UDT, SchH III, IPO III

Am. & Can. Ch. True Lee Copper v. Gunner, Am. & Can. CD, BH

Ch. Lyvngwerth's Devotion v. Ponca, CD

Ch. Tealaska Ringmaster's Espirit, CD, TDX

Nighthawk's Espirit, SchH II, BH

Ch. Ironwood's Cade

Am. & Can. Ch. Cannon River Destroyer, CDX, Can. CD, TD

Ch. Eagle Pt. Candi v. Immerlachen, CDX, TD, BH

Kaiser Rudolf v. Steinmetz, UDTX, Can. CDX

Am. & Can. Ch. Windrock Fanni von Richter

Tobant's Wotan, Am. & Can. CDX, Amer. TDX., Can. TD

Am., Can. & Mex. Ch. Perez's Amber von Roush, CD, PC

Baron OJ Von Yden, UD, Can. CDX, SchH I, B

Ch. Axel v.d. Marorie, CDX, Can. CD, SchH I, B

Ch. Helkirk Weissenburg's Chance

Am. & Can. Ch. True Lee Chelsea v. Gunner, Am. & Can. CDX

BIS, BISS, Costa Rican, Mex. & Am. Ch. Von Baker's Carbon Copy

BIS, BISS, Ch. Tobant's Grant

Macho v.d. Nedermolen, SchH III, B

Ch. Dago vom Kallenberg, CD

Rodsden's North Star von Eppo, UD, Can. CD

Ch. Farwest's Arizona, P.T.

Ch. Tina vom Bruhlhof Hawkhaven, CD, SchH I, B

Von Braders Liselotte, Am. & Can. CDX, TDX

Langhoffen's Havoc, CDX, TDX

Doroh's Orenda Von Arba, CD, Am. & Can. TDX

Ch. Black Jack von Dorrow, UD

Am. & Can. Ch. Blackwood Dante v. Lyvngwerth, Am. & Can. CD

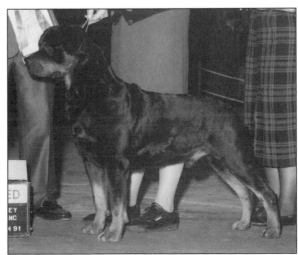

Ch. Von Gailingen's Matinee Idol, UDTX, Can. CDX, Agility 1 (Ch. The Fuhrer of Adamwald ex Von Gailingen's Lofty Ideals, CD), owned and trained by Cathy Thompson.

Ch. Winterhawk's Chief Justice, UDT, SchH I, MRC Hall of Fame member (sitting), Ch. Windrock's Flora v. Richter, CDX, TD MRC Hall of Fame (center) and Ch. Windrock's Fanni v. Richter, all MRC Hall of Fame members, owned and trained by Jane Justice.

Am. & Can. Ch. Lawler's Carly of Phantom Wood, CD, TDX, Can. CD

Ch. Nordike Breanna Gruppstark, Am. & Can. CDX

Ricklin's M One A One, SchH III, BH

HIT Walking H Dina Lee v. Deather, CD, PC

HIT Stefen Imzadie's Hannelore, CD, TDX, Can. CD

Gewitter's Argus, UD, TDX, Can. CD

Am. & Can. Ch. Windrock's Sophie v. Richter

Can. OTCH Tealaska Havoc at Dawn, UD

Am. & Can. Ch. Pico v. Hegestrauch, BH

Am. & Can. Ch. Von Boylan's Boldly Bridgette, CD, BH

Ch. Windrock's Jack Hammer

Ch. Vom Sonnenhaus Krugerrand, CD

Telem's Catherine the Great, CD, TDX, Can. CD

AMERICAN ROTTWEILER CLUB
GOLD PRODUCTION AWARD WINNERS (AS OF 1996)
(TITLES ARE THOSE LISTED BY THE ARC WHEN INDUCTED)
Gold Sires:

Ch. Birch Hill's Governor, CD

Ch. Birch Hill's Minuteman, CD

Ch. Birch Hill's Quincy, CD, TD

Brando vom Dattelner Hof, SchH II, FH

Ch. Cannon River Oil Tanker, CD

Ch. Dieter vom Konigsberg, CD

Ch. Donnaj VT Yankee of Paulus, CDX

Ch. Dux vom Hungerbuhl, SchH I

Ch. Eiko vom Schwaiger Wappen, CDX

Ch. Eppo von der Keizerslanden, CDX

Ch. Falco van het Brabantpark

Ch. Gasto vom Liebersbacherhof, CDX, TD

Ch. Goldeiche Ara von Brader, CD

Grave Kapenborgh, CD, SchH I

Ch. Igor von Schauer

Ch. Ironwood's Cade

Ch. Jack vom Emstal, CD, SchH I

Ch. Kokas K's Degen von Burga, CD, TD

Ch. Lyn-Mar Acres Arras v. Kinta

Ch. McCoy von Meadow, CD

Ch. Mirko vom Steinkopf, CDX, SchH III

Ch. Nelson van het Brabantpark

Ch. Panamint Otso v. Kraewel, UD

Ch. Quick von Siegerhaus, CDX, SchH I

Ch. Radio Ranch's Axel v. Notara

Ch. Rodsden's Ansel v. Brabant

Ch. Rodsden's Berte v. Zederwald, CDX

Ch. Rodsden's Bruin v. Hungerbuhl, CDX

Ch. Rodsden's Elko Kastanienbaum, CDX, TD

Ch. Rodsden's Kane vom Forstwald, CD

Ch. Rodsden's Kluge von der Harque, CD

Ch. Trollegen's Fable

Ch. Trollegen's Frodo, CD

Ch. Welkerhaus' Rommel, UD

Amboss v. Konigssiek, SchH III, IPO III, FH

Ch. Von Brader's Eiger

Ch. Von Hottensteins Hubabubba

Ch. Barto v't. Straotje, IPO III, TD

Ch. Cannon River Independence, CD

Oleo v.h. Schmidgall, SchH III, IPO III

Gold Dams:

Ch. Anka von Gailingen

Ch. Merrymoore's Imp von Dorow

Ch. RC's Gator Bel von Meadow

Rodsden's Gypsy

Ch. Rodsden's Lady Luck, CD

Ch. von Gailingen's Welkerhaus Cia, CD

Wyvonie van het Brabantpark, CD, TD

Ch. Aryan's USS Ursula, CDX, TDX, SchH I

BISS Ch. vom Sonnen-
haus Krugerrand, CD
(Belg. Ch. Grave Kapen-
borgh CD ex vom
Sonnenhaus Tanja v.
Vera), a Specialty winner
owned by
Joanne Cochran.

Ch. Roborotts Arco von Ilco, TD (Klubsieger Ilco v.d. Fusse Der Eifel ex Daggy v. Bierberger Winkel), a Specialty and all-breed BIS winner and Systems top winner, owned by Martin and Florence Thomson.

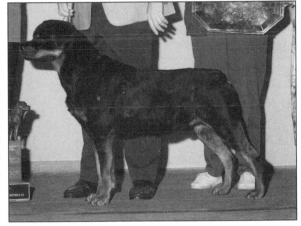

Ch. Nordike's Aluger v. Lindenwood (Scharf Elko v. Regenbagen, CDX ex Rodsden's Can. Ch. Lindenwood Lamia, CDX), owned by Thomas and Laura Wurstner, is a Specialty winner.

Ebonstern Bryt Promis v. Heller

Ch. Rodsden's Gay Lady, TD

Ch. Doro v.h. Kertzenlicht, CD

Ch. Tri-Lee's Champagne, CD

Not only did clubs and organizations present awards, but further honors were established in the names of famous dogs, some of which are still with us, but most of which have passed on. The Am. & Can. Ch. Donnaj VT Yankee of Paulus, CDX Memorial Trophy, the Ch. Anka von Gailingen Memorial Trophy, The Kato Bowl, and the Am. & Can. Ch. Birch Hill's Governor, CD

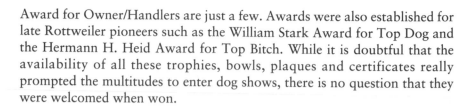

Award for Owner/Handlers are just a few. Awards were also established for late Rottweiler pioneers such as the William Stark Award for Top Dog and the Hermann H. Heid Award for Top Bitch. While it is doubtful that the availability of all these trophies, bowls, plaques and certificates really prompted the multitudes to enter dog shows, there is no question that they were welcomed when won.

SHOWS, SHOWS AND MORE SHOWS

Until the 1980s, a win at the CRC, MRC, GSRC and ARC Specialty shows assured the winning dog a place in history. These shows attracted the best of the Rottweilers being shown—and the most. Today, one isn't surprised to see entries at local dog shows rivaling those entries at early Specialties. There are dog shows somewhere in the United States every weekend of the year, with the exception of the Christmas and New Year's holidays, and at almost every show the Rottweiler has the largest breed entry. With all this competition, it is no surprise that exhibitors clamored for more Specialties. The local breed clubs responded by pursuing AKC recognition and eventually hosting their own Specialties, and the ARC created "regional Specialties" where the ARC supported a local breed club that had not reached AKC Specialty status by designating a show of the breed club's choice as an ARC regional Specialty.

With all these Specialties being held, one would think the original Specialties would be lost in the crowd. However, the CRC, MRC and ARC remain the largest Specialties, and in fact, the MRC Specialties for the last three years have been the biggest Rottweiler Specialties not only in the United States but anywhere in the world.

The "German-Style Shows"

If two Rottweiler enthusiasts with their dogs meet in a parking lot, they will soon be gaiting them around in friendly competition. So strong is the desire to compete that the Rottweiler owner is constantly on the lookout for new venues to prove his dog's value. The "German-style shows" were welcomed by many who felt that the rigid, somewhat sterile atmosphere of the AKC show could be improved upon. These shows, held outdoors in informal settings, with class descriptions copied from German shows and officiated by foreign experts, offered the exhibitor an enticement absent at almost all AKC shows—written critiques by the judges. Whereas a few Specialty clubs such as the MRC and GSRC had offered critiques at their Specialties when the judges had been foreign experts, it was these German-style shows that really promoted the idea of having the judge's evaluation on paper, in the exhibitor's hand before he left the show.

These shows began in the late 1970s with individuals or working dog organizations. The shows were well-attended and, without a doubt, listening to an expert give detailed critiques was an education well worth traveling a distance to receive. These shows were basically matches, because no titles or awards were recognized by anyone other than those hosting the events. The value of a match should not be dismissed, particularly in the case of the German-style shows where the exhibitor has an opportunity to have his dog evaluated through the eyes of an expert. The problem with the German-style shows was that fanciers began to take them too seriously.

German style shows began mushrooming around the country and at each there mushroomed a sieger (translated as champion) title. A major criticism of these U.S. shows is the use of the sieger title. In Europe, certain shows are designated as sieger shows, and the dog that wins is awarded the sieger title. This title is recognized by the *Federation Cynologique Internationale* (FCI) and consequently all the countries under the FCI, and the title will appear in the ADRK stud book if the dog is German.

It would appear that all American German-style shows are designated sieger shows. However, the sieger titles are recognized only by the organization running the show. Some of these shows are affiliated with national clubs that promote the working aspects of the Rottweiler and copy the ADRK system of breed testing and rules as much as possible. The American Rottweiler Verein and the United States Rottweiler Club are two examples; some of the shows are simply sponsored by a local group of fanciers. Great confusion arises when, in advertising, the "Ottumwa Sieger" or the "Peotone Sieger" is simply advertised as a "sieger," and one has no idea whether the advertiser is referring to a title awarded locally or in Europe.

Ch. Windrock's Jack Hammer (Ch. Pioneer's DJ Star Stuben, CD ex Ch. Windrock's Sophie v. Richter), all-breed BIS winner and Systems top winner, owned by Matt and Lorene Jones.

BIS, BISS Am. & Can. Ch. Windrock's Rolex (Ch. Goldeiche Brick v. Mikon, UD ex Ch. Windrock's Fanni v. Richter), a Specialty and all-breed BIS winner and a Systems top winner, owned by Bonnie Rosenberg.

BISS, BIS Am., Can. & Bda Ch. Pioneer's DJ Star Stuben, Am. & Bda CD (Ch. Ironwood's Cade, CD ex Ch. Pioneer's Das Bedazzled, CD) owned by Joan Eversole, a Specialty and all-breed BIS winner and Systems top winner.

So popular are these shows that it became apparent that foreign judges, particularly the ADRK judges, found themselves passing each other in the airways as they officiated at German-style shows all over the United States. The proliferation of these shows was not unnoticed by the ADRK and the German Kennel Club (VDH or *Verband fur das Deutsche Hundeswesen*) who found their judges increasingly "on vacation in America." The German Kennel Club responded by making a rule that German judges could officiate only at American shows sanctioned by the AKC. This left our American German-style shows with a problem as to where to fill the increasing call for foreign experts. Filling in for German judges came German breeders, retired judges, and judges from countries other than Germany. The German-style show became the "German-style show that may or may not be judged by a real judge."

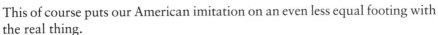

This of course puts our American imitation on an even less equal footing with the real thing.

As an entertaining alternative to AKC shows and, depending on the expertise of the judge, as a learning experience, these German-style shows will continue to offer something of value to the Fancy. Sometimes what they offer is to affirm our belief that our very best dogs can compete with the best of any other country anywhere in the world.

The Very Best

From our discussions with foreign breed experts officiating at both AKC and American German-style shows, our best are certainly competitive with theirs, yet few of our American dogs get to foreign shows. An example of a successful foray into the foreign show world is the first American-bred, International champion bitch, Int. Ch., Dominican, Puerto Rican, Mexican, South American, Champion of the Americas, 1988 World Siegerin & American Ch. Green Mtns. Flora, American, Puerto Rican/Dominican CD, Mex. TD (Am. & Can. Ch. Donnaj Green Mtn. Boy ex Rasmussen's Nasty Mounster) bred by Anthony Attalla and owned by Frank Fiorella. Frank also owned a dog whose exceptional attributes, first recognized in Europe, shone but too briefly in the New World. Int., Dutch, Luxembourg, Belgian, Am., Can. Ch. Barto v't. Straotje, IPO III, Am., Can. TD in a career cut short by cancer became an ARC bronze producer and MRC Hall of Famer. His most titled offspring is Select Ch. Boss v.d. Biestse Hoeve, CD, TD, SchH III, IPO III (out of Dagmar v.d. Biestse Hoeve) owned and trained by Ken Hemmerich. Imported from the Netherlands as a puppy, Boss has matured into a dog that we all would love to either own or say we bred, or say we trained! He is an example of a dog that has achieved success in both AKC and German-style shows.

During the Golden Age, we could reminisce about our very good dogs with firsthand knowledge. Today, no matter how frequently we judge, nor how far afield, we simply cannot have the pleasure of meeting all those Rottweilers worthy of being remembered as exemplary. So it is with regret that we must limit our discussion to a few of those dogs of which we have personal acquaintance.

Long-term influence is registered on a breed in two ways—through top show winners or top producers. So like the actor who wins both an Oscar and an Emmy, the Best in Show Rottweiler that is also a top producer is memorable, indeed. Ch. Ironwood's Cade, CD, owned and bred by George Chamberlin, Ch. Nelson v.h. Brabantpark (Simba v.h. Brabantpark ex Golda v.h. Brabantpark), bred by Tony Huyskens of the Netherlands, owned by Clara Hurley and Michael Grossman, and Ch. Rodsden's Berte v. Zederwald, CDX bred by Julie Wilson and Joan Klem and owned by Lew Olson all from the late 1980s and early 1990s gave their long-term influence to the Rottweiler.

BIS, BISS Ch. Andrecas Aramis von Der Mond, CD (Ch. Black Jack v. Dorow UD ex Cira v.d. Dorenburg, CD, SchH I), a Specialty and all-breed BIS winner and Systems Top Producer, owned by Robert Simmons.

Ch. Amberhaus Freyja, CD (Ch. Amberhaus Elijah v. Ara, CDX ex Ch. Sun-Burst Amberhaus Alexa, CD), a Systems top winner, owned by John and Diane Fugman.

Ch. Lindenwood's Bouncer, CD (Ch. Gasto v. Liebersbacherhof, CDX, TD, SchH I, ex Ch. Heika v. Forstwald, CD), owned by Linda and Bill Michels.

As top producers, these dogs have all sired Best in Show winners. In fact, Nelson is a BIS grandpa through son BIS, BISS Ch. Tobant's Grant (out of Tobant's Texas Tootsie) bred by Sheri Page and Sherilyn Sheridan and owned by Joseph and B.J. Thompson. Grant in turn sired BISS winner Ch. Serrant's Bannor (out of Ch. Tobant's Honey Bun v. Whelan), bred and owned by the Thompsons and Scott Russell. Two Nelson sons who have both vied for beauty wins in California are BIS winner Ch. Von Der Lors Braxx Nelson (out of Friendships Midnight Sadie), owned by Gloria and James Kepler and bred by Laura Worsham, whose kennel includes the lovely veteran bitch, Ch. Von der Lors Anastashia Cade (Ch. Ironwood's Cade, CD ex Friendships Midnight Sadie) and BIS Ch. Powderhorn's Mile of Wencrest (out of Ch. Babsy v. Reinaartshof) owned by Clara Hurley, Michael Grossman and Missy Taylor and bred by Clara and Mike. If it sounds like success runs in a family, it does. An example is Cade and two full brothers from a repeat breeding, Ch. Ironwood's Galahad, CDX owned by Maureen Bourgeois and Ch. Ironwood's Gremlin owned by Laura Catron of Beaverbrook fame. Laura is a double threat to those who compete against her as she has produced many outstanding dogs such as 1986 MRC Specialty winner Ch. Beaverbrook's Eisen v. Bruin and is also a superb handler.

Nelson, as we have mentioned, was not whelped here and proves that with all the Rottweiler imports to the United States, there were bound to be a few outstanding ones. Two imports who contributed significantly to the breed were both memorable movers. Klubsieger, Int., Am., Can. Ch. Bronco vom Rauberfeld, SchH III, FH (Int. Ch. Benno vom Allgauer Tor, SchH III, FH ex Centa vom Durschtal, SchH III) was imported by Felice Luburich in the early 1980s. To see him charge around the ring was to understand what is meant by reach and drive. Ch. Eiko vom Schwaiger Wappen, SchH III, CDX (Igor vom Kastanienbaum, SchH III ex Klubsieger, Bundessieger, Int. Ch. Anka v. Lohauserholz, SchH III, FH) is one of our ARC Gold producers and a dog of outstanding type. Sire of two BIS winners, Ch. Goldeiche's Ara von Brader, CD and Ch. Von Brader's Eiger, he also produced beautiful daughters such as Group placing Ch. Von Bruka's Fiona, CD (out of Von Bruka Alpha Girl) and Ch. Von Bruka's Indra v. Yden (out of Gundy v. Luckshof) for his owners Karen Billings and her late husband, Bruce.

An especially attractive import of the 1990s (now a veteran) in the American show ring is Ch. Pico vom Hegestrauch, BH (Arri vom Hertener Wappen, SchH III ex Gamba vom Giesenend, SchH I) owned by Diana Lane. Pico won the Stud Dog class at the 1995 ARC specialty, demonstrating again that one can never underestimate the influence of German bloodlines

In the 1980s, our involvement with imports came in the form of three males whose personalities could not have been more different. ARC Bronze producer Ch. Dux von der Blume, CDX, TDX, SchH III (Klubsieger, World Sieger, Bundessieger, Europa Sieger, Int. Ch. Nero vom Schloss Rietheim, SchH III, FH ex Gora vom Wildberger Schloss), owned by Peter M.

Ch. Epic's Adultress (Ch. Birch Hill's Governor, CD ex Ch. Donnaj Happy Hooker), owned by Bob and Rose Hogan.

BISS, BIS Am. & Can. Ch. Jade Hagen Kodiac, CDX, Can. CD (Ch. Von Brader's Eiger ex Liebs Kraus v. Baker, CD), owned by Ernest McDowell, a Specialty and all-breed BIS winner.

Rademacher, sired five champions including a Canadian BIS winner, Ch. Rodsden's Kraus Miller, CDX TD (out of Ch. Rodsden's Toni vom Forstwald, Am. & Can. CD), owned by Carl Faust. However, Dux was at his most memorable in the Schutzhund ring where his devotion to Pete and focus on the sport were undeniable. Whereas Dux was the happiest in the company of Pete on the working field, our next import simply liked being with everyone.

Ch. Gasto vom Liebersbacherhof, CDX, TD SchH I (Benno vom Amselhof, SchH III ex Dolli vom Liebersbacherhof) accompanied us home from a visit to Germany and right into our affections as one of the most agreeable Rottweilers we've ever known. "Grimm" became an ARC Gold producer. One son, Ch. Rodsden's Danzig v. Gasto, CD, TD (out of Ch. Rodsden's Toni v. Forstwald, Am. & Can. CD), owned by Gene Banta, was both a specialty and all-breed BIS winner.

Ch. Rodsden's Hester v. Forstwald, CD (Am. & Can. Ch. Rodsden's Elko Kastanienbaum, CDX, TD, Can. CD ex Ch. Asta v. Forstwald, CD), owned by Dr. Yvonne Fine.

If a picture is worth a thousand words, then there is no better description of ARC Gold producer Ch. Eppo v.d. Keizerslanden, CDX, Can. CD, BH (Fulko v. Tannewald, SchH III ex Walda v.d. Keizerslanden) than the picture taken of him which has appeared in many publications, including the cover of the ADRK's newsletter, *Der Rottweiler*. With limited socialization living on a dairy farm in Holland, Eppo moved into the Klem household and quickly adapted to suburban life. While never demonstrably affectionate, he was very tolerant of everyone and earned his CDX title as a middle-aged dog. For a dog who came so late to working, Eppo sired a great many dogs whose trainability found expression in numerous working titles. Two cases in point are sons Hardi von der Markenrichter, which was the 1985 working champion of Holland and our own MRC Hall of Famer Ch. Rodsden's Quito of Wylan, CDX, TDX, SchH III, IPO III, FH (out of Can. Ch. Wyvonie v.h. Brabantpark, CD, TD) owned by Ron Maloney and Sue Rademacher and trained and shown to his championship by Brian Meyer and his working titles by Ron.

One must always remember that successes on the working field are not just dependent on the natural ability of the dog but also on good luck in getting the right dog to the right owner. Case in point, Maryanne Butler's experience with training a dog began with her first Rottweiler, a Wyvonie son, Ch. Rodsden's Omar of Wyko, UDT, SchH III (by Am. & Can. Ch. Rodsden's Elko Kastanienbaum, CDX, TD, Can. CD). Finding she was as good at working Rottweilers as she was at giving elegant dinner parties, MaryAnne trained and seriously competed with her next Rottweiler, Ch. Inka v.d. Flugschneise, TD, SchH III (Bundessieger, Klubsieger, Int. Ch. Falko v.d. Tente, SchH III ex Konny vom Liebersbacherhof, SchH I). Now training her third Rottweiler, an Inka son, towards a SchH III, MaryAnne is a past president of the MRC

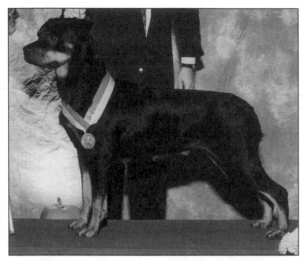

Ch. Helkirk Weissenburg's Chance (Ch. Mr. Impressive of Helkirk ex Ch. Weissenburg's Fury), a Systems top winner and MRC Hall of Fame member, owned by Ann Stroud.

Ch. Gamegard's Moonraker (Ch. Pioneer's DJ Star Stuben, CD ex Ch. Gamegard's Femme Fat'al), a BISS winner owned by Ellen Walls.

Schutzhund Verein. Owner/trainers like Ron Maloney and MaryAnne Butler do a great deal for their dogs' breeders' stature in the Rottweiler Fancy.

Periodically there is a call from the Fancy expressing the opinion that the working breeds should demonstrate working ability and that champions from breeds in the Working Group be required to also possess an obedience degree. The top-winning, top-producing Rottweilers who also have advanced AKC working titles are to be greatly admired. Dogs such as Ch. Rhomark's Axel v. Lerchenfeld, UDT (Ch. Elexi von der Gaarn ex Ch. Chelsea de Michaela, CD), owned by Ken and Hildegaard Griffin; Ch. Panamint's Otso v. Kraewel, UD (Black vom Golderbach ex Ch. Cilly vom Uhlbachtal), owned by Howard and Beverly Hendler; Ch. Welkerhaus Rommel, UD (Circle ML's Aster ex Wonnemund), owner Rita Welker; Ch. Dachmar's Adah v.d. Barenhof, UDT (Ch. Panamint Zyklon von Watzenhof, CD ex Ch. Barenhof

Ch. Rivera's Anka (Ch. Von Brader's Kalif, CD ex Von Brader's Orrie), owned by Jeff Long.

Amby of Arrow Ranch, CDX SchH II), owned by Charles and Mary Long and Donna Hames; Ch. Heidi v.h. Kertzenlicht, UD, Can. CDX, BH (Am. & Can Ch. Van Tieleman's Cisco, CD ex Ch. Contessa v.h. Kertzenlicht), owned by Jeff and Linda Gregg; Ch. Roja's A Gumbo File, UD (Ch. Koka's K's Degan von Burga ex Ch. Haserway's Regal Fancy), owned by Patricia Storer; Seren's Arabeske, UD, Can. CD (Am. & Can. Ch. Donnaj VT Yankee of Paulus, CDX ex Ch. Doroh's Fantastic Serenade, Am. & Can. CDX), owner San Brooks; Am. & Can. Ch. Von Gailingen's Dassie Did It, UDT, Can. CD (Ch. Srigo's Zarras v. Kurtz ex Ch. Anka von Gailingen) and Ch. Von Gailingen's Matinee Idol, UDTX (Ch. The Fuhrer of Adamwald ex Von Gailingen's Lofty Ideals, CD), owner/breeder Catherine M. Thompson, prove that being successful in the conformation ring or the whelping box does not preclude training and successfully competing for advanced titles.

Demonstrating working ability in their dogs is one tool that breeders and owners can use to dispell some of the public's apprehension regarding the strength and power of the guard dog breeds. The AKC statistics from 1994 point out that among the working breeds, the Rottweiler leads the field in almost all working categories. However, before patting ourselves on the back we should remember that 455 Rottweilers earning companion dog degrees does not look particularly impressive in an annual registration of over 100,000 dogs! Breeders must encourage their puppy owners to take their dogs through obedience and, of course, many do. It isn't luck that frequently dogs with the same kennel name also have working titles. Breeders like Jeff Gregg (Cimmerron), Janna Morgan (Gatstuberget-Evrmor), Joan Reifman (Haserway), Peter and Marilyn Piusz (Seren), Norma Dikeman (Nordike), Jane Justice (Windrock), Catherine Thompson (Von Gailingen), Walter and Esther Putirskis (Amberhaus), and Karla Kastern Ebert (Phantom Wood) practice what they preach and can be found active in the various phases of obedience competition.

Ch. Von Brader's Icelander, CD (Am. & Can. Ch. Birch Hill's Governor, Am. & Can. CD ex Ch. Von Brader's Elsa) a Systems top winner, and all-breed BIS winner owned by James and Eleanor Jackson.

Ch. Von Hottenstein's Up an At 'em (Ch. Von Hottenstein's Hubabubba ex Ch. Von Hottenstein's Sassafras), owned and handled by Nancy Reynolds.

Ch. Baron v. Roxer, CD (Ch. Weissenburg's Lucifer v. Roxer, CD ex Baroness v. Raschke, Am. & Can. CD), a BIS winner and Systems top winner, owned by Walter and Jan Stevens.

Being the only breed in the Working Group where there are substantially more dogs earning obedience degrees than championships, one would suppose that greater value is placed on earning working titles. However, among serious breeders—and by serious we exclude puppy mills that breed for profit, backyard breeders who simply choose the mates for their dogs by convenience and proximity and the sentimental breeder who breeds to produce that one puppy in hopes of duplicating the parent but has no idea what to do with the rest of the litter—the interest is in improving what is already there. To the serious breeder, a championship indicates that others in addition to the dog's owner and breeder deem the dog a quality specimen. This puts a burden of responsibilty on today's judges to honestly evaluate a dog's championship potential. This subject will be discussed in a later chapter, but suffice it to say that a championship is a major consideration when choosing breeding stock and a big factor when selling a dog. A championship title affects a dog's breeding future much as a college degree enhances a person's job prospects.

Unfortunately, as not all breeders are serious breeders, there is a great multitude of puppies being produced whose futures are anything but certain.

RESCUE

In the Golden Age we rescued Rottweilers; we just did it quietly and didn't call it rescue. Breeders took back those puppies that for some reason, and usually not the fault of the puppy, didn't fit in their new homes, or we found new homes for the older dogs who suddenly found themselves homeless, or for the few unfortunate who turned up in animal shelters or pounds, we traced them back to their breeders so that they could rescue their own stock. Rottweilers were a relatively rare commodity, so a lost one, an abandoned one or a mistreated one caused quite a stir in the Rottweiler community.

Today, with between 2,000-3,000 litters registered a month, with the average litter size at seven puppies, multiplication says that it is impossible to trace every abandoned dog back to his or her breeder, and Rottweiler rescue has become a nationwide concern. We doubt there is a Rottweiler club in the country that hasn't debated and formulated some policy regarding a rescue program. The bottom line for all the clubs is that breeders should be responsible for their own puppies. But from there on up to rescuing dogs whose backgrounds are totally unknown, bred by breeders whose interest in their puppies cease with their sale, policies vary and often heated arguments result.

Should all Rottweilers be rescued? Do all Rottweilers deserve to be rescued? Can the clubs afford to do it? What are the legal implications of placing rescue dogs? These are all questions that the clubs have asked themselves in developing rescue policies. It is little wonder that these policies vary greatly from club to club. And to quote one of our authorities on rescue, Marylou Stott, who chairs the MRC Rescue committee, "The Rottweiler does not rescue well." The Rottweiler is a strong character in a strong body and to evaluate the character of a dog whose background is unknown and place it in a new home takes a better expert than most of the owners and breeders are.

After many years of engaging in actual rescue, the Colonial Rottweiler Club's current policy is to present funds to those clubs and individuals active in rescue, thus aiding rescue without the club officially doing it. There are many truly dedicated Rottweiler fanciers, such as Sandra Gilbert, Jill Rudd, and Dr. Evelyn Ellmann, who engage in rescue for the noblest of reasons— because they love the breed. At the national Specialty for the American Rottweiler Club, the parade of rescued Rottweilers honors those who unselfishly open their homes to these dogs and the dogs fortunate enough to have found new homes.

The Houston chapter of the American Rescue the Rottweiler Foundation states it was formed for the sole purpose of rescuing, rehabilitating and placing abandoned, abused and destitute Rottweilers into loving and caring homes. It has been said that this organization has relocated over 300 Rottweilers. Most clubs fall somewhere between the CRC and the ARRF in their rescue programs, although there is little doubt that these programs are constantly being reevaluated.

With some bias we feel that at the present the most workable rescue program for a Rottweiler club, which would have limited funds for that activity, would be similar to the rescue program used by the Medallion Rottweiler Club. Therefore, we list the MRC Rottweiler rescue guidelines that were written by MRC rescue chairman Marylou Stott and the MRC Board of Directors.

1. If the breeder is unknown, the first step shall be to contact the breeder or the person from whom the dog was obtained.

2. Any Rottweiler that has bitten will be denied rescue.

3. Any Rottweiler that has a positive heartworm test will be denied rescue.

4. All Rottweilers will be character-evaluated by a selected committee.

5. Before a Rottweiler will be fostered or removed from a home, all owners of the dog must relinquish ownership.

6. All Rottweilers being turned over by current owners will be checked with the local health department for any registered bite.

7. Prospective owners must fill out the necessary forms and be interviewed by a selected rescue committee person.

8. All applications will be cleared through the committee chairperson.

9. Medical and/or other expenses incurred will be collected when the dog is adopted, from either the new owner or some recompense from the rescue fund.

Am., Can., Mex. & Int. Ch. Quick v. Siegerhaus, Am. & Can. CDX, SchH I (Ch. Birch Hill's Hasso Manteuffel, CDX, TD ex Ch. Maid v. Siegerhaus), a Systems top winner and MRC Hall of Fame member, owned by Tom and Carol Woodward.

Am. & Can. Ch. Von Boylans Boldly Bridgette, CD, BH (Ch. Pico v. Hegestrauch, BH ex Cora v.d. Waldachquelle), a Specialty and Systems top winner, owned by Diana and Robert Lane.

10. If in the event that a breeder is notified, refuses to help, and is an MRC member, all information regarding the dog and its ancestry will be published in the MRC newsletter.

We in the breed have to make many unhappy decisions—not to breed the beautiful but dysplastic dog, not to promote the handsome dog of dubious character, and not to rescue those dogs who may harm the breed's reputation or pose a possible threat to others. And it is that last decision that is the most controversial.

Ch. Gruppstark's Alex v. Bastille, CDX, SchH I (Ch. Borris v. Grenzlandring, CDX ex Legacy's Gretchen v. Bastille, CDX), owned by Arthur Grupp.

Am. & Can. Ch. Wisteria's Bismark v. Fruhling, Am. & Can. CDX (Ch. Gatstuberget's Maximus, CD ex Ch. Gaerta's Wandering Wisteria)—Best in Specialty Show from the Veterans Class, at eight years. Owned and handled by Nancy Hawkins.

What isn't controversial is the pride the Rottweiler Fancy feels for our genuine four-legged heroes.

THE HEROES

The Rottweiler who rushes into a house during a California earthquake and saves a child from a falling refrigerator, the Rottweiler who drags his handicapped mistress from a burning van, the Rottweiler who brings a phone to his fallen master, and those Rottweilers who despite cut and bleeding paws continued to search through the rubble in Mexico City and Oklahoma City when other search and rescue dogs had stopped are the heros we celebrate.

In the April 30, 1995 issue of the *Sunday Oklahoman*, an advertisement entitled "an open letter of gratitude" ran which read in part:

> In the midst of our sorrow over the tragic bombing, I want to pay special tribute to workers whose unflagging devotion has brought us both tears and inspiration. They have names like "Kodiak" and "Zeke." They have trusting eyes and they walk through broken glass and over sharp edges of concrete and steel on wounded paws looking for people who need to be found. And they never give up.

Like the human race, there are more good Rottweilers than bad ones It is just that we don't hear enough about the good and too much about the bad.

Today there are more areas for success within the breed thanks to the programs set up in the various Rottweiler clubs, more activities that one can try with a Rottweiler due to new events in and outside AKC performance formats, and hopefully a better awareness by owners and breeders of the moral and legal responsibilities of owning one or more of this remarkable breed.

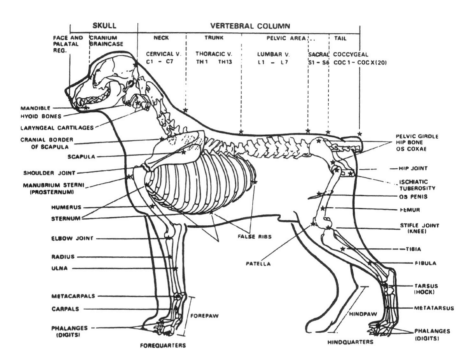

SKULL		VERTEBRAL COLUMN				
FACE AND PALATAL REG.	CRANIUM BRAINCASE	NECK	TRUNK	PELVIC AREA		TAIL
		CERVICAL V. C1 – C7	THORACIC V. TH1 TH13	LUMBAR V. L1 – L7	SACRAL S1 – S6	COCCYGEAL COC1 – COC X(20)

MANDIBLE
HYOID BONES
LARYNGEAL CARTILAGES
CRANIAL BORDER OF SCAPULA
SCAPULA
SHOULDER JOINT
MANUBRIUM STERNI (PROSTERNUM)
HUMERUS
STERNUM
ELBOW JOINT
RADIUS
ULNA
METACARPALS
CARPALS
PHALANGES (DIGITS)
FOREPAW
FOREQUARTERS

FALSE RIBS
PATELLA

PELVIC GIRDLE HIP BONE OS COXAE
HIP JOINT
ISCHIATIC TUBEROSITY
OS PENIS
FEMUR
STIFLE JOINT (KNEE)
TIBIA
FIBULA
TARSUS (HOCK)
METATARSUS
PHALANGES (DIGITS)
HINDPAW
HINDQUARTERS

ANATOMY OF A ROTTWEILER

(Reprinted from the Rottweiler in England, Midland Rottweiler Club 1985)

Chapter 4

A Comparison of Rottweiler Standards

In 1990 the American Kennel Club accepted the revised Standard as presented by the Rottweiler's National parent body, the American Rottweiler Club. Only the parent club in any AKC-recognized breed can submit changes or revisions to its breed Standard for acceptance by the AKC. And, what is a Standard? It is a written description of the ideal or typical specimen of that particular breed, including a description of the character and movement (gait).

As we have learned from the history of the breed, it was the ADRK in Germany that developed, nurtured and wrote the first "modern" Standard for the Rottweiler. You might call it the original parent club. Under the rules of the *Federation Cynologique Internationale* (FCI), the umbrella organization for kennel clubs in Continental Europe and a number of countries in other parts of the world, the country of origin of the breed establishes and can submit revisions to the FCI Standard. Through their wisdom and discipline and use of the breed in the ADRK, a marvelous working dog was developed for the world to enjoy. In the United States, we have a tremendous responsibility to maintain this marvelous breed and one way to do that is to keep the AKC-approved breed Standard as close as possible to the FCI/ADRK Standard. The 1990 revised AKC Standard does attempt to do that. Here is a comparison of the two 1990 Standards:

AKC REVISED STANDARD

Approved May 8, 1990—Effective June 28, 1990

In the late 1980s, the AKC decided it wanted to have all breed Standards conform to the same general format and use the same terminology, so it notified the "parent" clubs that they had to comply with these requirements as soon as possible. Many breed clubs objected to this arbitrary ruling and did not comply but the ARC had wanted an excuse to revise the Rottweiler Standard as the 1979 revision was not what the original committee had suggested. For one thing it allowed three missing teeth before the dog was disqualified. It had been patterned after the Doberman Pinscher Standard, which did and still does allow three missing teeth. (Very few Standards carry a tooth disqualification.) So the ARC seized the opportunity and revised the Standard as of June 1990.

Four years later, the AKC reversed itself on this, so only those who rushed to comply actually ended up doing it. Uniformity also meant very sterile, unimaginative Standards. It also did not allow for an Introduction or short historical summary and explanation of the function of the breed, which is so important for an owner, breeder or judge to understand. The authors would surely like to see the Standard revised again so that it could include some of the great descriptive German turn of phrase, which really helps articulate the essence of the breed to the novice. Maybe we could "sneak" in phrases such as Hans Korn's, "a dog with unfailing good humor . . . with willingness to forget unpleasant events." I would like to get "refinement" in there, as Herr Pienkoss writes,

Refinement implies in the dog, descent from forbears which rose above the average in form and working performance. A dog with refinement is also one which is beautiful, noble and proud looking. Size is not the main feature of the refined dog, but beautiful, clear outlines and a harmoniously proportioned body. Refinement does not express itself only in the form, but also in posture and character. Temperament without pushiness, courage without wildness, friendliness with a touch of reserve.

Oh, well, we will just have to work with what we have as of 1990!

INTRODUCTION
FCI STANDARD NO 147F
ROTTWEILER

Country of Origin: Germany
Specific Breed Suitability: Companion, Protector and Working Dog

FCI Classification

Group II (Schnauzer and Pinscher, Molossers and Swiss Mountain Dog varieties). Section 2.1: Molosser, Mastiff type.

Short Historical Summary

The Rottweiler is believed to be among the most ancient of breeds. His origin stems from Roman times, in which era he performed the duties of guard and drover dog. When the Roman Legions traversed the Alps, the dogs accompanied them, protecting the soldiers and driving the herds. Settling in the area of Rottweil, the Roman Army dogs came into contact with dogs native to the area. The natural result was an interbreeding of the two.

The principal duties of these hybrids remained the guarding and driving of large herds, and the defense of their masters and the masters' property. As there was a large concentration of the dogs in the vicinity of the Old German Empire City of Rottweil, the dog acquired the name Rottweiler-butcher Dog.

The butchers bred this type of dog solely for its working ability and for their personal use. With the passage of time, an outstanding guarding and drover dog, as well as cart dog, was the result. In addition, with the dawn of the 20th Century, when the police were soliciting service dogs, the Rottweiler was tested. It was readily recognized that the dog was admirably suited to this type of duty. As a result, in 1910 the Rottweiler was officially recognized as a police dog.

The objective in the breeding of Rottweilers is to produce a powerful yet vigorous dog, black with rust (mahogany) clearly defined markings, which despite its substance is stamped with an air of nobility and is capable of fulfilling the role of companion, guard and working dog.

AKC: 1.   General Appearance

The ideal Rottweiler is a medium-large, robust and powerful dog, black with clearly defined rust markings. His compact and substantial build denotes great strength, agility and endurance. Dogs are characteristically more massive throughout with larger frame and heavier bone than bitches. Bitches are distinctly feminine, but without weakness of substance or structure.

FCI: 1.   General Appearance of the Dog

The Rottweiler is a medium-large, robust dog, neither gross nor slight, nor spindly. In correct proportion he is compactly and powerfully built, indicating great strength, maneuverability, and endurance.

AKC: Size, Proportion, Substance

Dogs—24 inches to 27 inches, Bitches—22 inches to 25 inches, with preferred size being mid-range of each sex. Correct proportion is of primary importance, as long as size is within the Standard's range. The length of body from prosternum to the rearmost projection of the rump is slightly longer than the height of the dog at the withers, the most desirable proportion of the height

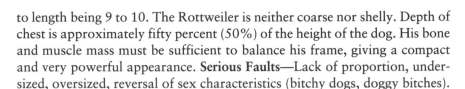

to length being 9 to 10. The Rottweiler is neither coarse nor shelly. Depth of chest is approximately fifty percent (50%) of the height of the dog. His bone and muscle mass must be sufficient to balance his frame, giving a compact and very powerful appearance. **Serious Faults**—Lack of proportion, undersized, oversized, reversal of sex characteristics (bitchy dogs, doggy bitches).

FCI: 2. Important Proportions

The length of the body measured from the point of the prosternum (breastbone) to the rear of the pelvic edge (ischial protuberance) should exceed the height at the highest point of the withers by 15%.

3. Demeanor and Character

He is descended from friendly and peaceful stock and by nature loves children, is affectionate, obedient and trainable and enjoys working. His rough appearance belies his ancestry. His demeanor is self-reliant, with strong nerves and fearless character. He is keenly alert to, and aware of, his surroundings.

AKC: Head

Of medium length, broad between the ears; forehead line seen in profile is moderately arched; zygomatic arch and stop well developed with strong broad upper and lower jaws. The desired ratio of backskull to muzzle is 3 to 2.

Forehead is preferred dry, however some wrinkling may occur when the dog is alert.

Expression is noble, alert, and self assured. **Eyes** of medium size, almond shaped with well-fitting lids, moderately deep-set, neither protruding nor receding. The desired color is a uniform dark brown.

Serious Faults—Yellow (bird of prey) eyes, eyes of different color or size, hairless eye rim.

Disqualifications—Entropion. Ectropion.

Ears of medium size, pendant, triangular in shape; when carried alertly the ears are level with the top of the skull and appear to broaden it. Ears are to be set well apart, hanging forward with the inner edge lying tightly against the head and terminating at approximately midcheek.

Serious Faults—Improper carriage (creased, folded or held away from the cheek/head).

Muzzle—Bridge is straight, broad at base with slight tapering towards tip. The end of the muzzle is broad with well-developed chin. Nose is broad rather than round and always black.

Lips—always black; corners closed; inner mouth pigment is preferred dark.

Serious Faults—total lack of mouth pigment (pink mouth).

Bite and Dentition—Teeth 42 in number (20 upper, 22 lower), strong, correctly placed, meeting in a scissors bite—lower incisors touching inside of upper incisors. Serious Faults—level bite; any missing tooth.

Disqualifications—Overshot, undershot (when incisors do not touch or mesh); wry mouth; two or more missing teeth.

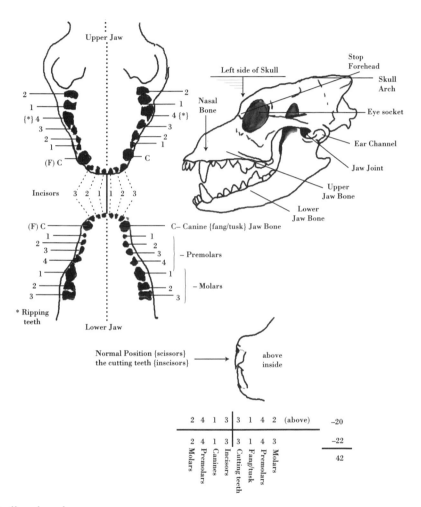

Skull and teeth.
From *The Regulations Regarding Breeding Matters for the Rottweiler Dog*, reprinted by permission of the ADRK.

FCI: 4. Head

4.1. SKULL

Medium-long, the backskull broad between the ears, the forehead line seen from the side only moderately arched. The occiput is well developed without protruding excessively.

4.2. FOREFACE

Nose—The bridge of the muzzle is straight, broad at the base and slightly tapering. Nose is large, rather broad than round, always black with proportionately large nostrils.

Muzzle—Must never be long or short in comparison to the backskull.

Lips—Black, close-lying with the corners closed; gums should be dark.

Jaw—Strong, broad upper and lower jaw.

Cheeks—Pronounced cheek-bones (zygomatic arch).

Dentition—Complete (42 teeth) bite is strong with the upper incisors closing like a scissors over those of the underjaw.

Eyes—Medium-large, almond shaped, of dark brown color with tightly fitting lids.

Ears—Medium-large, pendant, triangular, set well apart and high. When brought forward, well-placed ears will broaden the appearance of the backskull.

AKC: Neck, Topline, Body

Neck—Powerful, well muscled, moderately long, slightly arched and without loose skin.

Topline—The back is firm and level, extending in a straight line from behind the withers to the croup. The back remains horizontal to the ground while the dog is moving or standing.

Body—The chest is roomy, broad and deep, reaching to elbow, with well-pronounced forechest and well-sprung, oval ribs. Back is straight and strong. Loin is short, deep and well muscled. Croup is broad, of medium length and only slightly sloping. Underline of a mature Rottweiler has a slight tuck-up. Males must have two normal testicles properly descended into the scrotum.

Disqualification—Unilateral cryptorchid or cryptorchid males.

Tail—Tail docked short, close to body, leaving one or two tail vertebrae. The set of the tail is more important than length. Properly set, it gives an impression of elongation of the topline; carried slightly above horizontal when the dog is excited or moving.

FCI: 5. Neck

Powerful, moderately long, well-muscled, slightly arched, without dewlap or throatiness.

6. Body (Trunk)

Back—Straight, strong, tight; loin is short, strong and deep.

Croup—Broad, medium-long, gently sloping, neither flat nor steep.

Chest—Roomy, broad and deep (approximately 50% of the height of the dog at the withers) with a well-developed forechest and well-arched ribs.

Abdomen—Flanks not drawn up.

Tail—Docked short so that one or two tail vertebrae remain.

AKC: Forequarters

Shoulder blade is long and well laid back. Upper arm equal in length to shoulder blade, set so elbows are well under body. Distance from withers to elbow and elbow to ground is equal. Legs are strongly developed with straight, heavy bone, not set close together. Pasterns are strong, springy and almost perpendicular to the ground. Feet are round, compact with well arched toes, turning neither in nor out. Pads are thick and hard. Nails short, strong and black. Dewclaws may be removed.

FCI: 7. Quarters

7.1. FOREQUARTERS

Overall—Seen from the front, the forelegs are straight and not set close together.

Seen from the side, the lower leg is straight. The shoulder angulation should approximate 45%.

Shoulder—Well placed.

Upper Arm—Lying correctly on the body.

Forearm—Strongly developed and muscular.

Pasterns—Somewhat springy, strong and not steep.

Feet—Round, well closed and well knuckled, pads hard, nails short, black and strong.

Authors' note—ADRK Standard directs breeders to leave the front dewclaws on to achieve as natural a dog as possible. We feel leaving the dewclaws on can lead to injuries to the dewclaws, as well as, the fact that novices often forget to trim these extra nails. Further, the front legs appear cleaner without those nobby dewclaws in place.

AKC: Hindquarters

Angulation of hindquarters balances that of forequarters. Upper thigh is fairly long, very broad and well muscled. Stifle joint is well turned. Lower thigh is long, broad and powerful, with extensive muscling leading into a strong hock joint. Rear pasterns are nearly perpendicular to the ground. Viewed from the rear, hind legs are straight, strong and wide enough apart to fit with a properly built body. Feet are somewhat longer than the front feet, turning neither in nor out, equally compact with well arched toes. Pads are thick and hard. Nails short, strong and back dewclaws must be removed.

FCI: 7.2. HINDQUARTERS

Overall—As seen from the rear, the rear legs are straight and not set close together. In a natural stance, the articulation between the upper thigh and the lower thigh forms an obtuse angle.

Upper Thigh—Moderately long, broad and very muscular.

Lower Thigh—Long, powerful and heavily muscled, sinewy with strong tendons, well-angulated, not steep.

Feet—Somewhat longer than the front feet.

AKC: Gait

The Rottweiler is a trotter. His movement should be balanced, harmonious, sure, powerful and unhindered, with strong forereach and a powerful rear drive. The motion is effortless, efficient and ground-covering. Front and rear legs are thrown neither in nor out, as the imprint of hind feet should touch that of forefeet. In a trot the forequarters and hindquarters are mutually coordinated while the back remains level, firm and relatively motionless. As speed increases, the legs will converge under the body toward a center line.

FCI: 8. Movement

The Rottweiler is a trotter. The back remains firm and relatively motionless. The gait is harmonious, positive, powerful and free with long strides.

9. Skin

Skin on head is tight-fitting but allowance is made for some wrinkling when dog is alert.

AKC: Coat

Outer coat is straight, coarse, dense, of medium length and lying flat. Undercoat should be present on neck and thighs, but the amount is influenced by climatic conditions. Undercoat should not show through outer coat. The coat is shortest on head, ears and legs, longest on breeching. The Rottweiler is to be exhibited in the natural condition with no trimming.

Fault—wavy coat. **Serious Faults**—Open, excessively short or curly coat; total lack of undercoat; any trimming that alters the length of the natural coat. **Disqualification**—long coat.

FCI: 10. Coat

10.1. QUALITY

Consisting of outer coat and under coat. The outer coat is medium long, coarse, thick and straight. The under coat must not show through the outer coat. On the back of the rear legs the hair is somewhat longer.

AKC: Color

Always black with rust to mahogany markings. The demarcation between black and rust is to be clearly defined. The markings should be located as follows: a spot over each eye; on cheeks; as a strip around each side of muzzle, but not on the bridge of the nose; on throat; triangular mark on both sides of prosternum; on forelegs from carpus downward to the toes; on inside of rear legs showing down the front of the stifle and broadening out to front of rear legs from hock to toes, but not completely eliminating black from rear of pasterns; under tail; black penciling on toes. The undercoat is gray, tan, or black. Quantity and location of rust markings is important and should not exceed ten percent of body color.

Serious Faults—Straw colored, excessive, insufficient or sooty marking; rust marking other than described above; white marking any place on dog (a few rust or white hairs do not constitute a marking). **Disqualifications**—Any base color other than black; absence of all markings.

FCI: 10.2. COLOR

Black with sharply defined dark reddish-brown markings on the cheeks, muzzle, under the neck, on the chest and legs and also over the eyes and under the tail.

11. Height and Weight

HEIGHT OF MALES 61 TO 68 CM

61 to 62 cm = small (61 cm = 24 inches)

63 to 64 cm = medium

65 to 66 cm = large = ideal size (66 cm = 26 inches)

Weight: about 50 kilos (about 110 lbs)

HEIGHT OF BITCHES 56 TO 63 CM

56 to 57 cm = small (56 cm = 22 inches)

58 to 59 cm = medium

60 to 61 cm = large = ideal size

62 to 63 cm = very large

Weight: about 42 kilos (about 92 lbs)

AKC: Summary

Lack of proportion, undersized, oversized, reversal of sex characteristics (bitchy dogs, doggy bitches). Yellow (bird of prey) eyes, eyes of different color or size, hairless eye rim. Improper carriage (creased, folded or held away from the cheek/head). Total lack of mouth pigment (pink mouth). Level bite; any missing tooth. Coat fault—wavy coat. Open, excessively short, or curly coat; total lack of undercoat; any trimming that alters the length of the natural coat. Straw colored, excessive, insufficient or sooty marking; rust marking other than described above; white marking any place on dog (a few rust or white hairs do not constitute a marking). **Faults**—The foregoing is a description of the ideal Rottweiler. Any structural fault that detracts from the above-described working dog must be penalized to the extent of the deviation.

FCI: 12. Faults

Overall—Light-boned, poorly muscled, insufficient leggy appearance.

Head—Houndy, too narrow, weak, too short, too long, or too coarse, shallow forehead (faulty or insufficient stop).

Foreface—Long or pointed muzzle, ram or split nose, convex or concave bridge of the muzzle, light or spotted nose.

Lips—Open, pink-colored or flecked lips or lips with open corners.

Jaw—Narrow underjaw.

Cheeks—Overly prominent cheeks.

Bite—Level or even bite.

Ears—Too low-set, heavy, long, leather too thin, pulled back in such a manner as to stick up, and ears that are not properly carried.

Eyes—Light, protruding (lids not fitting tightly) too deep set, too big or too round eyes.

Neck—Too long, thin, poorly muscled neck, dewlap or throaty.

Body—Too long, too short, narrow.

Chest—Flat-ribbed rib cage, shallow rib cage.

Back—Too long, weak or swaybacked, roach backed.

Croup—Steep croup, too short, too flat or too long.

Tail—Too high-set or too low-set.

Forequarters—Narrow-set or crooked forelegs. Straight shoulder, faulty or deficient elbow placement; too long, too short or too straight upper arm; weak or straight pasterns; spread toes, too flat or too arched toes, stunted toes, light nails.

Hindquarters—Poorly muscled thighs, sicklehocked or cow-hocked or bow-legged, too little or too much angulation. Dewclaws on.

Skin—Wrinkled head skin.

Coat Condition—Soft, too short, too long or curly, lacking under coat.

Color—Incorrect color, poorly defined, too extensive markings.

AKC: Disqualifications

Entropion, ectropion. Overshot, undershot bite (when incisors do not touch or mesh); wry mouth; two or more missing teeth; Unilateral cryptorchid males. Long coat. Any base color other than black; absence of all markings. A dog that in the opinion of the judge attacks any person in the ring.

FCI: 13. Disqualifying Faults

Overall—Obvious reversal of sex characteristics (bitchy dogs or doggy bitches).

Demeanor—Anxious, shy, cowardly, gushy, vicious, excessively suspicious (distrustful), nervous animals.

Eyes—Entropion, ectropion, yellow eyes, two eyes of different color.

Dentition—Overshot, undershot, dogs with missing premolars or molars.

Testicles—Unilateral cryptorchid or cryptorchid males. Both testicles must be well-developed and properly descended.

Coat—Exceptionally long and curly coated.

Color—Dogs that do not have the typical black ground color in combination with correctly placed brown markings; white marks.

CLOSING THOUGHTS ON THE STANDARD

The FCI Standard, as you can read, does not give instructions to the handler in the show ring, or the judge. Its emphasis is instructional toward breeding as the Standard is, of course, a part of the breed rules under the breed warden system of the ADRK. This is allowable because the ADRK carries its own stud book.

The AKC, on the other hand, while not being able to enforce any breed rules (any litter will get registered if the sire and dam were registered), it does tell the judges when to excuse and/or disqualify. The AKC Standard stipulates that while an aggressive or belligerent attitude towards other dogs should not be faulted, a judge shall excuse from the ring any shy Rottweiler and if a dog, in the opinion of the judge, attacks any person in the ring the dog shall be disqualified. Although the latter is not mentioned in every Rottweiler Standard, any dog that attacks a person in the ring will be disqualified in every country in the world.

As we read through and compare the two Standards, it is nice to realize that they have, indeed, been describing the same dog. This same vision of a breed makes it infinitely easier to import Rottweilers for breeding or to judge them in foreign countries.

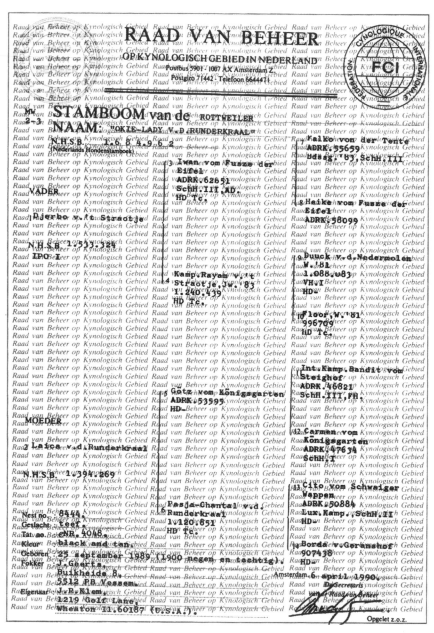

The Dutch pedigree of Okie-Lady v.d. Runderkraal, bred by J. Geerts and imported by Joan R. Klem.

Experiencing Our Changing AKC

Every person involved with purebred dogs has had some experience with the American Kennel Club, even if only to register the family dog with the AKC so that it will have "papers." But if you are interested in owning a purebred dog, or expect or want to become actively involved in the sport, you must know as much as possible about the purebred dog umbrella organization—the American Kennel Club. If the general public knew just a little more about the AKC, it would be a big help to dog owners; perhaps it would dispel some of the misunderstandings and criticisms of what the AKC does or is able to do, and what the AKC does not or cannot do.

The American Kennel Club was established in 1884 as a nonprofit organization devoted to the advancement of purebred dogs. It had two primary goals: to maintain a registry of recognized breeds, and to adopt and enforce rules and regulations governing dog shows and performance events. Over the years, its scope of interest has expanded, as has its number of registrations, dog shows, performance events and rules. But the AKC only has jurisdiction over the areas stated in its charter. In other words, AKC can suspend, fine or expel people and clubs from AKC privileges for violations to its rules, but it cannot close down kennels or related operations for health reasons or for inhumane treatment of dogs; only a local or county government has the authority to do that. If, upon inspection for an AKC rule or registration violation, unhealthy situations are found, the AKC representative can alert local authorities.

If a person registers ten or more litters during a year, the AKC sends an inspector to check on that person's record keeping and his "dog keeping."

The AKC admits clubs as members, not individuals. Most member clubs (Specialty clubs, all-breed and Group clubs, Obedience clubs and field trial clubs) elect officers and directors, who elect or appoint a delegate to attend quarterly AKC meetings. The delegates, in turn, elect a Board which meets every month and, together with its committees and the AKC staff, discusses, researches, elaborates on and applies the rules, regulations and policies under which the AKC operates as the recognized umbrella club for the sport of purebred dogs in the United States. (Not all clubs are members; many are sanctioned by AKC to hold events but have no official voice in AKC policy-making.)

Today, the AKC fosters and encourages interest in the health and welfare of purebred dogs in addition to promoting responsible dog ownership. Approximately 170 members of the 400-person staff are located at the AKC headquarters in New York City, while another 185, including the staff of Registration and Information Services, are located in Raleigh, North Carolina. The remaining personnel support the AKC's dog shows, performance events and inspection programs in the field throughout the United States.

Not all of the AKC rules pertain directly to the Rottweiler, although just about everything the AKC does or doesn't do affects all of us involved with purebred dogs in some way. Since this book is concerned only with Rottweilers, we intend to make you aware of only those rules that have a direct impact on the Rottweiler breed.

CHANGING RULES AND ATTITUDES

Registration of Imported Dogs

A perfect illustration of the ways in which the growth in the number of Rottweiler registrations has affected AKC registration rules is the new difficulty an owner faces registering dogs that were bred in Germany. In the 1960s, the AKC required only a properly signed ADRK *Ahnentafel* showing the transfer of ownership from one party to another. An Ahnentafel is a pedigree registration certificate, with space for transfer of ownership and a record of shows and Schutzhund Trials all on one certificate.

In the 1970s, as owners of increasing numbers of imports were seeking registration for their dogs, AKC requirements for registration became more stringent. The AKC application now included a space for photos.

If we were to give a title to the last decade and a half it would be "The Commercialization of the Rottweiler," with the subtitle, "The Age of the Import." Calls from the ADRK inquiring whether we had any knowledge about persons who were asking for duplicate Ahnentafels indicated to us that the ADRK was beginning to have suspicions about exports. The AKC was also suspicious, because now the AKC no longer accepts the transfer signature on an Ahnentafel as proof of ownership; now it also requires a letter on ADRK letterhead from the office of the ADRK showing official Transfer of Ownership and date of transfer.

The most recent pamphlet describing the registry services provided by the AKC lists the requirements for the registration of imported dogs. According the the AKC, a dog whelped outside of the USA may be eligible for registration in the AKC Stud Book when imported into the USA, given the following conditions:

A. The imported dog is of a breed eligible for individual registration in the AKC Stud Book.

B. The imported dog was registered in its country of birth with the registry organization designated on the Primary List of Foreign Dog Registry Organizations BEFORE it was exported from its country of birth.

C. The Pedigree for the dog issued by the foreign registry organization contains at least three generations of ancestry, establishing that each dog in the three generations was of the same breed and registered in its country of birth with one of the registry organizations on the Primary List. Each dog named in the three generations must be identified by its registered name and registration number. The pedigree, or any other official documentation issued by the foreign registry organization, must also include the official Transfer of Ownership and date of transfer to the American importer, verifying that the transfer was recorded with the foreign registry organization.

D. The owner who applies to register the imported dog is a resident of the USA.

When completed and submitted, an *Application to Register an Imported Dog with the AKC* must be accompanied by the ORIGINAL official foreign pedigree.

Two (2) color photographs providing close-up front and side views of the dog in a standing position are required. The photographs should be no smaller than 3 × 4 inches in size.

The fee to register an imported dog is $25. (Of course, the fees have also gone up through the years.)

The Primary List of Foreign Dog Registries includes these countries:

Australia	Mexico
Austria	Monaco
Belgium	New Zealand
Bermuda	Norway
Canada	Panama
Columbia	Philippines
Czech Republic	Portugal
Denmark	Singapore
Finland	South Africa
France	Sweden
Germany	Switzerland
Holland	United Kingdom (including
Hungary	Northern Ireland)
Ireland	Venezuela
Italy	

You do not have to buy a dog from one of these countries if you plan to use it for breeding purposes only because, as the AKC rule states, "A dog imported into the USA that is not eligible for registration in AKC's Stud Book (not owned by a resident of the U.S., for instance) may be eligible for ENROLLMENT FOR BREEDING PURPOSES ONLY. Litters produced by such an enrolled dog *may* be eligible for AKC registration provided the litter is the result of a mating with a dog individually registered in AKC's Stud Book and acceptable in all other respects."

Limited Registration

Owners of litters now have the option of granting *full* or *limited* registration to the individual puppies from that litter. *Full* registration is just what the word implies; the puppy is eligible to participate in all AKC events and to have its progeny registered with the AKC. *Limited* registration limits the eligibility of the puppy to compete in AKC conformation shows. It may not compete in conformation, but may compete in any AKC performance event (obedience, tracking, agility, herding etc.). It also precludes eligibility of any progeny from an individual with a limited registration to be registered with the AKC. The good news is that the limited registration can be rescinded by the breeder if a dog turns out better than expected. (Our personal requirement to rescind a limited registration includes breed quality in conformation and character, and a good or excellent OFA report if the dog is too young for OFA certification.)

The Registration Certificate Enhanced

Inclusion of Orthopedic Foundation for Animals, Inc. (OFA), and Canine Eye Registry Foundation, Inc. (CERF), numbers on AKC registrations is now a practical reality. In 1992, the AKC computer and the OFA computer began a dialogue. This high-tech cooperation between the OFA and the AKC, and also with CERF, led to the inclusion of OFA and CERF numbers on certain classes of AKC registration paperwork, registration certificates and three- and four-generation certified pedigrees. OFA now has a registry for elbows, which will surely be included in future AKC documents.

CHANGES IN DOG SHOW RULES

Imports Eligible for Puppy Classes

For those who import dogs, the first change in show rules, allowing imported puppies to be shown in puppy classes, was a fair and welcome change. Originally, imports, regardless of age, had to be shown in the Open class. When AKC developed a new age class, the 12 to 18 month class, it was also opened to imports.

Lowering the Jump Heights

In the 1980s, the AKC acted on appeals from obedience exhibitors to lower the jump heights to those currently reflected in the regulations. For Rottweilers, it means jumping one and a quarter times the dog's height as measured from the high point of the withers to the ground, with a maximum height of thirty-six inches.

When obedience was recognized as a competitive event by the AKC in 1936, the height required for all dogs was twice the height at the withers, with a maximum of forty-two inches. At that time, obedience rings were much larger.

During the 1940s and '50s, the AKC Board approved smaller ring sizes, and it became evident that some of the very large breeds no longer had enough distance for the takeoff and landing necessary to negotiate the forty-two inch height. As a consequence, the jumps were lowered to one and a half times the dog's height at the withers, with a maximum height of thirty-six inches.

During the 1960s, an independent, informal study was conducted by owners of certain breeds and by the AKC Board in response to a request to lower the jump heights for the short-legged, massive and disproportionate breeds. As a result, these breeds were permitted to jump their height. (The Rottweiler Standard calls for neither short-legged, massive nor disproportionately built dogs. Quite the contrary!)

In all these decisions, the Board tried to balance the arguments of exhibitors with different points of view; some said a high jump was too demanding on a dog, and others maintained that an obedience-trained dog should demonstrate some level of athletic prowess, as reported in the April 1995 *AKC Gazette*.

Few things spark more heated debate in the Rottweiler world than lowering jump heights. In April 1995, the Board was again approached with a request to lower the jump height for Rottweilers to just the height at the withers. This request was denied. The jump height for Rottweilers in AKC Obedience Trials remains at one and a quarter times the height of the dog as measured from the highest point of the withers to the ground with a maximum of thirty-six inches.

Changes in Appearance by Artificial Means in Conformation

In 1993, the AKC approved changes of the DOG SHOW RULES, addressing changes in appearance by artificial means. An incident concerning the exhibition of a Rottweiler in the Veteran Dog class after cruciate ligament surgery may have helped bring the issue to a head, so that the AKC set up a committee to define "artificial" means.

The committee compiled a list of procedures undertaken strictly to restore the health of a dog that would not, in and of themselves, affect a dog's show eligibility, and a list of those procedures that would make a dog ineligible for shows. Procedures undertaken to restore the health of a dog which would not affect a dog's show eligibility would include, but not be limited to, the following:

1. Repair of broken legs, even if it involved the insertion of pins, plates or wires.
2. The removal of damaged cartilage.
3. The repair of ligaments that have ruptured or been torn.
4. Caesarean sections.
5. The repair of umbilical hernias.
6. The removal of tumors or cysts.
7. Gastric torsion/bloat surgery.
8. Splenic torsion.
9. Tonsillectomy.
10. Correction of "cherry eye" (which involves the gland of the nictitating membrane).
11. Debarking.
12. The removal of dewclaws if it is a regular practice in the breed.

The list of procedures that would make a dog ineligible is so long that it includes "most all others," excluding the above. The use of drugs was not addressed.

Foreign Dogs Competing in AKC Events

On September 10 1996, the AKC delegates voted on the following rule: An unregistered dog with an acceptable foreign registration that was whelped outside the U.S. and that is owned by a resident of the U.S., or of a country with a foreign registry organization whose pedigrees are acceptable for AKC registrations (see "Primary List of Foreign Dog Registries") may, without special approval, be entered in licensed or member dog shows that are held not later than 30 days after the date of the first licensed or member dog show in which the dog was entered, but only provided that the individual foreign registration number and the name of the country of birth are shown on the entry form; and provided further that the same name (the name on the foreign registration) is used for the dog each time.

Although we doubt we will see a great influx of Europeans coming over to show their dogs in AKC events, this rule points out how vital it is to view the Rottweiler breed in global terms and how fortunate we all are to have standards that, essentially, describe the same dog.

AKC Policy on Schutzhund and Protection-Like Events

In 1989, the AKC approved a policy which prohibited any club that is eligible to hold AKC events from sponsoring any type of activity in which a dog is expected to act in an aggressive manner toward a person. This included Schutzhund, as well as any other activity involving the biting, grabbing or attacking of a person. Advertising these trials in an official AKC document (premium list, judging program or catalog) is also prohibited. The AKC believes that any exercise in which a dog attacks, bites, grabs or is aggressive toward a person creates a public perception that is counterproductive to its efforts in combating breed-specific vicious dog legislation. Failure to comply with this policy will result in the revocation of a club's show and/or trial-giving privileges.

While we understand the AKC's position and concerns, we feel singling out a sport shows a lack of understanding of that sport. Schutzhund trials are under as rigid rules and restrictions by its umbrella organization as obedience by the AKC is. Correctly taught, Schutzhund does not teach aggression. It teaches control! What was surprising about the AKC statement was that it went unchallenged by American Schutzhund organizations. At the time, they seemed very unconcerned about what effect an AKC statement would have on their sport. They were wrong; it has had an effect. Although it would not have changed the AKC policy, many felt that those involved in the sport should have gone on record with the AKC and the public stating that Schutzhund is a sport encompassing tracking, obedience and protection, not aggression.

Chapter 6

A Whole New World . . . New Performance Events—AKC Sanctioned and Unsanctioned

THE CANINE GOOD CITIZEN PROGRAM

In 1989 the AKC initiated the Canine Good Citizen Program (CGC). The introduction and purpose of the program is best summed up by the AKC's own statement:

> When man took the dog from the wild as his companion, he assumed responsibility for the dog's care and upbringing. Over time, man taught dogs to perform certain tasks and to comply with household rules so that life together would be mutually satisfying. Today, dogs in this country must have good manners to live harmoniously within families and to survive the increasing challenges of anti-canine advocates. The purpose of the Canine Good Citizen Test is to demonstrate that the dog, as a companion to man, can be a respected member of the community and can be trained and conditioned always to behave in the home, in public places, and in the presence of other dogs in a manner that reflects favorably on the owner and the dog.

The CGC is not an official title of record given by the AKC, because any AKC club or qualified dog training organization, as well as 4-H Clubs, private trainers, and others may hold a CGC Test. The Judges or evaluators do not have to be certified by AKC but should be experienced in working and training dogs, with considerable knowledge of dog behavior and a keen awareness of the public's attitude toward dogs. Although no records of pass or fail are kept by the AKC, the AKC is now asking for a report of the Tests to be sent to them. One wishes it had been done in the beginning so that we would know how many Rottweilers and other breeds, as well as mixed breeds (any dog can enter a test) had participated and/or passed. We do know that at our various Rottweiler club-sponsored CGC Tests, the pass record is very high.

Before the evaluator passes the dog (the test is "pass-fail"), he or she considers whether this is

1. The kind of dog you would like to own.
2. The kind of dog that would be safe with children.
3. The kind of dog you would welcome as a neighbor.
4. The kind of dog that makes its owner happy and is not making someone else unhappy.

In order to qualify, the dog must pass each of the ten test categories. The dog need pass the test only once to receive a CGC Certificate.

The Tests are as follows:

1. Accepting a Friendly Stranger
2. Sitting Politely for Petting
3. Appearance and Grooming
4. Walk on Loose Lead—Out for a walk
5. Walk Through a Crowd
6a. Sit and Down on Command
6b. Stay in Position (Sit or Down)
7. Praise/Interaction
8. Reaction to Another Dog
9. Reaction to Distractions
10. The Dog Left Alone

Never have so many had such a great responsibility as do Rottweiler owners to make sure that their dogs are indeed Canine Good Citizens. Irresponsible breeders selling to irresponsible owners have caused terrible public relations for responsible Rottweiler breeders and owners. You can help combat this bad PR by readying your dog for this relatively simple test for a well-bred, well-socialized Rottweiler. So be sure to give it a "priority red" status for your sake, your dog's and that of the entire breed.

Legislative Recognition for Canine Good Citizens

The AKC informs us that in 1991, Florida became the first state to pass a Resolution supporting the Canine Good Citizen Program. Since then, other states have followed suit. To find out if your state has a Resolution

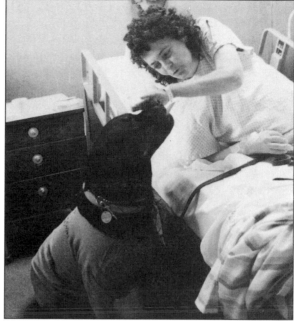

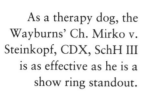

As a therapy dog, the Wayburns' Ch. Mirko v. Steinkopf, CDX, SchH III is as effective as he is a show ring standout.

supporting the AKC Canine Good Citizen Program, contact your State Representative. If your state has no CGC Resolution, and, if you belong to a dog club, ask the other members to write or call their State Representatives, too. The more people making the request, the faster the legislators act.

THERAPY ROTTWEILERS

The therapeutic value of pets has been acknowledged for more than thirty years but the chartering of organizations devoted to testing, certifying and registering dogs as Therapy Dogs is more recent. About 1982, terms were defined related to therapy and service animals by the legislature, and legislation was drafted to allow elderly people in care facilities the opportunity to have residential animals, provided that the animals had been trained by recognized training schools.

This paved the way for dogs to be used on a visiting basis as therapy dogs in hospitals, nursing homes and residential care homes. Organizations arose to train evaluators and to certify and register the dogs. Therapy Dogs International is the oldest registry for therapy dogs in the U.S. TDI is a nonprofit organization and visitations of Therapy Dogs are a voluntary service, so no charge is made to the institution or individual for whom this function is performed. As you would expect, members wishing to represent TDI to the public (at public fairs, shows or to the media) must request permission to do so from TDI. A number of our Rottweiler clubs combine the CGC Test with TDI certification as long as they have an approved evaluator available.

TDI dogs are to be used solely for emotional therapy and are not used for physical therapy of any sort, or pulling patients on gurneys or wheeled vehicles. It is sort of too bad that our TDI and cart-pulling Rottweilers aren't allowed to do this, but one understands the problem it might cause with insurance. The purpose of a therapy dog is to provide comfort and companionship. And when a sweetheart of a Rottweiler puts its head in the person's lap asking for a pat, there is nothing more comforting.

Perhaps the following article will help us better understand the therapy concept. It was printed in an ARC Newsletter written and experienced by Beth Fitzgerald and her Rottweiler, Liberty (Shadetree-Stonycreek Liberty, CGC, TDI), who sometimes takes a day off from therapy and competes in conformation at dog shows.

THE CANINE CONNECTION

He never smiled . . . trapped inside a body whose electrical impulses had gone awry—it was so difficult for him to make it respond, he had given up. The deep shell he had withdrawn into made it impossible to reach the youngster within. The staff and therapists who treated Christopher had exhausted their skills and the expansive knowledge of the medical field to no avail. So they brought in the dogs!

On the first visit, the warm tongue and soft nose brought about a small smile. So small, a stranger might not have even noticed, but Christopher's caretakers noticed and were amazed. With each visit the breakthroughs were large and quicker. A smile and giggle turned to twinkling eyes and a full, hearty laugh. Arms that for many months had remained clenched close to his body began to reach outward. Each jerky attempt was rewarded with a doggy kiss or the loving touch of a soft nose.

Today Christopher sits up in his wheelchair and can feed himself, but he enjoys giving little treats to the animals that come to visit him even more. They have broken the shell that was once his world. It s hard to tell who is happier, the therapy dogs, Christopher or the hospital staff. Christopher laughs as little Cody sits on the tray of his wheelchair and entertains him. He rewards Liberty with a doggie cookie as she sits beside him when he motions to her. Another signal from him and she lies down. Visitors may not understand Christopher's garbled speech but the dogs understand him perfectly. Liberty dances with delight when Christopher giggles and claps. He now can not only control his own body better, but he also sees the animals respond to his wishes. The joy he feels is contagious . . .

In the right hands and with proper temperament and training, Rottweilers can and have made a contribution in therapy work. Good training results in a dog that is under good control at all times, and good temperament results in a dog that relates well to people. A Therapy Dog title behind your Rottweiler's name and his participation in a program makes a great statement about the dog and the owners. They are marvelous ambassadors for the breed and for responsible dog ownership.

The working Rottweiler can still bring in the cattle . . .

. . . and the sheep, too, for that matter.

AKC HERDING EVENTS—SANCTIONED

The AKC began its herding program in 1990 with what it considered a logical decision—allowing only those breeds in the Herding Group to compete. Samoyed fanciers persuaded the AKC to open the events to their breed, asserting that they had wanted the Samoyed to be included in the new Herding Group all along when AKC split the Working Group. The Samoyed remained in the Working Group, but AKC went along with Samoyed people and opened Herding events to their dogs, too.

The Rottweiler fancier could not make that case, as we had never wanted to leave the Working Group. It is just that the Rottweiler could "work" at so many duties. And we could make the case that in its earliest history, herding was the first job at which this developing breed had demonstrated proficiency. Furthermore, although this was a new AKC program, the Rottweiler had been successfully passing AHBA (American Herding Breeds Association) and

Herding Instinct Certifications (HICs), and the Medallion Rottweiler Club and other Rottweiler clubs and groups had been holding HICs for three years. In the fall of 1993, the ARC Herding Committee and its most active member, Carol Krickeberg, formatted a presentation for the AKC to allow our breed to compete in AKC Herding events.

Each AKC Herding breed has a written herding standard that describes the way the dog works. Carol, whose family started the herding movement in the MRC, felt that the herding standard for the Rottweiler proposed in the June/July 1990 issue of *Rottweilers in Canada,* the official publication of the Rottweiler Club of Canada, was and is a terrific standard. It was well written and showed a great deal of insight about how and why a Rottweiler works stock the way he does. So, now, are you ready for another Standard?

Herding Standard for the Rottweiler

Introduction: The Rottweiler was developed as a multifaceted herding and guard dog that should work all kinds of livestock under various conditions, i.e., town or country. He is intensely concerned with gathering and controlling and can be very protective of "his" stock.

The Rottweiler is only one of several herding breeds developed in the same general area in Germany from the same or similar base stock. The others are still used in their original function and have not become known in the Americas.

Trainability: The Rottweiler is highly trainable when he can see a purpose to his actions. If bonded to his handler, the desire to please is excellent. Young males especially should be started young on ducks to gain confidence and to condition them to working off the stock. Adolescent males can be difficult to start. Because of their assertive character and youthful lack of confidence, they often feel the need to exert too much force and dominance. This usually results in their total loss of control of the stock, which in turn causes an even more forceful dominant reaction and eventual total frustration.

Keeping the dog off the stock initially with a long pole seems to be the most successful method because a line or long lead increases force and frustration. Once the dog realizes that he has more control working off the stock, the battle is won. His great desire for control and his good natural balance will keep him working back where he is most effective.

The female is normally much easier to start as an adult, being more receptive to discipline and less inclined to excessive force. A large number of females are not forceful enough to work cattle initially and should be started on ducks or sheep.

Training to gather is easy since herding instinct is very high and the Rottweiler gathers naturally. There is seldom a need to punish for gripping or biting as the Rottweiler is unusually inhibited in using the mouth on stock

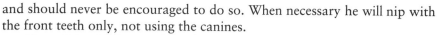

and should never be encouraged to do so. When necessary he will nip with the front teeth only, not using the canines.

If possible, the Rottweiler is best started as a puppy on ducks and then graduated to sheep and trained in much the same fashion as a Border Collie. They can then be moved to cattle. Some may never be able to work cattle.

The more confidence a Rottweiler has, the less forceful he becomes (unless it is needed) and the easier he is to train.

WORKING STYLE

1. They should show a natural gathering style with a strong desire to control.

2. They generally show a loose eye and have a great amount of force while working well off the stock. They make much use of their ability to intimidate.

3. The Rottweiler will often carry the head on an even plane with the back or carry the head up but have the neck and shoulders lowered. Some females will lower the entire front end slightly when using eye contact. Males will also do this when working far off the stock in an open field. This is rarely seen in males when working in indoor arenas.

4. The Rottweiler has a reasonably good natural balance.

5. He force-barks when necessary and when he is working cattle uses a very intimidating charge. There is a natural change in forcefulness when herding sheep. When working cattle he may use his body and shoulders, and for this reason should never be used on horned stock.

6. When working cattle, he will search out the dominant animal and challenge it. Upon proving his control over that animal, he will settle back and tend to his work.

7. The Rottweiler has little power from behind for driving cattle and therefore is best utilized as a control along the sides to turn stock, and to gather strays.

8. If worked on the same stock for any length of time, he tends to develop a bond with the stock and will become quite affectionate with them as long as they do as he directs.

9. The Rottweiler shows a gathering/fetching style when working sheep and learns directions easily. He drives sheep with ease.

Endurance: The Rottweiler is a natural trotter and, if built correctly, can trot for long distances. Hot weather bothers these dogs, particularly the males. His great force and control over sheep allow him to expend minimal amounts of energy when working this type of stock. When working cattle (especially strange cattle), he will often seek out the dominant animal and establish his own dominance, thereby allowing himself to relax as he works later. Since he does not use the mouth, he expends great amounts of energy in his intimidating charges and periodic tackles to control unruly cattle. It is therefore necessary for him to establish his control at the start.

UNDESIRABLE TRAITS

1. Biting without strong provocation.
2. A dog that cannot be taught to work off the stock, but continues to use excessive force.
3. Extremely hard dogs that do not learn to avoid being kicked or dogs that viciously attack stock after being kicked.
4. A dog that lacks the desire to control and dominate since a large part of the Rottweiler's working ability comes from this desire.

With the tenacity of a Bulldog, the determination of a Bloodhound and the stubbornness of a Rottweiler, the ARC Herding Committee prevailed with the wholehearted approval of every herding judge who had ever judged the Rottweiler. The AKC approved the entry of Rottweilers into Herding events as of June 1, 1994!

AS REPORTED BY CAROL KRICKEBERG:

On June 1 entries closed at noon for an AKC Test and Trial to be held on June 19th at Shadybrook Farm in Oregon. There were four Rottweilers entered. Three were entered at the Pre-Trial Test level. They entered once under each Judge, Shannon and Gayle Oxford from California. One was entered in Herding Started. At the end of the day, Risgar's Resa Von Webber, TD, owned and handled by Chris McMahan; Ch. Farwest's Arizona, owned by Dave and Ellen Minturn, handled by Ellen; and Can. Ch. Rolo's Altera CDX, Can. CD, owned by Roger and LoAnne Maier, handled by LoAnne; had all earned their PT (two legs under two different Judges). Paragon's Maserati, owned and handled by Barbara Davenport, had earned the first leg toward his HS by WINNING the class. He finished his HS with two firsts and a second. What a good way to say thank you to the AKC!

And, what a good way to say, We told you so, AKC!
Every time we add new events or programs we of necessity need to add to our vocabulary those words and definitions that describe them. HS, HI, HTD, HCT sounds like a foreign language! We have had some good laughs over the many acronyms which we Rottweiler people value as titles. So to help us make Herding titles less foreign, Carol Krickeberg has defined and summarized them for us as follows:

AKC TITLES: HS (herding started), HI (herding intermediate) and HX (herding excellent). Titles are earned by qualifying in three trials with three different Judges. A Herding Champion title may be earned after a dog has achieved an HX. The dog must acquire 15 points from a schedule based upon number of dogs defeated in the Advanced Trial class, working either sheep or cattle. Currently, no championship points are available from the duck arena. The Herding Champion will have placed first at least twice, with one of the first place wins worth at least three points. AKC does not recognize any difference in stock when awarding trial titles, so if an HS is earned on ducks, that title cannot be repeated on sheep or cattle. Besides the trial titles, AKC offers two test titles, HT (Herding Tested) and PT (Pre-Trial Tested). The Test titles each require the dog to be certified by two different Judges.

AHBA TITLES: HTD I, II and III (Herding Trial Dog) followed by a small letter indicating the kind of stock upon which the title was earned: *s* for sheep, *c* for cattle, *g* for goats and *d* for ducks. Each title level is earned for only the one kind of stock. So you could see a dog's name printed as Bosco HTD Is, HTD IId with Bosco having a first level title earned on sheep and a second level title earned on ducks. (Go for it, Bosco! How about an HTD III scgd?)

Two legs earned under two different Judges are required for each title. AHBA has a sanctioned testing program consisting of a two-leg HCT for dogs who have no experience with livestock, and a pre-trial title of JHD. The HCT program is the best way we know of to introduce a dog to livestock.

The Australian Shepherd Club of America (ASCA) titles include: STD (started trial dog), OTD (open trial dog) and ATD (advanced trial dog). Small letters designate the kind of stock and each title is earned separately on ducks, sheep and cattle. Earning a title requires two legs under two different Judges.

All the organizations change the trial courses to increase the difficulty for each title. The first-level trials (AKC's HS, AHBA's HTD I and ASCA's STD) are primarily *fetching* courses. After an initial outrun, in which the dog goes from the handler to get the sheep and brings them back toward the handler's position, the handler is able to walk through each obstacle in front of the sheep with the dog fetching along behind the stock. For the intermediate class (AKC's HI, AHBA's HTD II and ASCA's OTD), the dog does the outrun, and then drives the stock, with the handler remaining at a specific position called the handler's post on the course, through some of the obstacles. The handler is allowed to assist with usually the last one or two, which allows the dog to fetch (bring the stock toward the handler). The highest level of difficulty, the advanced classes (AKC's HX, AHBA's HTD III and ASCA's ATD) require the dog to drive the entire course, with the handler remaining at the handler's post until it is time to open the gate to pen the stock.

You should recognize from the above descriptions that it is more difficult to teach your dog to drive than it is to teach him to fetch. Rottweilers are almost always fetchers, and once they have learned that skill well along with the commands AWAY (circle counter clockwise), COME BYE (circle clockwise, "by the clock"), OUT (go out away from the sheep), WALK UP (slowly come closer to the stock), WAIT (stop), and LOOK BACK (look behind you, you lost one or more), they can be taught to drive. Handlers and dogs as well must learn this whole new language.

Thank you, Carol, for the explanation.

On May 26, 1995 in Perry, Georgia, in conjunction with the ARC National Specialty, the American Rottweiler Club held the first sanctioned AKC Herding Trial for Rottweilers only. There were seven total entries. Two were entered in the HT and five in the PT. Of the seven entered, one passed the HT. So we enter her in the record books as the first Rottweiler to pass at our first Rottweiler AKC sanctioned Herding Trial, Eagle Point's Elke v. Immerlachen, bred, owned, trained and handled by Mary Ann Roberts.

Once you and your Rottweiler have learned the language, Herding Trials can become an obsession. We could define "a herding obsession" as that response which puts one again and again in a pen, usually muddy, with sheep smelling as they do of lanolin, in all kinds of weather, praying that your dog will remember the language and declaring, "There is nothing like Herding!" You are right about that!

Von Gailingen's Toot Sweet taking the window jump in Novice Agility.

AGILITY—SANCTIONED

On July 1, 1994, sanctioned Agility Trials under AKC-approved rules could officially begin. But, actually, Agility was begun in England as an equestrian-type obstacle event for dogs as entertainment between Group judging at Crufts Dog Show in 1978. The creative mind of this event was John Varley, a committee member of Crufts. The enthusiasm for this event spread across England so that by 1980 The Kennel Club granted official recognition to the sport.

A few years later, an American, Kenneth Tatsch, liked what he was seeing in English Agility and was convinced there was potential for the sport in the U.S. "I was in awe of what I was seeing," he said; "the cordial social environment, the intensity of the dogs working and the joy they were having doing this." After many demonstrations by Tatsch and his colleagues, the United States Dog Agility Association, Inc. (USDAA) was established in 1986, basing rules and regulations on the British standards that emphasized speed and precision control.

As with any new idea, there was room for more variation. Charles (Bud) Kramer introduced the National Club of Dog Agility, NCDA, in 1987. This provided another distinct style of agility to ensure success for more breeds of dogs. Kramer was also hoping to provide guidelines for the AKC should it include the sport in the performance repertoire by sanctioning events. After meetings and discussions with Mr. Kramer, NCDA Judges and AKC representatives, the AKC began offering Agility as an AKC-sanctioned event beginning July 1, 1994. (Thanks to Susan Traynor for the historical input.)

And just what is "Agility?" What do the dogs have to do? Well, have you seen a new park playground recently? Imagine this playground set up inside a large ring at a dog show. You will see an A-frame, a dog walk (a heavy board about twelve inches wide and ten feet long mounted about four feet off the ground with exit and entrance ramps), a see-saw, an open tunnel set in a "U" shape, a closed tunnel made of dark material, and a crawl tunnel. You will see jumps of all kinds imaginable—a circle jump, a spread jump (longer than it is high), a solid wall jump, a double bar jump, and sometimes, a picket fence jump, a brush jump, a window jump, a tire jump (of course, the Rottweiler requires a larger window and tire to jump through), a water jump and several platform jumps, and even a Sway Bridge, depending on whether the ring is for Novice or Advanced classes. In the middle of all this you may see six to twelve, three-foot flexible poles mounted about twenty-one to twenty-four inches apart, called *weave poles*. (Wish for the 24-inch spread if you are performing with a Rottweiler, because sometime during the course your dog will have to weave through them!)

What does your dog do in this ring? He moves as fast as he can over, under, into, across or through the obstacles required of the class he has entered. In order to qualify, the dog must complete the course within the

As with so many other things they do well, Rottweilers are "naturals" in Agility.

Von Gailingen's Painted Lady, CDX clearing the wall en route to winning her class and proceeding to High in Trial. The accomplished Agility Rottweiler was trained by owner Michael Dembeck.

required time. His score is based on his time, less deductions for refusals to go over, under, into, across or through an obstacle. Of course, the handler goes right along with the dog. As Cathy Thompson, whose Bayshore Companion Dog Training Club sponsored the first East Coast Trials, put it, "The newest AKC fitness and weight loss program has now become a reality. It's called Agility . . . all you have to do is run 100 yards in fifty-five seconds or so while talking your dog over the course in the right order. . . . "

The AKC Agility Regulations begins with a statement of purpose. The purpose of AKC Agility Trials is to afford owners the opportunity to demonstrate a dog's willingness to work with its handler under a variety of conditions. (That does sound like a Rottweiler, doesn't it?) The program begins with basic entry-level agility and progresses to more complex levels that require dogs to demonstrate higher levels of training and interaction with their handlers. Agility results in a better-rounded, conditioned dog, provides good basic training for search and rescue dogs, demonstrates good training and citizenship and has excellent spectator appeal. An Agility Trial is a sporting event and all participants should be guided by the principles of good sportsmanship both inside and outside the trial course. As an active participant in the sport, Susan Traynor, puts it:

Jeanne Irvin's Von Gailingen's Tammy Whynot successfully scales the A-frame.

The weave poles.

The bond that develops between dog and handler is incredible. You can see the confidence, problem-solving abilities, and trust grow. Yes, trust! Your dog will learn that you will never ask anything that is not possible. That is the basis of the most incredible bond you can have with your dog. From my personal experiences with rescue/second-hand/abused dogs, I have found that this type of training produces better results than our traditional obedience training.

The first thing you notice about Agility Trials is the roar of the crowd. Obedience Trials and conformation shows are relatively quiet by comparison. You don't want to distract the dogs and the Judges. But no amount of shouting of encouragement and delight seems to bother the dogs or Judges in Agility. Agility is truly a spectator sport!

Rottweilers are successfully competing in Agility Trials probably because we have noted in all the articles and reports and books that the word "fun" is used over and over again. And as a bonus, this fun thing to do with your Rottweiler may earn him another AKC title.

Remember, please, that the AKC is forever changing, updating, adding to and deleting from its rules and regulations. We are grateful to the many pamphlets and brochures available from the AKC on all the sanctioned events and the articles and updates given in the *American Kennel Club Gazette* from which we have gathered much of this material. But since by the time you read this book many of the rules and regulations may have been changed, updated, added to or deleted from, do write the American Kennel Club, 51 Madison Ave, New York, NY 10010 for the latest rules and regulations before getting seriously involved in any of the events discussed in this chapter.

FLYBALL COMPETITION—NOT SANCTIONED BY AKC

Flyball competition and Agility have a great deal in common. For one thing, they both have the roar of the crowd to signal that the games have begun. They both are great spectator sports. They both take an athletic Rottweiler in good physical condition and very special equipment to set up the course. If you have the Rottweiler and the course, there is hardly anything that is a greater crowd pleaser, and better PR at the same time, than Agility or Flyball or both. In our experience the Rottweiler that does one of them often migrates into the other. At the International Kennel Club in Chicago and similar big shows around the country, your Rottweiler may do both on the same weekend.

Flyball competition is a team sport rather than an individual competition. Think of the hurdle track competition for people, only the competitor hurtling down the track and over a series of low jumps is not a person but a dog. Human track stars, however, do not have to step on a lever which makes a tennis ball fly out of a hole, catch the ball in their mouth and hurdle back down the track over the jumps to the finish line as another teammate starts down the course, possibly barking.

One does not usually picture a Rottweiler in Flyball competition. But the medium-sized athlete whose attention can be focused entirely on bringing the ball back and not on the other team's dogs of various breeds racing side by side can do it and be a dependable team player. Just ask Susan Traynor and her Agility and Flyball champion, Rodsden's Margot de Quiche, CD.

As Susan Traynor tells us, Flyball, THE sport for all tennis ball-loving dogs, began as an obedience class graduation exercise developed by Californian Herbert Wagner in the 1970s. He was invited to give a demonstration on the *Tonight Show,* and this new sport was embraced by several dog training clubs in the Toronto and Detroit areas. After introducing the idea in demonstrations at a few dog shows, the first tournament was held in 1983.

To keep records of tournaments and to standardize rules, the North American Flyball Association (NAFA) was formed in 1985 by a group representing twelve teams from Ontario and Michigan. Interest and participation has soared since its beginning and is now enjoyed throughout North America and the United Kingdom. NAFA now has more than 200 member clubs with more than 4000 registered dogs.

For an NAFA Rule Book send $10.00 in U.S. funds to

North American Flyball Assoc. Inc.
PO Box 8, Mt. Hope, Ontario
Canada LOR 1WO

Flyball demonstration at a Medallion Rottweiler Club Mini-Clinic.

DRAFT DOG AND PARADE CARTING—NOT SANCTIONED BY AKC

For the Rottweiler, carting demonstrates and preserves one of the most important early functions of the breed. As we have learned, herding was the first use to which the Rottweiler was put and pulling a cart as a draft animal was the second. Possibly, carting was not the second as, sometime in between, the breed's protective and guarding instincts were noticed and used. Our early Rottweilers had to work for a living, and hauling a cart with whatever produce the owners put in it became a part of their lives. The Rottweiler was built for hard work and had the temperament that allowed him to be used without ruining his unfailing good humor. The Draft Tests and Parade Exercises and the vocabulary used reflect this early commercial use. Freight Load, Freight Haul, Gee and Haw become part of our new Draft Dog vocabulary.

Specialty Cart and Wagon Exercises and Draft Tests were designed by the Medallion Rottweiler Club Draft Dog Committee, Wayne Budwick, Chairman, based on the Newfoundland and Bouvier des Flandres Club Exercises and Tests. They were approved by the MRC in January 1989 but the MRC had been sponsoring them on a trial basis before then. The MRC presents at least two Draft Dog events each year and exhibitions of Draft Dogs featuring Rottweilers have been held with all-breed dog shows and community fun days. Rottweiler owners have been carting in parades unofficially for many years all over the country and we now see them doing it all over the world. The American Rottweiler Club has established a Draft Dog committee, chaired by the aforementioned Wayne Budwick. Now that the AKC has sanctioned Rottweilers as herding dogs, perhaps it might be interested in developing a Draft Dog program. The more titles our Rottweiler can get, the better! Some have titles that already fill two lines of text. But that is what our breed is all about, the working dog that really works!

Carting for the whole neighborhood—"Rhett Butler" and the gang.

Putting on the harness . . .

. . . attaching the cart . . .

. . . and away he goes—
not bad for the first time!

For further information on carting and draft dog tests, write

Wayne Budwick
7847 49th Ave.
Kenosha, WI 60050

WEIGHT PULLING

Our first introduction to weight pulling competition was in the 1970s when young Alex Rothacre called to tell us that his Rodsden's Phalz v. Hungerbuhl had won a contest. Weight Pulling competition was promoted by the sled dog clubs and traditionally limited to the sled dogs, but Alex had talked the Malamute Club holding the test into letting him enter his Rottweiler, never supposing he would give them any real competition. Alex and Phalz were both built like weightlifters and trained accordingly. So as they developed the skills to become really competitive, it became more difficult for Alex to find a test that would allow him to compete with his Rottweiler. But all things change

Weight-pulling on a covered concrete surface.

Weight Pulling weigh-in; Countyman's Deutsch-man, CD weighed in at 120 lbs!

and some for the better. Today Rottweilers have no trouble finding competition, as Mary Lou Stott reports:

It was with the help of the Malamute Club that I was able to learn about the sport and work my own Rottweilers in the sport of Weight Pulling.

As Mary Lou describes it, you and your dog approach the chute. As soon as the dog is in harness and ready, you walk away a distance of eighteen feet, turn, and on a signal from the Judge give the command, HIKE! The clock starts ticking. The dog arches his neck and with one foot off the ground at a time begins to pull the weight cart, loaded with more than 2,000 pounds of bagged, dry dog food, toward the finish line sixteen feet away. Your dog's muscles ripple; he has been in training for months. He feels good about himself. The crowd starts cheering but the dog is focused only on your command to HIKE. He has sixty seconds to pull the cart a distance of sixteen feet to the finish line.

Weight pulling seems a natural extension of carting and, actually, carting is how you keep your dog in shape for pulling in the off-season. The weight pull season is usually from October through March. We believe there are wonderful, exciting activities for Rottweilers and their owners to enjoy together in every season of the year. These further enhance what should always be a mutually gratifying relationship.

Chapter 7

Introducing the New AKC Programs

JUDGES' EDUCATION

In every breed, the most universal complaint about dog shows is not about the size of the ring, the human amenities or the ring stewards, it is about the judging. Rottweiler exhibitors are no exception. The AKC responded to these complaints by initiating the Judges Institutes, changing the rules for approval and encouraging each club to appoint a Judges' Education chairperson and/or committee, JEC.

The purpose of the Judges' Institute is to provide judges with an intensive, week-long exposure to everything relating to the judging process—from AKCs application requirements, to managing a ring, to studying new breeds. (Attendance at the Judges' Institutes is not mandatory, however.) These Institutes typically ask the local Specialty clubs to provide examples of their breed for hands-on study, which may include how to approach and examine the dog, how to count the teeth and check the bite, how to critique the dog and how to evaluate gait. They provide a chance to practice with the breed.

Hands-on is a phrase that came into use when the AKC decided that applicants for judge positions would have to take a test requiring them to place a group of dogs, just as one would in an actual show, and then (not just as in an actual show), explain why they had made their decisions. A breeder/judge, a Group judge and an AKC field representative conducted the test. The AKC soon realized that this was impractical as a test. In the Rottweiler breed, for instance, there were then only about six breeder/judges to cover the whole United States! Hands-on was a poor test for many reasons, but it is a great teaching tool and is now used at the Institutes and at breed seminars. Skip ahead to the chapter on judging to read what a judging applicant must do today.

JECs are more active at the national level than at the local level in terms of organizing and promoting judges' education. The AKC requires that a Judges' Breed Study Seminar be given in conjunction with National Specialties. The AKC is also developing a Mentor Program in cooperation with parent (National) breed clubs. The ARC, in cooperation with the AKC, re-taped the video about the Rottweiler, incorporating the 1990 revised Standard; the tape is currently available. The ARC has also produced a new *Illustrated Standard* which was sent to all Rottweiler judges and is available for sale. But for arranging the actual events and providing the dogs, the handlers and the ringside tutoring at the Specialties need local JEC and club cooperation and support. Nearly every populous area in the U.S. will have local Judges' Breed Study Groups for all breeds which meet monthly and are supported in many ways by the AKC.

The AKC is trying to improve the quality of judging; the local clubs are also trying to do what they can in this direction, but they will never satisfy everyone. Actually, AKC judges are well educated in the sport and do a very good job—even if we do say so ourselves.

Public Education Coordinators—THE EIGHTH GROUP

In 1990, the American Kennel Club requested each sanctioned AKC club to appoint a Public Education Coordinator, or PEC. The AKC considers this effort so important that it calls it the *Eighth Group*. And in no breed is public education more important than in the Rottweiler. The local Rottweiler clubs actively promote public education in many places and in many ways. Schools, dog shows and matches are the most popular forums for teaching responsible dog ownership, followed by veterinarians' offices, obedience classes, fairs and parades. PECs also educate through their club newsletters, via visits to nursing homes, 4-H and Scout groups, local supply stores, parks and churches, and through participation in Oktoberfests, Pumpkin Parades,

Large, well-attended dog shows provide a wonderful showcase for breed clubs to educate the public. This is the Medallion Rottweiler Club booth at the International KC show in Chicago.

Dog cart rides for kids were a big hit at the International.

Christmas Parades, Pet-a-Thons, health clinics and tattoo or microchipping clinics.

Through the PECs, the AKC provides copious materials and support and has developed very successful children's programs which Rottweiler clubs and individuals have utilized to teach responsible dog ownership and, along the way, responsible Rottweiler ownership. The Best Friends Video and supporting materials, the Kid's Corner Newsletter, the coloring books and activity sheets, the Canine Ambassador Directory and program, the Poster Contests, T-shirt Contest, bumper stickers (e.g., A dog is for LIFE . . . Not just for Christmas!), Calendar (Every Dog Deserves . . .) and Buttons (Puppies are NOT stocking stuffers) are available.

To further encourage public education, the AKC introduced a Community Achievement Merit Award Program in 1993, recognizing outstanding public education efforts in local communities. Ron Sidler of the Southwestern Rottweiler Club of San Diego was one of the first recipients. Remember that public education is not just structured programs; every time Rottweiler owners are out in public with their dogs, they are performing a service of public education. Therefore, they should make sure they give the world a positive impression of the Rottweiler breed.

LEGISLATIVE COORDINATOR

The last ten years have been a decade of canine legislative activism. In response to this, the AKC asked each breed club to appoint a Legislative Coordinator. The AKC and the American Dog Owners Association have both

Library time at the local school.

A Rottweiler demo dog helps teach 4-H kids beginning obedience.

become better organized and better funded, and have become active in opposing unduly restrictive legislation. Each has a newsletter which covers proposed dog legislation (and resulting litigation in the case of ADOA). The AKC has established a Canine Legislation Department and Hotline (1-800 AKC-TELL), and provides public relations, financial and other assistance to local groups of dog fanciers.

As Mike Rowan, MRC Legislative Coordinator, points out, the types of dog legislation which can have the greatest impact on the Rottweiler, such as the dangerous dog laws, regulate the ownership and activities of dogs exhibiting behavior deemed dangerous to people or other animals. Regulations in these laws might include muzzling, additional liability insurance, additional registration and fee requirements, fencing or other forms of confinement, forfeiture of the dog and euthanasia. However, the most controversial type of regulation found in these laws has been breed-specific; i.e., the ownership of certain breeds or types of dogs is either prohibited or subject to restrictions not imposed upon other breeds or non-purebred dogs. While the so-called pit bull type is the first target, the Rottweiler is or will be second. Dog

Pumpkin Day Parade with "witch Klem." Some say the senior author is "type" cast. Hmm!

Practicing for Chicago's Christmas Day Parade with the Candy Cane sleigh.

fanciers have, in many cases, been successful in convincing their legislators to enact non-breed-specific laws. In some instances they have been able to enact, at the state level, non-breed-specific laws which preempt, or override, breed-specific ordinances that local municipalities have enacted. Everyone is in favor of NON-breed-specific dangerous dog laws. These protect people from bad dogs while preserving the rights of purebred dog owners, since no breed is inherently vicious or bad. The Rottweiler has often been the target of adverse media, including the incessant reporting of any injuries or deaths caused by Rottweilers even though, when investigated, the causes are usually due to human error. Negative portrayal in movies and television commercials and programming, use of Rottweilers by drug dealers and other criminals for guard or attack purposes, careless and/or unethical breeding practices and improper homes for the puppies by the fast buck elements in our society, and the activities of animal rights groups, have all contributed to this targeting.

More threatening dog laws are those which have imposed restrictions on our right to breed dogs. The animal rights movements, led by such well-organized and well-funded groups as People for the Ethical Treatment of Animals (PETA), are responsible for promoting such laws. The legislative efforts of the movement are by no means limited to breeding restrictions on dogs. The movement has a 12-point agenda which, in order to be met, will require Draconian legislation on a wide variety of subjects. The movement's ultimate goal is to end the ownership and use of all animals, in any way, by humans.

THE NATIONAL BREED CLUBS ALLIANCE, INC.— NOT AFFILIATED WITH AKC

The National Breed Clubs Alliance, Inc. was formed in response to a movement by the Association of Veterinarians for Animal Rights, who were trying to get the American Veterinary Medical Association to oppose cropping and docking. The Alliance was started by the American Boxer Club and the Doberman Pinscher Club of America. The Veterinary Medical Association has rejected this proposal twice.

The Alliance now represents twenty-eight National Breed Clubs. The American Rottweiler Club is one, with membership (including the members of member clubs) of over 20,000 exhibitors, breeders and dog lovers. While there are some forty-nine breeds that would be directly affected, the Board of Directors of the Alliance has voted to open the membership to all National breed clubs.

As AKC Judge John Connolly, President, says

> We must stand firm against any cropping ban, as this is just the first step in the activists' program, next is docking, then controlled breeding and finally the elimination of pets. They have objected to the ownership of animals by humans without considering that these animals would not exist without human ownership. They target cropping (soon docking) as a controversial issue that can stir up support from the public and even many dog owners. They have been successful in many other countries because the dog Fancy

was not paying attention. One of the goals of the Alliance is to keep the American dog Fancy informed of these actions.

Ear cropping and tail docking are prohibited in Scandinavia. Ear cropping is prohibited in Great Britain and, although tail docking is still allowed, it may only be done by licensed veterinarians, and many refuse to do the procedure. Regulations almost sneaked through in the Netherlands, but any decision was tabled until the entire European community of nations makes a decision. The pressure is on all over Europe, and the ADRK is on the alert and taking a very positive stand against the banning of tail docking. (The European community of nations has put off making any decision on laws about docking and cropping until the year 2000, so there is a reprieve for a little while, but it has not gone entirely away.)

Tail docking is often mentioned in the same breath as ear cropping, and either would surely be included in the regulation even though the procedures are completely different. Tail docking is done when the puppies are only a few days old, before the nerves are mature enough to register pain. The puppies seldom experience discomfort, and infections are rare. Surgical scissors are usually used to snip off the tail, but there is an alternate method which some breeders use; they put rubber bands around the point where they wish the tail to be docked, and the tails gradually shrivel up and drop off painlessly.

The purpose of tail docking is breed-specific, in some cases to provide a firm handle to grab and in others to eliminate that handle. Boxers, Dobermans and Rottweilers have docked tails so intruders have less to grab. Some Sporting breeds, such as Cocker Spaniels and English Springers, that work in the bramble thickets are docked to avoid serious and painful injury to long tails (not to mention getting the long tails caught in doors!). Terriers' docked tails were originally used as handles to extricate the dogs from vermin tunnels

Just in case you ever wondered what Rottweilers with tails look like, here are some dogs in Denmark to show you. The dog on the right was docked—but not enough!

if necessary. An old tale of the tail that has been passed down to us is that docking or bobbing, as in the Old English Sheep Dog, was done to identify working stock dogs exempt from taxation. We are pretty sure that this is one reason why the old German burghers docked the tails on their Rottweilers.

There are other reasons why the Rottweiler should remain a docked breed. Because the Rottweiler is a square breed, nine tall to ten long ideally, and is what some call a "rear wheel drive" dog, a tail would be a detriment to co-ordination during function. For the Rottweiler's early functions as a drover dog and as a draft dog, a tail would have been an inconvenience and would have gotten in the way. Aside from the historical perspective, the breed has, since the beginning of registrations and Standards, not been bred for the tail to conform to a specific form. As a result, when we do see Rottweilers with tails, those tails have no uniformity. Some tails curl over the back, some are longer than others and carried down, some are held to the side, some have no excess hair and others have some feathering. Requiring a tail would mean adjustments to structure, top line and croup which would have to be written into the Standard and then bred for. Of course, the immediate result would be a change in the Rottweiler's whole appearance and, thereby, the character of the breed that we think of as a Rottweiler.

The American Kennel Club does not take a position on ear cropping and tail docking. Instead, it leaves the issue to breed parent clubs to decide. The issue of cropping and docking is not going to go away, so we in the Rott-weiler Fancy must be ever-alert to all its present and future implications for the breed.

Chapter 8

Working Goals for Your Rottweiler

In 1982, the American Rottweiler Club held its first AKC Tracking Test on a ranch north of San Francisco. Because this event was a "milestone in the breed," we wanted to support the test, and, although it was a bit extravagant to go 2,000 miles to Track, we entered Ch. Wasatch Rock v.h. Brabantpark, CDX. The terrain for the Tracking Test consisted of recently vacated cattle fields, and our "city dog" was interested in the gopher holes and water holes, but he was downright fascinated with the cow patties. It seemed unlikely that he would settle down to track, especially as the temperatures were high and we had drawn the last track in the hottest part of the day. Four Rottweilers passed that day, and the last to do so was our Rocky. The thrill of finding that glove at the end of the track was something we can't begin to describe. Training a dog, working out the problems and succeeding in the trials builds confidence, furthers understanding of the relationship between man and dog, and creates a bond between partners. And that's just how we *humans* benefit!

No breed benefits from training more than the Rottweiler. Bred to work, the Rottweiler is naturally intelligent, quick to learn and much happier with a job to do. The breed began this century as police and military dogs. A natural offshoot of police training was the sport of Schutzhund, designed originally for the German Shepherd Dog. Today it continues as the primary working sport for the Rottweiler in Europe, and as an increasingly popular sport here in the United States.

Schutzhund

The sport began in Europe in the late 1890s as a way of testing and preserving those skills and abilities required of a protection dog. Schutzhund trials

The Ultimate Goal: High Protection In Trial, won here by Ch. Inka v.d. Flugschneise, SchH III, owned, trained and handled by Mary Ann Butler.

are as common in Germany, for example, as our AKC Obedience Trials are here. Schutzhund began in North America in 1969 with the formation of the North American Schutzhund Association (NASA), which combined German, international and American AKC rules (NASA's unique rules proved a deterrent to the club's later progress). The German Shepherd Dog Club of America was also forming its own organization at this time. A split in that group resulted in the United Schutzhund Clubs of America (USA). A further split within USA resulted in the formation of the American Landesverband of the Deutscher Verband der Gebrauchshundsportvereine (DVG).

DVG is the oldest and largest Schutzhund training organization in the world, beginning in 1903 as a German police and service dog club. The DVG is comprised of eleven geographic regions, ten of which are in Germany; the eleventh is the American Landesverband.

Most Schutzhunders competing with Rottweilers belong to either USA or DVG clubs. Both the American Rottweiler Club and the Medallion Rottweiler Club had sponsored DVG trials prior to the adoption of the current policy of the American Kennel Club regarding the sport. The United States Rottweiler Club and the American Rottweiler Verein, as non-AKC clubs, continue to support Schutzhund and, combined, have an estimated 1,000 members training in the sport.

Schutzhund encompasses three areas of training—tracking, obedience and protection work. It is the last phase, the bite work, that has been misunderstood and has caused the most criticism of the sport. The tracking and obedience sections are similar to exercises in advanced American obedience. Titles offered are SchH I, SchH II and SchH III which all include tracking, obedience and protection, but on increasingly advanced levels. The FH (*Fahrtenhundprufung*) title is the advanced tracking degree, similar to the AKC's TDX degree. The BH (*Begleithundprufung*—traffic secure dog) title includes many of the same exercises as in beginning AKC obedience levels, as well as the current AKC Canine Good Citizen test. To promote friendly, stable dogs and trainers already demonstrating the ability to control their animals, the BH title is now required before any dog can earn other Schutzhund titles.

Schutzhund exercises are graded on a scale, with 300 points being a perfect score (100 points each for tracking, obedience and protection). To pass,

The retrieve over the one-meter high jump (almost forty inches).

The retrieve over the scaling wall (almost six feet high).

a dog must earn a minimum of seventy points each for tracking and obedience, and eighty points for protection. Schutzhund I (SchH I) is comprised of a 300–400 pace track (see diagram), and heeling on leash and off, including through a milling group. During the obedience routine, a gun is shot to check for gun shyness. The dog is also required to retrieve a dumbbell on the flat ground as well as over a one-meter jump. The obedience phase ends with a go out and down. The protection phase features a hold at bay and bark, bite to defend handler, and ends with a courage test in which the dog is sent out after an agitator. Following the protection phase in SchH I, SchH II and SchH III, the dog is awarded a Pronounced, Satisfactory or Insufficient rating for courage and hardness in protection.

SchH II exercises are similar to SchH I in the obedience phase but include the addition of a six-foot A-frame the dog must go over to retrieve the dumbbell. The tracking is slightly more difficult. The protection phase now includes a search through six blinds for the agitator, finding and barking, an escape and defense, a transport where the agitator again attacks the handler and the dog defends, and then a courage test in which the agitator is transported back to the judge.

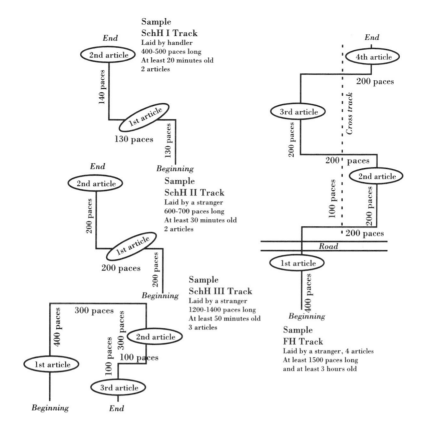

In SchH III, the track is more difficult and includes another article to find. The obedience and protection segments are the same as in SchH II. What really separates SchH I from SchH II and SchH II from SchH III is the amount of control required by the handler of the dog, and the precision the dog demonstrates in executing the exercises.

Our acquaintance with Schutzhund began with those dogs that had Schutzhund titles when we imported them. The first trial we entered was over twenty years ago, with the most gentlemanly of dogs, Ch. Arco vom Dahl, CDX, SchH III, who was also handled in junior showmanship. Perhaps because Arco exemplified what was wonderful about the sport, we became enthusiasts. Our appreciation was further increased as we watched our nephew and brother, Peter Rademacher, compete with his Ch. Dux von der Blume, CDX, TDX, SchH III. We have bred dogs that, partnered with exceptional owner/trainers, have been credits to the sport. Without a doubt, the sport of Schutzhund most demonstratively tests both the physical and mental capacities of the dog and the resolution and dedication of the trainer. It is a sport not to be entered into lightly, and for that reason we recommend

The courage test.

that Rottweiler owners first attempt AKC Obedience and Tracking titles before venturing into Schutzhund work.

Schutzhund is also a sport dependent upon the quality of training available. If one has the desire to embark on Schutzhund training, we cannot stress too emphatically the importance of finding a good working club with a reputation for turning out competition-level dogs. We also recommend the following sources of additional information on Schutzhund work:

Schutzhund: Theory and Training Methods by Susan Barwig and Stewart Hilliard, 1991, Howell Book House.

United Schutzhund Clubs of America
729 Lemay Ferry Rd.
St. Louis, MO 63125-1427

DVG America Magazine
3333 S. Bannock, Suite 950
Englewood, CO 80110

Barking at the blind after
the search.

Obedience

In *The Complete Rottweiler* (New York, Howell Book House, 1983), author Muriel Freeman was kind enough to say, in the section on distinction in Obedience, "In reading this section on outstanding Obedience dogs, one cannot fail to notice that almost all of them carry the Rodsden Kennel prefix. . . . Great credit must go to this kennel for their active promotion of all phases of the working Rottweiler as well as the correct phenotype."

Credit has to go particularly to Pat Rademacher, because his enthusiasm for Obedience was infectious.

Because of our interest in the working aspects of the breed, we have been fortunate to meet those in the breed who are more talented in areas of training than we are. One such person is Duane Pickel.

Although we had corresponded with Duane for many years, we first met him in 1987 when he and his wife Miriam came to the MRC specialty and won High In Trial with their Arko von Pickel, UD. Duane's experience as a handler and trainer covers thirty years. With eight years in the military K-9

On the command of *aus* (out), the dog releases the sleeve.

service, Duane approaches training with the thoroughness of one whose life has depended on the training of one's dog. Following military service, Duane served twenty-two years with the Tallahassee, Florida Police Department where he started the Tallahassee Police Department K-9 Unit and supervised that unit from 1971 until his retirement in 1993. In 1978, his German Shepherd dog was the number one police dog in the nation. For four years, Duane was also vice-president of the United States Police Canine Association.

During his career, Duane has trained in excess of 15,000 military, police and citizen dog teams, including over forty-nine winners of AKC titles, eleven of which were nationally ranked. Training and working with Rottweilers from Vietnam to the AKC Obedience ring, Duane's understanding of the "inner workings" of the Rottweiler is unparalleled. An author of articles on training that have appeared in the *AKC Gazette*, *Dog World*, *Off Lead*, and *Front & Finish*, we are pleased to present "a private lesson" with Sergeant Duane Pickel!

Obedience competition's ultimate goal is the achievement of an Obedience Trial Championship. Shown here is Carla vom Kasseler-Hof, owned and trained by Emmy Verkozen, one of eight OTCH Rottweilers, two dogs and six bitches, who had earned the title at the time this book was written: The others are OTCH Mondberg's Donnamira v. Beier, OTCH Way-Mar's Disco Dawg,

OTCH Dolly v. Odenwald, TD, SchH I, OTCH Magnum von Meadow III, TDX, OTCH Waymar's Rocky Raccoon, OTCH Masty Sunde vom Tanzenfeld, OTCH Summers Glory Da Bratiana.

Am & Can. Ch., Canadian OTCH Von Brader's Jem of Phantom Wood, UDTX, JHD taking the Utility Bar Jump, owned and trained by Karla Kastern Ebert.

OBEDIENCE TRAINING AND THE ROTTWEILER

by Sgt. Duane Pickel
VONPICKEL K-9, Inc.
2570 Chaires Crossroad, Tallahassee, FL 32311

This chapter on obedience is not going to be a "How-to," but rather will deal with the "What, Why, When and Who." There are many how-to books and publications on the market; however, none will do any good unless you understand the following: what obedience is, why obedience train, when should I start and whom should I use for instruction.

First, let's explore the Rottweiler. The Rottweiler is an outstanding breed. They are beautiful, regal, loyal, protective and an excellent deterrent to crime for our homes. That's why we purchase them.

What most people won't tell you is that the Rottweiler is also strong-willed, arrogant, self-centered, and his main priority in life is to satisfy himself, not you! The Rottweiler's body is large-boned, heavily muscled with a large powerful head, capable of speeds in excess of thirty miles per hour, jaw pressure of 1,800 pounds per square inch, and pound for pound is twice the strength of a man. Rudolf Schimscha, retired trainer, German Customs Canine Unit for forty-seven years, states that the Rottweiler is seldom used in his employ because they tend to train the handlers more than the handlers train them. The Rottweiler, in law enforcement circles, is considered the forty-four magnum of the dog world.

All of the above is not intended to be negative, but is merely stating the facts. The Rottweiler needs a lot of training and attention, and before purchasing such a breed, one must evaluate the time and energy factor involved. The Rottweiler must be a house dog and a part of the family. When trained correctly, there is no greater reward than owning a Rottweiler or being owned by a Rottweiler.

Obedience training is a term that is applied to animals, but it is nothing more than an educational process. One would never say that my children are in school being trained, although sometimes that should apply. So when people think of training a dog, they think that there is some magic to the process. But that's not the case, it's only an educational process. Parents raise and educate their children without much thought, but when it comes to the family dog, we are lost as to what to do. Why? Because we aren't thinking in the proper terms. A child, prior to entering school, learns the whole English language, the do's and don't's of life, where to go to the bathroom and where not to, to respect their parents, come when called, remain when told and when to be quiet. Just equate this common sense with your dog.

The dictionary gives the meaning of *education* as developing the faculties and powers of (a person) by teaching, instruction or schooling. So parents should start thinking in terms of education instead of training. Remember that the difference between dogs and children is the fact that your dog basically ages a year every two months, so everything is accelerated.

"Watch me!"

"Front."

For example, the terrible two's come between four and six months. The good thing is that they can be potty-trained in a few months instead of a few years. Also, a dog reaches the mental age of twelve and stops. Meaning you won't have to worry about him wanting to borrow your car—or stealing it.

ELEMENTS AND PHASES OF TRAINING

Before starting the specifics of the elements and phases of training, I think it's important to talk about the handler's attitude during a training session. One must become an actor or actress in order to train a dog. You must make a dog think and believe that this instructive time together is more fun than eating spaghetti or having sex. You can't teach a dog something that you don't know, so you must learn your training session and then teach it to your make-believe dog before bringing out your Rottweiler. I feel that a Rottweiler is one of the most intelligent breeds in the dog world, and that in itself makes this educational process very difficult. For if you don't display confidence in your instruction, then he will not follow. A good example is the situation one encounters in the military.

I spent eight years in the military service in Vietnam, and twenty-two years with the Tallahassee Police Department, which is a paramilitary organization. If sent on a patrol with leadership that lacked confidence and knowledge of the task at hand, then nobody in their right mind would follow without a great deal of caution and distrust. Well, training a dog is the same thing. That Rottweiler will not take your lead unless he has confidence and trust in you. So until you establish confidence in what you are doing, the fake-it-until-you-make-it rule is in order. Go over the training session many times in your mind. Then practice the new exercise many times with your imaginary dog before introducing it to your dog. This is called visualization training. It really works and it carries over to the practice field. A builder of a house will build the house many times in his or her mind before actually picking up a hammer. Building a puppy is no different. Now, let's go on to the elements and phases of training.

For years, in my dog obedience classes, I've taught my students that there are four critical elements to successful training. Those elements are love, communication, consistency and persistence. Without the others, each of the elements is incomplete.

Love is an emotion and is impossible to teach or even to explain. However, this emotion must be present and genuine, or your Rottweiler will know. Rottweilers work on a fifty-fifty relationship of love and respect. Some males require a forty-sixty relationship of love versus respect. However, the love must be shown and not just spoken. As stated before, Rottweilers are very intelligent and tend to learn very quickly, but after becoming proficient in a routine such as for the Companion Dog test, they become bored and only perform because of their love for you and the fact that this makes you happy. That is why this expression of love is so important.

A handler can be successful by using consistency, persistence and good communication skills. This has been demonstrated by many professional trainers who train and show large numbers of dogs. However, for the maximum success in training to occur, there is another critical variable, love. Love facilitates good communication with a dog and when the handler loves the dog, it is much easier to be persistent. We aren't so likely to give up on those we care about. Operationally defined, love is the ability to put your dog's needs above your own. You've had a long day and you are tired, but your dog has been inside all day. The dog's needs come first, so you go outside with your canine friend. This expression of devotion on your part is not consistency, persistence or communication. But it is invaluable to the training experience. This is the part of the training relationship that teaches the dog, "you and me . . . we're a team." Loving a dog and taking care of the dog's needs results in bonding and develops trust that can benefit training.

With dogs, love means that you need to put your money where your mouth is. If you truly love this dog, give it a good quality of life. The way to do that (in addition to meeting basic needs) is to provide it with training. Love won't stand alone in training, however. You can love your dog all day long, but you will not be a successful trainer without the other elements—consistency, persistence and good communication skills.

Ch. Rodsden's Quito of Wylan, CDX, TDX, BH SchH III, IPOIII FH (Ch. Eppo v.d. Keizerslanden, CDX, Can. CD, BH ex Can. Ch. Wyvonie v.h. Brabantpark, CD, TD), MRC Hall of Fame member, owned and trained by Ron Maloney and co-owned with Sue Rademacher.

Ch. Dillon v. Wacissa, CD (Ch. Adolf v. Kresta ex Marlon Brando's Vendetta), a multiple Specialty and BIS winner, Systems top winner, owned and handled by Robert Pandolfi.

This top-winning brace consists of Am. & Can. Ch. Shadowdale's
Headliner, Am. & Can. CD, CGC and Shadowdale's Skye Watch. They
are owned by Rebecca Kucharski. *Robert Skibinski*

Ch. Oakbrook's Caliber v. Doroh (Ch. Von Lida's Class Act, CD ex
Ch. Solitaire v. Oakbrook), owned by Arthur Twiss and Eric and
Amelia Jimenez and bred by the Jimenezes and Dorothy Wade, made
history as the youngest Rottweiler to win a Specialty. He is shown here
in the win at the 1993 CRC Specialty under Mrs. Robert Forsyth. He
was but eighteen months old at the time.

Rottweilers give a good account of themselves in Search and Rescue (SAR) work.

Rodsden's Wotan v.d. Harque, CDX, TD, owned by Jane Wiedel, was the first Search and Rescue Rottweiler. He is shown here doing the work that distinguished him.

Introduce your Rottweiler to the love of water and the joys of swimming. Teaching him to retrieve from the water is great fun and good exercise.

When he learns to love the water, he really, really loves the water. This is Grace Acosta's Ch. Acosta's Oro Negro Johansson, CD, CGC, RTD, TT, HIC.

Ch. Heidi v.h. Kertzenlicht, UD Can. CDX, BH, owned, trained and handled by Jeff Gregg

Ch. Rodsden's Vikon v. Eppo, CDX, TD, SchH I, nationally ranked Obedience performer, owned, trained and handled by Angela Schroeder. *B. Love*

Communication

So a trainer is consistent and persistent. Does that guarantee success? No. A person can consistently reinforce the same things, and they can be persistent and practice at the same time every day for ten years, but if they lack the skills needed to effectively communicate with the dog, training effects will not be maximized. Good trainers know what makes their dogs tick. They know how to get that dog wound up and how to calm it down. Beginning handlers often need the help of obedience teachers to learn to effectively communicate with their dogs. Communication begins with getting the dog's attention, and continues with learning how to maintain that attention. Communication also relates to the vocabulary that we teach a dog. Experienced trainers know that DOWN and OFF are two different words. Being a good handler means being a good communicator.

In communicating with your dog, remember that your relationship must be well-defined. Your relationship must be that of a parent rather than a friend. The Spock method of child instruction is not effective on people or dogs. If you allow your dog to develop itself as suggested by Spock, it will have only instinct to function on rather than education. Through education, Rottweilers need to learn a clear-cut and well-defined direction to take. If your relationship becomes only one of a friend, then remember, friends don't tell friends what to do. And you must.

Consistency

It is important in training to be consistent. Animals learn faster when the rules stay the same. Whether they know the scientific language or not, handlers who do a good job at being consistent are handlers who understand the principles of operant conditioning. Goals and objectives are set for each training session, and the dog is consistently reinforced for appropriate behavior. Corrections, when needed, are also consistent and are given by good handlers in an unemotional fashion. However, if you consistently make the same handling errors, the dog will not learn the skills you've introduced. Consistently making the same reinforcement errors may actually shape undesirable behaviors. The saying "practice makes perfect" isn't true; only "perfect practice makes perfect."

Consistency can be applied both in teaching new skills and in maintaining skills that have been previously learned. For example, when teaching a new exercise such as down, the dog is reinforced for being in the down position. A good handler will not get tired, assume a close enough attitude, and begin to reinforce the dog when only the front end is down.

One of the hardest training skills for beginning students to acquire is the ability to be consistent with regard to maintaining previously taught skills. For example, a dog has gone over the bar jump, and it finally looks like directed jumping is falling into place. The dog returns to the handler, sits in front in the most crooked sit the world has ever seen, and receives enthusiastic praise and hugs. Many days of letting the crooked sits go unattended will result in training problems that need to be undone.

Consistency is also important in teaching behaviors related to family living. Some owners feed the dog at the table at almost every meal. Then, when company arrives they look absolutely mortified when the dog shows up at the table begging for steak and potatoes. By the way, I let my dogs beg at the table and I just tell my company that it took months of training to get the dogs to look that sad when not given a piece of food.

Consistency relates not only to reinforcing the correct or desired behaviors of the dog, it also relates to handler behaviors. Handlers must

Rodsden's Wilma of Bamar, CDX, co-owned by trainer/handler Howard Bernier.

Rodsden's Orrie of Cadan, CD with co-owner/trainer/handler Nanette Kirby.

learn the rules of the obedience game and abide by them. Stepping off on the left foot means heel. Stepping off on the right foot means stay. Beginning handlers, not realizing the importance of footwork, sometimes make the mistake of stepping off on the right foot to begin heeling. Inconsistent handling techniques will confuse a dog. A handler must understand that the left hip means position, and the left foot means heel or go, which is direction. Consistency in body movement affords the dog a lowered reaction time to respond. Reaction time is the time between when the dog sees your movement and when it responds to it. Try heeling beside another handler and you will understand what you are asking the dog to do. This is similar to trying to learn a new dance step. If you were in the sport of boxing, the last thing you would want to do is to telegraph your punches. However, in handling a dog, you always want to telegraph your moves.

Persistence

Persistence can be defined as the ability to hang in there. Being persistent is sometimes hard for beginning handlers, especially those who have a difficult dog. Unfortunately, in dealing with hard-to-manage dogs, things often get worse before they get better. A dog who has a long history of calling the shots may resist a new regimen that involves training and being compliant. When there is resistance, impatient handlers often give up. It is these people who say, "I tried obedience training and it didn't work."

Being persistent may also be difficult for handlers who have already trained one dog and acquired a title or two. This can be due to factors such as boredom or handler burn-out with foundation or basic work. There are many people who have had one great dog, but in training a second or replacement, fall short because they forgot how much time it took to get that great dog. As handlers, we all need to remember that if we expect our dogs to be disciplined, then we must be disciplined too. Good handlers will stay on a problem until it is solved. A handler may be perfectly consistent, abide by all of the rules of operant conditioning and never make a single reinforcement error, yet still experience failure at training due to a lack of persistence. Persistence is the ability of handlers to follow the rules. When the training gets tough, the tough keep training

PHASES OF TRAINING

For training to be successful, one should be aware of the three elements of training in addition to the elements of training. The three phases of training are *instructional, motivational* and *corrective*.

Instructional Phase

The instructional phase involves new teaching skills. It is in this phase that the behavioral principles of shaping, fading and chaining are used.

In shaping, the handler reinforces successive approximations of the desired behavior while gradually raising the standard until the desired behavior is met. For example, in initial scent discrimination work, a dog may be reinforced for simply looking for an article. Later, the reinforcement will be delivered when the correct article has been located.

Fading involves the gradual fading of stimuli used to control the dog's behavior while a new skill is being taught. In teaching the Go Out, some

First Lady Brenna von Wertz, CD, owned, trained and handled by Liz Wertz.

Ch. Iolkos v. Dammerwald, CD, owned, trained and handled by Joan Klem.

handlers have the dog go out to the desired location and sit on an area that has been marked by a box, lines, etc. As the dog learns the task, the lines and visual stimuli are faded.

Chaining can be either backward or forward in nature. In chaining, a series of behaviors is chained together to make a complete task such as go out, turn, sit, approach the correct jump, etc. It is never appropriate to use punishment techniques when teaching a dog a new skill. The instructional phase should always be one of guidance and positive reinforcement.

A good example of instructional training is to pretend that you are trying to teach a Mexican child to sit in a chair. This child speaks no English, and you speak no Spanish. Just saying the word sit will mean nothing, even if you say it fifty times. You must pantomime sitting in the chair as you repeat the word sit. Then place the child in front of the chair and push on the back of the knees as you assist in a downward fashion and repeat the word *sit*. Too much force coupled with a lack of trust will cause resistance.

Motivational Phase

The motivational aspect of training should continue throughout a dog's education. Look at your training from the dog's point of view. What do you need to do to make this fun for your canine companion and yourself? Good handlers make learning new things fun, and they use motivational techniques to prevent the daily training session from becoming a chore. Think of the great teachers you've had in your life; most likely they were excited about what they were teaching. A good handler will know the dog's reinforcers. Does the dog work best for a food reward, or would he rather have hugs and praise? Sometimes all of the above. Remember that there is a big difference in food training and food rewarding. I don't believe in food training. In order to build long-term motivation, each training session should end on a positive note. Following the training, there should be some play time. You choose the training session routine; the dog should have the opportunity to choose preferred activities during the play time.

Corrective Phase

The corrective phase is the least understood phase in dog training. Discipline is not a hardship, but merely a habit, and when cultivated, it means a well-regulated life or a well-trained dog. Corrections range from a facial expression of disappointment to verbal corrections (e.g., "no") or corrections with a leash. The most important thing is that correction should never be given with emotion; praise with emotion, but never correct with emotion. Once corrected, a dog should be given a chance to repeat the exercise, and when the correct behavior is exhibited, it should be followed with praise. Discipline is on a scale of one to ten with ten being the highest and one being the least. I use a "no" as a level three. A four is a lead correction in the form of a snap release. One and two can be "leave it" or "stop." As your dog continues to ignore your demands after you know that it understands the exercise, then you must climb to the next level of discipline. Dogs are like children in this regard, and will test the limits out of need for their definition. Seeing how far they can go is natural.

Summary

Training a dog is much like the educational process that we apply to very young children. Parents use instinct and common sense; they teach their children a great deal in their first six years of life. Apply the same common sense to your dog in the first year. A good example is that when a two-year-old child crawls toward the hot oven, you remove the child and say "hot." If the child approaches the oven again, then you slap his hand and say "No, hot," and put him in the play pen to remove him from this danger. A puppy running away and not coming is the same thing. Climbing the ladder of discipline faster is called for because of the danger present. A dog will run into more trouble running away than he will ever encounter by remaining.

COMMUNICATION SKILLS AND WORDS

The single most important aspect of the training world is the communication skills you employ with your dog. To communicate with your dog, you will use words, hand signals and body language. This section will cover the words and their meaning. The following list of K-9 vocabulary will be discussed at length after you review the list. Make sure that you are consistent with these words, and persistent. Check them off as you program yourself to recall them. Remember that a dog cannot understand why a single word has multiple meanings. So don't use a word that means two things. Always keep in mind that you are working a Rottweiler, not a Golden Retriever. The Rottweiler's bite is worse than his bark, and if you are unfair in training, he will let you know. Also, the Rottweiler must know that there is an end to an exercise. If one repetition is done correctly, then never make him repeat it. The only time an exercise is repeated is when it's not done correctly. Your dog will then learn, "Well, the sooner I do this correctly, the sooner I get it over with and reap the rewards."

BASIC COMMANDS AND COMMUNICATION WORDS
K-9 VOCABULARY

Sit	Leave it
Down	Stop
Stand	Go to bed (crate)
Stay	Get it (toy, sticks)
Wait	Toy
Come	Ball
Heel	Good (very good)
Finish	Bad
Ready (Preparatory)	Better
Front (Specific)	Off
Heel (Recall to Heel)	Supper time

continues

Watch me	Are you hungry?
Fetch it	Time to eat
Give	Cookie (treat)
Hold	Pee (urinate)
Jump (fall on back side)	Hockey (defecate)
Up (no fall—climb)	Outside (specific or general)
Over (length)	Home (let's go home)
Find it	House (get in the house)
Sit right (straight)	Put your clothes on (collar)
Mark (direction by hand signal)	Hi-hello
Okay (release)	Good night
Move (change location)	Play (no play or let's play)
Hurry (faster)	Hold still (grooming or nails)
Easy (caution or slower)	Go for a ride
No sniff	Take your clothes off (collar)
No dog	Charge (utility go-out)

The seven basic commands taught for obedience are what I call the magnificent seven. They are sit, down, stay, stand, come, heel and finish. And they are self-explanatory, except that we must define heel position. The American Kennel Club defines correct heel position as being the tip or end of the dog's nose to the dog's shoulder being even with your hip bone. Now that means that when the dog is standing, the distance between the two points on a large dog will be eight inches in length. However, when the dog is in the sitting position, that distance will be cut in half. Any dog that is in front of this position is forging, and any dog that is behind this position is lagging. To make this position easier to recognize, remember that if the ear is even with the seam on your pants then the dog is correct.

The word "stay" means don't move a foot, so don't demean this word by improper usage. Use the word "wait" when you want the dog to just remain behind, such as going out the door. When working on the sit stay and the down stay, make sure that the emphasis is on the word "sit" or "down" and not the word "stay." Otherwise, your dog may stay, but not sit stay; it may lie down. This is the biggest problem with the sit stays.

On the famous recall words, I use three recall words which have different meanings. The first taught is the word "come." This is a very nonspecific word and just means "come to me." As the educational process becomes more involved, then I become more specific. "Front" means, "come sit front." Then in the Utility class we add another recall to the heel position by saying "heel." However we don't wait until the Utility level to teach it; it's taught early as we complete the recall come and front. The word "finish," which I use as a definition rather than a command, means go to the left side (heel position) from the front position or any position. I find that using a special word to have the dog go from the sit front to my left side (heel position) is a waste of a command word. Remember, the dog only has a capacity of 400 words, so we don't want to waste any.

I'm not going to bore you with going through these commands or words in your K-9 vocabulary, but I will touch on the important ones. However, the concepts behind these words are important, such as the word "No." This is a corrective command, and is not to be demeaned by over-usage. For example, when a human child gets in the terrible two's, then you feel like all you do is say "no-no-no." Well, it gets just as trying to the dog. Save "no" as a higher level of correction.

Teach "leave it," instead of the word "no," for when your dog picks up something that it is not supposed to. "Leave it" is a very good command. Another good substitution for "no" is the phrase "stop it" or just "stop." When your dog is licking or bothering a guest, then say "stop it" instead of the "no." Use the words "hold still" for grooming, examining the ears, brushing the teeth, etc.

Teaching your dog to go to the bathroom on command is a tool that is very helpful later on in life. So I use "pee" for urinate and "hockey" for defecate. When you are in a hurry and your dog wants to read the paper outside instead of relieving itself because of the distractions, then you can remind your dog what it is outside for. Start by saying "good boy, pee," when urinating and "good boy, hockey," when defecating. As time goes on, the words will be committed to memory.

One of the best commands you can teach, and they all have an application, is the word "hurry." This simply means faster, and it applies to heeling, recalls, retrieving, etc.

Other commands such as "put your clothes on, take your clothes off," are just other ways of increasing the vocabulary, and every time you expand on the brain you make your dog more human. Plus, before going outside to work or for a ride, you set the stage for control, rather than have the enthusiasm overpower the experience. You don't want to lose control before you start.

When teaching the stand, it's much easier to start each day as you groom your puppy. When time comes for the formal stand, then the word will already be known. My philosophy is that it is easier to prevent a problem than to cure one.

INSTRUCTORS

I receive six calls a day about canine training classes, but the question never asked is "What qualifies you to train me and my dog?" I can't understand why this is never asked. If you were going to take a college course, you would ask about the professor, would you not? However, most people want to know "how much does it cost" and "how long does it take!" When looking for a canine instructor, ask to see his dog perform and watch his students. Also, if the instructor doesn't have experience with the title that you are training for, he can't show you how to do something he has not done. The kind of breeds the instructor is working also makes a difference. A person who only has worked Goldens can't help you with a Rottweiler.

I would like to explain the canine hierarchy of positions in the police dog world. First from bottom to top handler, instructor, instructor-evaluator and trainer. A handler, after completing a 640-hour course, becomes certified as a handler. After three years in that position, a handler can apply for the instructor program. Upon completion, he is certified as an instructor. With three years of experience in that position and after training twelve certified teams, this instructor becomes an instructor-evaluator. With fifteen years of experience he becomes a trainer.

Looking for an instructor for AKC levels of training is not as clear-cut as in the police world. However, I would surely want to work with someone with experience in the Utility title and someone that has trained several students through the level I was seeking. Also ask for references from students.

AMERICAN KENNEL CLUB TITLES

WHY? WHEN?

ARE THEY COMPETITION?

The Utility Dog title differs from Schutzhund and hunting titles by the mere fact that the UD is not self-motivating. Schutzhund and hunting routines give the dog variety in exercises that accentuate the genetic function bred into the breed. Schutzhund adds tracking and protection work for Working breeds. Hunting has pointing or retrieving for those breeds. They were bred for these tasks, so doing what they were bred for isn't really training but directing. The same goes for herding. A hunting dog is not trained to hunt, but how to hunt. A Rottweiler is not trained to do protection work, but how to and when to. Again, Tracking dogs are not trained how to track, but are taught to do so on command and what to track.

The Utility Dog routine has nothing in it that is self-motivating. So the motivating must come from the handler, and that's why it is so valuable. It makes you and your dog a true team.

The American Kennel Club offers three titles in Obedience—Companion Dog (CD), Companion Dog Excellent (CDX) and the Utility Dog (UD). I refer to these titles as the Bachelors, Masters and Ph.D. of the dog world because they take about as long to obtain for your first dog! The Utility Dog will complete ninety-seven commands by hand signal which include directed retrieving, directed jumping and scent discrimination in a twelve-minute routine. I consider a trained dog and a responsible partner one that is trained to the CDX level, plus knows household training communication words. This training approaches eighty-one words. Once you have trained and lived with a Utility Dog, then you will never be able to live with a less educated dog again.

The reason for seeking these titles is the mere fact that if you don't seek the titles, then you won't get to that level of training. People are very goal-oriented, and if you establish these goals, then you will obtain them. But if you don't establish goals, then it's easy to brush off the training and re-place the time with something else. If you ever stop and take a break be-tween titles, then more than likely you won't return. It's kind of like with our own education; how many of you finished your Bachelors and said to yourself that you wanted to take a break from school, to get a job and have something you couldn't afford as a student. How many said, "I'm tired of living on peanut butter but will return to school." How many of us really did return? I'd say most did not and if you did, it was much harder than if you had just stayed in school. Your dog's education is the same.

The AKC titles are the same, and are certification of the education your dog has received. When I train, or train others, we work to the CDX level and beyond, in part to the Utility level, before testing for the CD title. Then I can test for the CDX title while I'm training for the UD. Once completed, then I'll polish the UD and test for that title. If you don't test for the title, which means you must go to three Obedience Trials and successfully pass to obtain the title, then you can't prove your dog is really trained to this stated level. Once done, then your dog is certified by a national organiza-tion that can vouch for your dog's temperament and educational level. There is a big difference between a run-through at home and a clean run at a trial. When the handler gets nervous, everything changes. A police handler con-ducting a building search in training has no nervous energy being displayed, but in a real building search looking for a bad guy that might hurt you, adrenaline flows. The dog must perceive that nervous adrenaline flow as "tighten up, because this one counts," instead of "I've screwed up," thereby doing nothing or going through his repertoire of tricks. AKC trials are the same, thus an educational process unequaled.

How long does it take to obtain these levels of training? To be blunt, it takes two hundred hours for the CD, four hundred hours for the CDX and two hundred hours more for the UD title. Now this is for your first dog! As you become more consistent and learn where you are going, then you can cut the time in half. This total of eight hundred hours can be com-pleted in eight months if you can put that much time in during this short period. Or it can take you eight years; that's up to you and your calendar.

Are the American Kennel Club titles competitive? The answer to this question is NO, but they can be. When a person is seeking the titles, then it should be looked at as a testing process. In this testing process, one can pass with an A or a D; that's up to the handler and to how much time you have to put into training for the title. The titles themselves are very mean-ingful, and when completed, no one ever asks for the score. Just like when you finish a college level, the degree at the end speaks for itself, and the grade-point average isn't relevant. Thank goodness!

Now if you have your titles and you are going back to run the dog through the routines for placements of first through fourth, then it's

We track in the winter, too. The dog follows the scent, *not* the footsteps.

Rottweilers at work searching luggage for illegal drugs on an airport carousel in Guadalajara, Mexico. The Rottweiler's excellent nose qualifies him as an excellent narcotics and bomb detection dog.

competition. But generally speaking, the AKC obedience ring is not competitive. You are competing against yourself, and each time you take the test, you try to better your score. I feel that this is the best way to approach it. It's just like in the martial arts that I've participated in for the past forty years. You are not considered a player until you've earned the black belt rank. Prior to that rank, you are a student, after which, you become a competitor. The dog world is very similar in the respect that the dog is the student seeking the levels, degree or titles. Then it becomes a player and thus a competitor if you so choose.

The UDX is the Utility Dog Excellent title, and it shows consistency in performance. This is the hardest title to obtain. Your score really doesn't matter; however, one must earn a qualifying score in both the Utility class and the Open class on the same day, ten times. This title is a real accomplishment.

The OTCH is the Obedience Trial Championship and is pure competition. Points are only awarded for first and second places in the Utility B and Open B classes. There are only sixty to eighty-four of these titles earned each year throughout the United States.

All Rottweilers should either have earned a CDX or have been trained to CDX level to make a fundamental difference in the public's perception of the breed. The Rottweiler is an outstanding member of the purebred family, and its salvation will occur through a positive image change. This can only be realized through responsible ownership, which must include obedience training and proper education.

TRACKING

We began this chapter by relating a story about Tracking, and it is appropriate that we close the chapter with a discussion of this sport because Tracking is an activity which can commence at the beginning or at the end of a dog's career. It is not unusual to see six- or seven-month-old puppies and nine or ten-year-old veterans competing in Tracking events.

Rottweilers are very good trackers! In 1994, more Rottweilers earned AKC Tracking Dog (TD) and Tracking Dog Excellent (TDX) titles than all the other Working breeds combined. Following the MRC's lead, the CRC and ARC now annually conduct Tracking Tests. These Tests are a real service to the breed, for spaces in all-breed Tracking Tests are dear, and often one has a long wait before getting into a Test.

The AKC's preliminary Tracking Test to earn the TD degree consists of a track, laid by a stranger to the dog, of 450-500 yards in length. It has at least two approximate 90° turns and has aged anywhere from thirty minutes to two hours before the dog is brought to it. At the end of the track is an article (usually a glove) which the dog must identify. The following is an example:

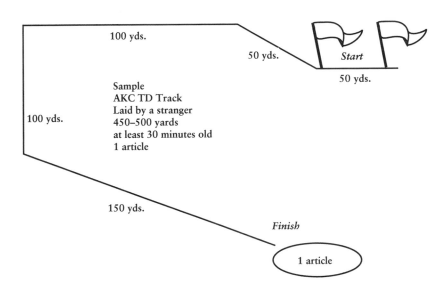

The TDX Test is longer (800-1000 yards), has any number of turns, and has additional cross-tracks which the dog must not follow. This TDX track is aged three to four hours, and there are three articles to locate. The TDX is

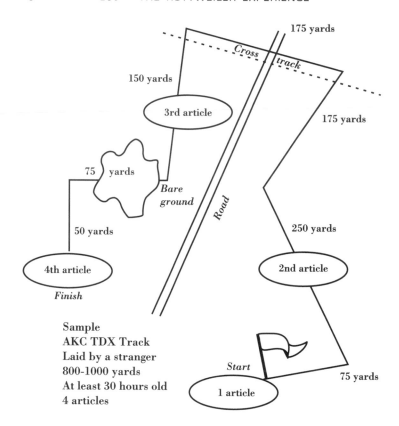

175 yards

Cross track

150 yards

3rd article

175 yards

75 yards

Bare ground

Road

50 yards

250 yards

4th article

2nd article

Finish

Sample
AKC TDX Track
Laid by a stranger
800-1000 yards
At least 30 hours old
4 articles

Start

1 article

75 yards

a big jump in difficulty over that of the TD, which is why, in 1994, twenty-seven Rottweilers earned TD degrees but only ten earned TDX degrees. It is not that the Rottweiler finds the TDX level daunting, but rather that the amount of time and space needed to train for the TDX is daunting to the handler!

The AKC has recently created another tracking competition called Variable Surface Tracking (VST). The VST track is 600-800 yards, includes from four to eight turns, one article each of metal, plastic, leather, and fabric, and is aged like a TDX track. In our area, our authority on this new exercise is AKC TD/ TDX judge, MRC member, and fellow Rottweiler breeder, Walter O'Brien. In comparing the differences between VST and TDX, Wally wrote, "The most notable difference, obviously, is the fact that the dogs are tracking on surfaces without vegetation. This includes concrete, mud, asphalt, various sizes of gravel, mulch and sand."

With some justification, we refer to VST as "urban tracking" because it was designed for a tracking test which could be conducted in industrial parks, on fairgrounds, in school yards, or in areas where urban and suburban sprawl rule out large areas of open fields. The third dog and first Rottweiler to be awarded the title of Champion Tracker (CT) is Rodsden's J Socrates of Quira, CDX, TDX, VST owned, trained and handled by Jack Hlustik.

You can start tracking with a puppy as soon as the puppy is old enough to walk on a lead, and has begun to show interest in ground scent. The equipment you need is minimal—a non-restrictive tracking harness, light, twenty to forty feet of weatherproof line, tracking stakes with flagging (to begin a puppy one only needs tomato stakes), and an article to be found, such as a glove or wallet. For guidance, you can contact one of the Rottweiler clubs. A number of these clubs have members who are also tracking judges. Tracking is a sport where everyone hopes the dog will pass, and there is not a more supportive group of fanciers in any sport than in Tracking! We also recommend the following literature:

Tracking Regulations—an AKC booklet
(Single copies free to individuals)
The American Kennel Club
51 Madison Ave.
New York, NY 10010

Koehler Method of Training Tracking Dogs by William Koehler
Howell Book House
1633 Broadway
New York, NY 10019

Tracking Dog: Theory and Methods by Glen R. Johnson
Arner Publications, Inc.
8140 Coronado Lane
Rome, NY 13440

Scent and the Scenting Dog by William G. Syrotuck
Arner Publications, Inc.
8140 Coronado Lane
Rome, NY 13440

Tracking: A TD Field Guide
Advanced Tracking: A TDX Field Guide
The Tracking Club of Massachusetts
438 Lowell St.
Wakefield, MA 01880

To quote Wally again, "The key to tracking is motivation." You motivate your puppy with short tracks and something rewarding to find, such as a toy or food. You motivate yourself by remembering that Tracking is a sport that requires the least participation by you because it depends on the natural ability and willingness of your dog. And like a stroll through the park, it is an enjoyable outdoor activity to share with your Rottweiler—but so much more useful! Our AKC tracking judges and search and rescue teams all began with a field, a line, a dog and that first track.

Although they continue to live in perfect health, dogs affected with a loss of pigment turn white or frosted. At 28 months of age, this Rottweiler's nose turned white/pink, then his testicles went pink, and he developed white hairs all over his body, white toenails, and a bubblegum-pink mouth. There is no common denominator (parentage, food, climate, etc.) in this dog's background and that of others with this condition. We strongly suspect "stress" as a contributing factor.

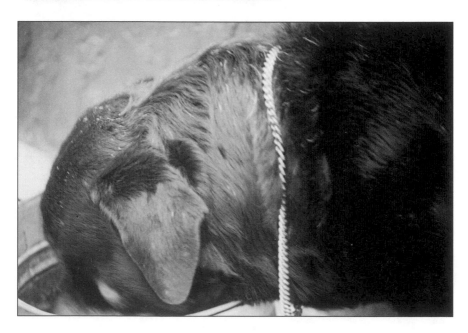

Chapter 9

Health Concerns for Rottweilers and Their Owners

The Rottweiler is a very "natural" dog. Through the years, selection for breeding has been based on working qualities and this, perhaps, accounts for its few hereditary and congenital problems. Canine hip dysplasia is the one developmental problem found in the breed with any statistical frequency. . . . As with any large, heavy breed, shoulder injuries may result from too much rough play with older dogs, or forced exercise, such as jumping, during the formative first year. Ectropion and entropion have been controlled in the Rottweiler by careful breeding so it is a possible, but not a significant, factor. There are few health problems that are unique to the breed.

Marthajo Rademacher and Curtis Giller, DVM, our veterinarian, wrote the preceding for *Medical & Genetic Aspects of Purebred Dogs*, Veterinary Medicine Publishing Company, Edwardsville, Kansas, in the early 1980s. How much of that still holds true today?

The Rottweiler is still a very natural dog, but with such a radical increase in the Rottweiler population we were bound to see new health problems cropping up. One clue to the state of Rottweiler health is found in the advertisements for stud dogs. For example, *Champion I'm A Healthy Rott, OFA, Elbows "Normal", CERF "Clear", VWD "Clear", Thyroid "Normal", Heart "Normal"* tells us more than that this is a dog which has been examined many, many times. It reveals the presence of those conditions which worry us today.

The big problem, unfortunately still with us from the past, is canine hip dysplasia.

HIP DYSPLASIA

The puppy that limps, the dog having difficulty rising, the young dog that can't manage slippery floors and the obedience dog struggling over the jumps could all be showing the symptoms of canine hip dysplasia (CHD).

Canine hip dysplasia was first reported by Dr. G.B. Schnelle as early as 1935. Through research it was found to be an inherited disease of polygenic character where there is faulty conformation of the head of the femur and the acetabulum. While no environmental cause has been found, it appears that environmental factors may influence the degree of expression of the genes within an individual. The only current means of reducing the genetic frequency of CHD is by selectively breeding for normal hips. Enter the OFA.

When you see numbers on a pedigree beginning with the initials RO (for ROttweiler) listed for the parents of your dog, you know that those parents have been certified free of hip dysplasia by the Orthopedic Foundation for Animals (OFA). It does not mean the parent will not produce offspring with hip dysplasia, but it does mean that the breeder is participating in a program to selectively breed for normal hips.

The OFA is a not-for-profit foundation established in 1966 (originally at the University of Pennsylvania and now at the University of Missouri) with the following objectives:

1. To collate and disseminate information concerning orthopedic diseases of animals.

2. To advise, encourage and establish control programs to lower the incidence of orthopedic diseases.

3. To receive funds and make grants to carry out these objectives.

Rottweiler fanciers welcomed a central authority to review and pass on hip X-rays and, led by the Golden State Rottweiler Club, the various breed clubs adopted codes of ethics requiring OFA certification prior to breeding. Starting with Muriel Freeman's Ch. D'Artagnan of Canidom, CD, RO-1, almost thirty years later we see RO numbers in the 40,000s! Much credit goes to those Code of Ethics club members and individuals, like Mrs. Freeman and Clara Hurley, who championed the cause of OFA X-raying and led by example. However, as the population of the breed increased, the influence of the COE clubs and single individuals diminished.

In 1991 the OFA issued a progress report on the fight to eradicate CHD in Rottweilers based on ratings (the OFA gives three ratings for what they consider hips free of dysplasia and four ratings for those considered dysplastic):

Number Evaluated	Free of Hip Dysplasia				Dysplastic			
37,497	Excellent	Good	Fair	Borderline	Mild	Moderate	Severe	
	5.9	51.3	17.8	1.7	10.3	10.9	2.1	

By January 1993, 46,047 Rottweilers had been evaluated, with 6.2% found to have excellent hips and 22.9% found to be dysplastic.

Over the decades there have been changes at the OFA which have affected the Rottweiler. A significant change was increasing the age of the dog for submission for an RO number from twelve months to twenty-four months. A recent development is the affiliation of the OFA with the AKC. Integrating the OFA information with the dog's permanent AKC records will, we hope, encourage more breeders to participate in the program.

Orthopedic problems are certainly not limited to hips. In November 1989 the OFA initiated an elbow registry. Although elbow dysplasia occurs in Rottweilers, we believe it is not nearly as prevalent as hip dysplasia and as yet not addressed in the various codes of ethics of the major clubs.

The Second edition of the OFA booklet *Hip Dysplasia—A Guide for Dog Breeders and Owners* presents an excellent explanation of hip dysplasia and the means for controlling it. It is available by making a donation to the OFA for the purpose of supporting further research (suggested donation $5.00). Write:

Orthopedic Foundation for Animals, Inc.
Nifong Blvd.
Columbia, MO 65201-3856.

RUPTURED ANTERIOR CRUCIATE LIGAMENT

Limping in the rear end does not always indicate hip dysplasia. The anterior cruciate ligament is an important structure in the stifle (knee) joint of the dog because it helps stabilize and strengthen the knee during movement. When this ligament ruptures (tears), it causes instability in the knee which in turn causes inflamation and damage to the joint.

The Rottweiler is a prime target for this condition because as the largest and heaviest of the German utility breeds, the breed's agility and bulk work at odds with each other.

The rupture can occur after a period of gradual degenerative changes in the ligament or by a blunt traumatic accident. Diagnosis is dependent on veterinary evaluation, and surgery is required to repair the damage. Usually surgical repair will result in a reduction of lameness and possibly a delay in degenerative changes causing arthritis in the joint. However, the surgically repaired knee may never be as strong as it was before the rupture, and it is not uncommon for the cruciate ligament in the other knee to rupture later.

CANINE EYE REGISTRY FOUNDATION, INC. (CERF)

Now, along with OFA certification appearing on the AKC records for Rottweilers, CERF certification is also being included in a dog's documentation.

Canine Eye Registry Foundation, Inc. (CERF) is an organization at Purdue University, established in 1974, whose goal is to reduce the incidence of inherited eye diseases in dogs. In order to be registered with the foundation, a dog must be examined by a diplomate of the American College of Veterinary Ophthalmologists.

Entropion (where the eyelid, along with the eyelashes, rolls into the eye, leading to possible ulcerations of the cornea) and **ectropion** (where the eyelid rolls outward and also causing irritation to the cornea) are conditions that must be corrected surgically. They are also disqualifications under the Rottweiler breed standard. Dogs with either entropion or ectropion should never be bred.

An eye problem that is more insidious and probably more prevalent is **cataracts.** At the eighth conference of the IFR in 1991, one of the reports covered hereditary cataracts in Rottweilers. The study was conducted in Oslo, Norway where 111 Rottweilers were examined to reveal that forty-one (36.9 percent) of the dogs had cataracts possibly of an inherited nature. (*Progress in Veterinary & Comparative Ophthalmology, Vo. 1, No. 1, 1991*). The lecturer at this conference, Dr. Ellen Bjerkas of The Norwegian Veterinary College, Oslo, also stated that in 1979 CERF reported twenty-five cases of what they considered to be inherited cataracts in 121 Rottweilers.

Cataract refers to any opacity of the lens or its capsule. There are different types of cataracts, such as developmental cataracts, which can be either congenital (present at birth) or juvenile, which develop as the dog matures. Congenital cataracts are not common; unfortunately juvenile cataracts seem to be more prevalent. This has led some of the breed clubs to sponsor CERF clinics, although the matter of requiring CERF certification has not been addressed in the present codes of ethics of the various clubs. There are still questions regarding the inheritability of the various cataracts.

PARVOVIRUS AND CORONAVIRUS

Two diseases *we know* the Rottweiler is susceptible to are parvovirus and coronavirus. Parvovirus burst upon the Fancy in 1978 with a dread akin to the black plague. Diarrhea and vomiting were symptoms that came on suddenly, and if this highly contagious disease was not treated immediately the results were frequently tragic. The University of Pennsylvania collected data on this outbreak and it was found that Dobermans, English Springer Spaniels and Rottweilers—especially young Rottweilers—were the most at risk.

Coronavirus was isolated in 1971, and like parvovirus, it spreads rapidly. Afflicted dogs will experience a loss of appetite, act lethargic, and eventually exhibit vomiting and diarrhea that is yellowish-green to orange in color and is very rank. Dehydration is a serious problem with both diseases.

Vaccines are now available against both diseases, although one still hears of outbreaks of corona and parvo. When purchasing a puppy, be sure to check with the breeder regarding vaccinations the puppy should have had and check with both your breeder and your veterinarian on what vaccination program you should establish for your puppy. Both diseases continue to be studied and new vaccines are made available.

CANINE HYPOTHYROIDISM

Lethargy is also a symptom of a much less alarming disease—canine hypothyroidism. Other symptoms are loss of hair, weight gain, and skin disease. Often the disease is discovered when, in trying to breed a bitch, she is found to have irregular cycles. A blood test is performed and, if the dog is found to have hypothyroidism, therapy is begun with thyroid medication.

A disease that is exacerbated by hypothyroidism is canine Von Willebrand's disease (VWD), which is an inheritable bleeding disorder.

VON WILLEBRAND'S DISEASE

The disease has been detected in as many as fifty-four breeds. Signs of the disease include mucosal bleeding, still births, neonatal deaths (fading puppies), prolonged estrus or postpartum bleeding, and lameness. The defect involves both platelet and coagulation function. Diagnosis is by a blood sample and therapy by the adminisration of therapeutic agents or by blood transfusions. *(Textbook of Veterinary Internal Medicine, Diseases of the Dog and Cat, Vol. 2, 1989, W.B. Saunders Company, Philadelphia.)*

We, personally, have had no experience with VWD; however, the fact that many Rottweilers are advertised as being tested for this disease would seem to indicate that other Rottweiler fanciers have had to deal with it.

ACUTE GASTRIC DILATATION (BLOAT)

A condition we have had experience with, and one traumatic to both the owner and the dog, is bloat.

Bloat is a condition where the stomach over-distends with gas and can actually flip upon itself (torsion). It is a condition especially prevalent in large, deep-chested breeds, including the Rottweiler. Anyone who has had a dog bloat and rushed the poor creature to the veterinarian will not soon forget it. Early signs of bloat are restlessness and abdominal discomfort. Vomiting or retching commence, although nothing appears except saliva or mucus. As the retching and abdominal distress increase, the dog becomes weaker, breathing is labored, the tongue becomes blue, until finally the dog collapses and dies.

Obviously bloat requires early recognition and immediate treatment for relief of the gas pressure and returning the body to normal.

Since food sitting too long in the stomach causes gas, we recommend that Rottweilers be fed smaller meals twice a day rather than one large feeding. It has also been suggested that you not feed your dog within an hour before or an hour after exercise—rather like the advice we all heard as kids about staying out of the water right after eating. A consistent diet minimizes stomach upset. And be sure to watch that your dog doesn't suddenly drink a great deal of water.

SUBAORTIC STENOSIS (SAS)

The "new disease on the block," or relatively new to the Rottweiler, is SAS or subaortic stenosis.

SAS is a congenital defect of the heart that impedes blood flow and is inherited in several breeds including the Rottweiler. Among the clinical signs are exercise intolerance, fainting or collapse. Shortened life span and sudden, unexpected deaths are also associated with SAS. (*Journal of Veterinary Medicine, May–June 1993.*)

Detection is determined by a cardiologist listening to the heart. If a murmur is detected, further investigation is warranted. The Medallion Rottweiler Club, in association with the University of Illinois, has sponsored several heart clinics as has the Colonial Rottweiler Club with the assistance of the University of Pennsylvania. At this time, investigations are underway to determine the extent to which the breed is affected by this disease.

There are, of course, many other ailments which the Rottweiler shares with all breeds of dogs—from relatively minor conditions such as eczema to fatalities from cancer. However, what the breed has going for it is that the Rottweiler was developed to be a hardy dog with few exaggerations in physical form that would lend themselves to obvious physical problems—a "natural dog." As patients, they are usually fairly stoic, so it is up to the owner to be vigilant in watching for medical problems that might arise.

Chapter 10

Bringing Home the Right Puppy

Caring for your dog begins with planning before you even bring the puppy home. Perhaps the most crucial decision you will make is "from which breeder do I choose a puppy?"

HOW DO YOU CHOOSE A BREEDER?

Even if the Rottweiler puppy you want will primarily be a pet, companion and protector for your family, and you have little interest in showing or breeding, you should look for the very best-bred litter you can find, one raised by experienced and dedicated hobby-breeders. The local Rottweiler clubs can provide you with lists of breeders, or better yet, you can attend club activities and personally meet Rottweiler fanciers in your area. Visit dog shows and study the catalogs, and attend obedience trials where breeders are likely to be exhibiting. The American Rottweiler Club has a breeder's list, or you can call 900-407-7877, which is the AKC's Breed Referral Program.

One of the first questions to ask a breeder is, "What are your club affiliations?" Participation in clubs, especially clubs with a code of ethics, demonstrates a greater interest in the Rottweiler than personal involvement in one's own dogs. The next question is "What have you done with your own dogs?" The breeder you buy from will not only have bred your puppy, but should be your primary source of information on the Rottweiler. The broader the experience your mentor/breeder has had, the more information he or she can pass on to you.

An AKC championship title or championship points indicates that someone besides the owner believes that those dogs physically conform to the Rottweiler Standard in beauty and have none of the disqualifying faults listed therein. Working titles are an additional way of documenting pedigree traits such as dependability, self-confidence, desire to please and, above all, trainability. Although titles cannot guarantee perfection, they do say something about the character of the dog who carries them, and of the owner's commitment to the breed.

We always wonder about breeders who, with little experience in either showing or training, state confidently that they can pick a puppy with potential conformation and trainability. Beware the "instant expert" as there is no shortcut to good breeding!

The pedigree provided by the breeder should contain as much background information on the ancestors of your puppy as possible, for this pedigree serves as the puppy's family history. We try, as you can see in our example of a Rodsden pedigree, to list all the conformation titles, American or foreign, in front of the dogs' names, and all the working titles, American or foreign, behind the dogs' names. In addition, we also include such extra data as eligibility for the various Rottweiler clubs' honor systems, especially noteworthy show wins such as all-breed and Specialty Bests, and hip X-ray information, either OFA or foreign. You can order an AKC certified pedigree for your puppy, but you will find that it includes only the American titles of ancestors and, until recently, no indication of hip status for any dogs named. There are numerous pedigree services available which can provide more detailed pedigrees if your breeder is unable to do so. MRC member Valerie Volker of Volkerstrasse Pedigree Service is an example of someone who does have the foreign studbooks available to trace all those foreign titles which probably appear in your puppy's pedigree—if only you knew it!

It is especially important to search the pedigree for OFA-certified ancestors in a puppy's pedigree, and to discuss with your prospective breeder

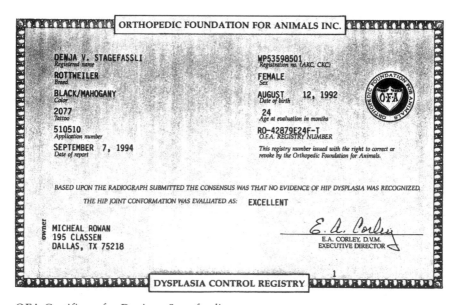

OFA Certificate for Denja v. Stagefassli.

AMERICAN KENNEL CLUB

RODSDEN'S RAVEN OF CADOK	WP548110/01
NAME	NUMBER
ROTTWEILER	FEMALE
BREED	SEX
BLACK & MAHOGANY	NOV 13 1993
COLOR	DATE OF BIRTH
CH IRONWOODS CADE	
SIRE WF640526 (10-87) OFA24 CERF103	
OKIE-LADY V D RUNDERKRAAL CDX	
DAM WG550109 (2-93) OFA24G CERF42 (NET)	
BOBBY ONTIVEROS & CHANDRA KLEM	
BREEDER	
NANCY MCCULLOUGH	JUN 28 1994
PO BOX 836	CERTIFICATE ISSUED
WEST LIBERTY, OH 43357-0836	

IF A DATE APPEARS AFTER THE NAME AND NUMBER OF THE SIRE AND DAM, IT INDICATES THE ISSUE OF THE STUD BOOK REGISTER IN WHICH THE SIRE OR DAM IS PUBLISHED.

THIS CERTIFICATE ISSUED WITH THE RIGHT TO COR-RECT OR REVOKE BY THE AMERICAN KENNEL CLUB

See Transfer Instructions on Back of Certificate

REGISTRATION CERTIFICATE

AKC unlimited individual registration Certificate for Rodsden's Raven of Cadok.

Rodsden's Rottweilers, REG.
PEDIGREE

WP461206/07	*Rodsden's O.Henry of Cadan*	WP461206/07
AKC Reg. No.	Registered Name of Dog	Individual Reg. No.

Date Whelped *December 29, 1992*   Sex *Male*

Breeder *Susan C. Rademacher*   Address

Owner *Susan C. Rademacher*   Address

PARENTS	GRANDPARENTS	GREAT-GRANDPARENTS	GR-GREAT-GRANDPARENTS
SIRE: CHAMPION **Ironwood's Cade,** C.D. RO-10845T (good) WF640526 *Select Champion Best In Show Winner MRC Hall of Fame ARC Gold Producer of Merit A.K.C. Canine Good Citizen Award*	CH. **Donnerschlag v Kertzenlicht,** C.D.X, T.D., RO-4413, *MRC Hall of Fame ARC Bronze Producer of Merit*	A/C CH. **Rodsden's Elko Kastanienbaum,** C.D.X., T.D., Can. C.D., RO-1448, *MRC Hall of Fame, ARC Gold Producer of Merit*	INT. CH. **Elko vom Kastanienbaum,** SchH I, HD-free ADRK
			CH. **Gundi vom Reichenbachle,** RO-846T, MRC Hall of Fame
		Phara vom Hause Kertzenlicht, C.D., RO-2036	CH. **Dux vom Hungerbuhl,** SchH I, RO-234, MRC Hall of Fame
			CH. **Rodsden's Frolich Burga,** C.D., T.D., RO-649, MRC Hall of Fame
	CH. **Disco van het Brabantpark,** RO-5813T *MRC Hall of Fame ARC Silver Producer of Merit* Dutch Import	**Simba van het Brabantpark,** HD-free Utrecht	**Igor vom Kastanienbaum,** SchH III, FH, HD-free ADRK
			DUTCH CH. **Odessa van het Brabantpark,** HD-free Utrecht
		Quarta v Hagenbach, HD-free Utrecht	**Lord v Emerich**
			Bella vom Allgauer Tor
DAM: CHAMPION **Susan van de Hoeve Cor Unum,** C.D. RO-26362T (good) WG320801 *MRC Honor Roll Dutch Import*	INT. CHAMPION **Glenn vom Markgraflerland,** SchH III, IPO III, FH HD +/- ADRK	INT. CH., BS/ES/KLUBSIEGER **Dingo vom Schwaiger Wappen,** SchH III, HD-free Utrecht	INT. CH. ES **Ives Eulenspiegel,** SchH III, HD-free ADRK
			Anja vom Schwaiger Wappen, SchH I, HD-free ADRK
		VDH CH., ITALIAN CH., ES/KLUBSIEGERIN **Yvonne vom Markgraflerland,** SchH III, HD-free ADRK	**Amur v Klingenrain,** SchH III, HD-free ADRK
			Queen vom Markgraflerland, SchH I, HD-free ADRK
	Lona van de Hoeve Cor Unum, HD-free Berne	INT. CH., DUTCH CHAMPION **Duuck v d Nedermolen,** SchH III, HD-free Utrecht	**Axel v d Nedermolen,** SchH II, HD Tc Utrecht
			Nuschka vom Rodehof, HD-free Utrecht
		Corona van de Hoeve Cor Unum, HD-free Utrecht	**Igor vom Kastanienbaum,** SchH III, FH, HD-free ADRK
			Qury van het Brabantpark, HD-free Utrecht

Pedigree of Rodsden's O. Henry of Cadan.

certification from the OFA. Ask to see the originals (or photocopies) of the OFA certificates for the sire and dam of the litter. Certification of the parents does not guarantee that your dog will be free of hip dysplasia, but it does tilt the odds in his favor. It is mandatory for dogs to be OFA-certified before being used for breeding in COE clubs, and it is unconscionable for any Rottweilers to be bred without this certification. Of course, this does not mean that all OFA-certified Rottweilers have the other breed qualifications and should be bred. It does mean that all Rottweilers used for breeding should have an RO number. Do not accept anything less. We also suggest that you discuss with breeders those health concerns we touched upon in the health section of this book. It is especially important that the breeder is up to date on which inoculations are needed for Rottweiler puppies.

Be critical of the advertisements you read. For example, ads that only state size seem to imply that there are few other positive characteristics of the dogs that could be used to promote the litter. Stating in the ad that both parents are on the premises is not necessarily a good recommendation, since knowledgeable breeders try to mate their bitches with the best possible stud dog, who may be across the country. However, we do suggest visiting the Rottweilers at the breeder's home and seeing the mother of the puppies, for she not only provides half the genetic material to the puppies, but it has been her disposition to which the puppies have been exposed. Also, her physical condition is indicative of the care the breeder has given to the litter in general.

The more knowledgeable you are and the more knowledgeable you sound, the more respect your inquiry will get. A responsible hobby breeder has socialized and watched these puppies from birth. You must trust your breeder. The hardest thing about success of a litter is matching the right pup to the right people.

A successful breeder will have part of the litter reserved in advance. Those on the breeder's waiting list who are interested in getting more involved in conformation showing and/or a breeding program will also rely on the breeder to select the more promising puppy for them. These puppies will cost more, but they will be from the same litter with the same genetic potential as the less expensive puppy the breeder might select for you.

Successful and respected breeders don't breed "pets." They only breed those dogs who have no disqualifying faults, have good temperaments, are sound and have won, or could win, on a given day in a conformation show. But large dogs usually have large litters, so they are not all offered at the higher prices. Those puppies not intended for showing and breeding should be sold with an AKC limited registration (see Chapter 5), which means that no offspring from them will be eligible for AKC registration, and they are not eligible for AKC conformation shows. They can, however, compete for any of the AKC obedience and other working titles. The sales contract you receive, which is also required from COE club breeders, will spell out which registration you will get.

Looking at the Litter

We have found the average Rottweiler litter to contain seven puppies, with the average weight of a puppy at birth to be between twelve and fourteen ounces. What strikes one when seeing a Rottweiler litter for the first time is how small the puppies are compared to their ultimate size. We have also found that the smallest puppy at birth does not necessarily turn out to be the smallest, and the largest puppy may easily be surpassed in size by siblings as the puppies mature. When looking at a really good litter, all the puppies should be uniform. The breeder can tell them apart, but you may not be able to! If a litter has only one "pick puppy," then it is not an exceptional litter, and we would not repeat that breeding. Under no circumstances should you be told that differences in temperament determine which puppy is a pet and which is not. All the puppies in a litter should be outgoing, friendly and responsive to human contact. Sometimes the enthusiasm and energy in which the traits are expressed vary from puppy to puppy, but their general attitudes should be as even as their conformation.

What a breeder should be striving for is a very good over-all litter—uniform, with only very minor differences. This is the best insurance that you will get that special pup, whether you are buying it as a pet, or have more serious intent for its future.

Discuss with the breeder the various puppies in the litter. Find out the differences in conformation and personality that the breeder sees in the puppies. There are some basic features an experienced breeder looks for in the puppies which can only be seen with any certainty after the puppies are six to seven weeks old. The puppy teeth will have come in by then, and the bites can be checked with greater certainty. The puppies should have scissors bites as required by the Standard. If a puppy is overshot, the upper incisors (front teeth) will extend over the lower front teeth so that there is a space between them. That pup automatically becomes a pet. The upper teeth should fit tightly over the lower teeth like scissors. Undershot is just the opposite, with the lower teeth extending over the upper teeth. In fifty years with Rottweilers, we have never personally seen an eight-week old puppy that was undershot. In our experience the undershot bite develops as the underjaw grows, usually after the permanent teeth have come in. The permanent teeth begin to emerge at about four months, and may cause some changes in the bite, sometimes up until a year of age.

Historically, early Rottweilers often had patches of white on their coats, especially a spot or streak on the chest, sometimes extending between the legs. Today this is considered a serious fault (unless it is just a few white hairs), and such a pup would automatically be sold as a pet. If the spot is very small,

Long coats are not common, but they do appear.

"Your breeder's selection is still the best bet." Ch. Yden's Chase Manhattan, CD, BH, HCT at five months.

it could disappear and this puppy might eventually become the handsomest puppy in the litter. The puppy with white markings would go to its new home with a limited registration, as would the pup with an incorrect bite.

Seven- to eight-week-old puppies will not yet show the rich mahogany, but the color may be starting to deepen in the muzzle. The puppies will have a soft, somewhat fuzzy, puppy coat which changes as the puppy matures. Often the adult coat first shows up along the top of the back. If the pup has long hair on and about the ears, rear and stomach (and the coat seems to "flow" as the puppy trots around), this may be a long-coated puppy. Long coats are not common, but they do appear. A puppy with a long coat is, of course, a pet since a long coat is a breed disqualification. There are many other things an experienced breeder looks for that can be pointed out to the new owner, another reason to buy from a breeder you can trust.

Our puppies are not allowed many visitors before they have had their first puppy shots, including the parvo shot at six weeks. No matter how concerned you are about parvo, however, puppies should not be raised in a "bubble"; family members should become the socializers until the puppies get to their new homes. Proper socialization and handling from the time of whelping has been provided by your breeder. We can't stress enough how terribly important that is to the future of your puppy.

You may be seeing the puppies for the first time when you go to pick yours up, so you must realize that one observation is not equal to the constant observation the breeder has given the litter. The high-energy little devil in the litter might have just finished tiring himself out and be sleeping while the quieter, more easy-going one has just awakened! Some breeders do character testing which measures such qualities as dominance, retrieving instincts, energy level, sensitivity to touch and sound, and social interaction. But, again, any test is only as good as the tester. We have never found any significant differences in the puppies when we have done puppy character testing that carried over in adulthood to any degree. The breeder's selection is still your best assurance, and the breeder's success is measured by getting the right dogs to the right people.

BRINGING THE PUPPY HOME

Once you have located a breeder you trust and feel comfortable with (and, incidentally, who will be available to answer those inevitable questions connected with raising a Rottweiler), it's just a matter of being patient until your puppy is ready to become a part of your home. According to most animal behaviorists, the ideal time to get your puppy is when the puppy is between seven and eight weeks of age. Breeders will tell you that, by this age, Rottweiler puppies crave human companionship. They are much more interested in human interaction than playing with each other, and this is the time that the puppy should begin to bond with his new owner.

There is no breed where it is more important to establish a "pecking order" early than with the Rottweiler. The puppy must learn from the beginning that you are master, and that all your family members precede the puppy in the social hierarchy of the group.

Best bets . . . Ch. Rodsden's Parry v. Gunter, CD, TD at nine weeks.

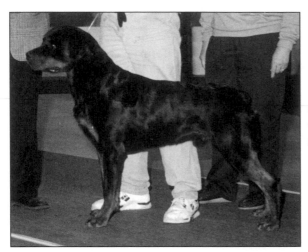

Ch. Rodsden's Parry
v. Gunter, CD, TD at
seventeen months.

One can get an older puppy at an age which fits right into the family, but if you want to have the greatest influence on your puppy's character, the best time to begin is at seven to eight weeks.

By seven weeks, the puppy will also have been weaned for about two or three weeks, and will be adjusted to a good commercial puppy food. The breeder should provide the new owner with a small supply of the food the puppy is accustomed to for the transition period from the breeder's home to the new home. In all likelihood, the breeder will have discussed food with the owner before the puppy leaves the litter.

What should you expect from the breeder when the "big day" arrives? When you pick up the puppy, the pup should be accompanied by American Kennel Club (AKC) registration papers. Papers usually take the form of a "blue slip," aptly named because it is blue in color. The blue slip is an application for individual registration provided by the AKC for each puppy after the entire litter has been registered. The blue slip lists the puppy's litter registration number, and has a place to print the name chosen for the puppy and an area where ownership can be transferred from the breeder to the new owner. All American-bred puppies follow this route of registration—from a litter application to a blue slip to a final individual AKC registration certificate. The blue slip allows the breeder to register the puppy directly to his or her own name, transfer ownership to a second party, or specify a limited registration from a breeder to a second party. The AKC registration certificates are color coded—a regular registration certificate has a purple border, while a limited registration certificate has an orange border.

With the papers comes the need to have decided on the puppy's registered name. We wish everyone who decides on a name for his or her Rottweiler puppy would remember that the word "noble" is often used to describe the breed. The AKC limits the name to a length of twenty-eight characters, and most often the breeder will require that the breeder's kennel name be part of the puppy's registered name. Your breeder's kennel name may be registered with the AKC. Registering a kennel name protects the breeder from the unauthorized use of that name (much as registered trademarks protect product names). To be able to register a kennel name requires breeding documentation over a long period of time in addition to a fee paid to the AKC.

German breeders, as well as many American breeders, name their litters alphabetically. These breeders require that all the puppies in the same litter have names beginning with the same letter so that years later, the dog's name will identify from which litter it came.

The health records should also come with the puppy. By seven weeks, the puppy should have had its first set of puppy shots and been wormed at least twice. The records should be complete and easy for the new owner to understand. The name of the breeder's vet should be included on the records for future reference by the new owner's vet. In the Rottweiler fancy today, there are serious discussions regarding the frequency of vaccinations. We recommend that new owners discuss vaccination schedules with both their breeders and their veterinarians.

Once the puppy has his individual AKC registration number, the new owner can request from the AKC a certified pedigree. However, breeders should always provide each puppy owner with their own three- or four-generation pedigree, which may be much more detailed than the AKC pedigree. Many

Introduce your puppy to your child under supervision. Never leave a child with a puppy, or grown dog, for that matter, without supervision.

If you teach your child and your Rottweiler to love and respect one another, they become buddies for life (and the kid always has her very own pillow).

of our dogs are only a generation or so away from European progenitors, and AKC certified pedigrees do not include foreign titles. We hope this will change in the future as the AKC and FCI come closer together. As the AKC only recently began to include information on hip dysplasia status, it is also quite possible that the AKC pedigree will include generations of earlier dogs whose hip status is not listed, but is known by the breeder. The pedigree provided by the breeder should be as complete as possible.

Feeding instructions and basic tips are a welcome addition to your puppy's "going home packet" because they offer help in getting through those first days in the new home. Helpful information on crate training, housebreaking, names of local obedience clubs, and other essentials offer answers to questions that may present themselves at all hours of the day and night. When in doubt, call your breeder (although perhaps not at all hours of the day and night!). The breeder is just as anxious as you are to have your puppy become a well-mannered and sincerely appreciated member of the family.

One common question asked by prospective owners as they take home their puppy is, "What size dog crate should be purchased for the puppy?" The practical answer is to purchase a crate large enough to serve a fully mature adult Rottweiler. Crate-trained dogs treat their crates like "indoor dog houses." It is a place to retreat for a nap or to just get out of the way. It isn't uncommon to see an adult Rottweiler happily sleeping in a crate with the door to the crate wide open and the choices of "softer" places at hand. If you are purchasing an airline crate, then you will need either a 400- or 500-size crate. However, we feel that for crate-training, a wire crate is preferable because, until the puppy comes to accept (and appreciate) his crate as his special place, the puppy will not feel so isolated in a crate from which he can observe what is going on around him.

Finally, the breeder should provide a contract which spells out what each party expects of the other and what is expected of the puppy. The better the

"Yes, Rottweilers get along well with kids and other dogs if they are brought up together."

"He loved my son; they grew together . . . my son could not have had a better friend . . . he was family; losing him was like losing a child. My son faced death for the first time; he misses his friend every day . . . "

understanding established between breeder and owner in the beginning, the fewer the opportunities for misunderstandings to crop up later on.

THE CASE FOR THE OLDER DOG

Over the years, we have imported many dogs that were no longer puppies. The advantage to getting a grown dog is obvious—you can see the "finished product." There is no guessing as to bite, eye color, clarity of markings and other features. If the dog is old enough, there is also no guessing as to hip status. Our experience has been that a dog with a stable, correct temperament makes rapid adjustments to new lifestyles, even to a new language. However, in acquiring an older dog you must remember that those forces which forged the character of the dog are unknown to you. The good and bad experiences the dog has matured through are unknown to you. And the dog's reactions to life's ups and downs are unknown to you—but not for long! The surprises may be pleasant, or they may not be.

CARING FOR THAT SPECIAL PUPPY

What often surprises new owners who bring home a seven- to eight-week old puppy is how much sleep the puppy requires, for puppies that age are truly babies, and must be treated as such. We immediately start crate-training a puppy with a wire crate placed in a corner of a room where it is out of the traffic flow, but still within the perimeters of family activity. The crate will eventually be the dog's safe haven, but in the beginning, the crate is simply a place to put a tired puppy, a puppy that is too much under one's feet, or a puppy that needs rescuing from over-enthusiastic children.

You should have received feeding instructions from the breeder and possibly a sample of the food the puppy is accustomed to. Our puppies have always done nicely on a good quality commercial puppy kibble, although many breeders recommend more elaborate diets. We do not recommend adding table scraps because not only do these "extras" throw off the balance of nutrients in the commercial food, but tend to make picky eaters of the puppies who will then prefer the extras to their regular food. Overfeeding does not make for a bigger Rottweiler. It makes for a fatter one. However, we remember the sad case of an owner who continued to feed his puppy the amount recommended at eight weeks and was alarmed that, as the puppy aged, it seemed constantly ravenous! Use common sense and, when in doubt, call the breeder. We feed our adult dogs twice a day because it seems to satisfy their hunger and serves as a precaution against bloat.

Elevated feeding dishes were practically unknown when we began in Rottweilers. (One remembers those very heavy crockery dishes that were in vogue which, while a struggle to carry full of food, were nonetheless easily demolished by a playful Rottweiler.) Elevated dishes are better because they force the puppy to stand up straight, strengthening its pasterns, and the dishes are infinitely lighter to carry. Such elevated feeding stations can be purchased at dog shows, from mail order catalogs, in pet shops, or, if you are handy about making things, can be of your own design.

A regular feeding routine greatly aids in housebreaking a puppy. Rottweilers are usually easy to housebreak if one is willing to devote the time (and patience) right from the beginning. Sometimes the housebreaking results are exceptional. Louise and Fred Pacelt's Rottweiler bitch, Webony, learned to ring a bell when she needed to go out. Webony never rang the bell to simply go out to play or because she wanted to go for a walk. It was an impressive demonstration of housebreaking!

Toys amuse the puppy, provide something acceptable to chew on, and serve as a tool for establishing pecking order in the family. The puppy is to rank below all human family members in authority and, consequently, should release the toy to any family member without protest. Again, common sense dictates that adults do not let children tease or torment the puppy. Likewise, all human family members should also be able to handle the puppy's food without the puppy guarding the food dish. Toys should be appropriate. You would be surprised how needle-sharp Rottweiler puppy teeth are, and how the "indestructible toy" disintegrates after a few hours of chewing. Balls and kongs are favorite toys, but must be of a suitable size not to be swallowed. A particularly tragic story is told of a young Rottweiler who loved to retrieve and, in catching a hard rubber ball, had it lodge in his throat. The dog suffocated before the owner could dislodge the ball.

A word about natural bones—dogs do love them, but there is a down side. Once we gave a litter, of about six weeks of age, some large bones to play with. Normally the puppies reacted in happy enthusiasm to the dog biscuits which we sprinkled in the pen. Reacting to these real bones, the litter turned into four-legged piranhas! It wasn't a pretty sight as they growled and snarled over the bones. We never did that again. We also had an older dog that nearly died when a bone splintered and impacted his intestine, so we personally do not recommend feeding natural bones to Rottweilers of any age.

Grooming

Grooming a Rottweiler is one area that is relatively simple thanks to the breed's hard, short coat. A curry comb or brush should do the trick to remove dirt. Our Standard states that Rottweilers are to be untrimmed. Nails, however, must be kept short. Rottweilers notoriously dislike having their feet handled, so the owner of the new puppy must establish a routine from the beginning of frequent nail cutting either with clippers or an electric grinder. Your dog may not like it, but he must submit to it. Drop ears also require careful scrutiny and proprietary cleaning to prevent ear infections.

Most of us try to eliminate as much stress in our lives as possible. We should do the same for our puppy. That is one reason breeders try to avoid placing puppies in new homes during the holidays. However, there are internal stress periods that almost all puppies go through. The first is at about three or four months when the puppy is teething. The deciduous (baby) teeth are falling out, and the permanent teeth are coming in. This is a good time to avoid trying situations with the puppy, although the teeth should be monitored to see that the baby teeth do, in fact, fall out. If a baby tooth is firmly in place and crowding the newly erupted permanent tooth, a veterinarian should be consulted.

An indication of stress during this period can be reflected in a change in either ear carriage or a weakness in the pasterns. Your veterinarian may recommend a vitamin/mineral supplement to your puppy's diet. Folded ears (in which a crease is suddenly noticed) are not that uncommon and demand immediate attention. Either the affected ear must be massaged, or the incorrectly folded ear can be taped. As breeders, we get the most questions about how to tape, so we would like to present the following technique recommended by breeder Dorothy Wade and previously reprinted in the 25th and later 30th Anniversary Books of the Medallion Rottweiler Club. As judges, we must say that it is always unfortunate when an otherwise lovely head and expression is spoiled by incorrectly folded ears.

DOROTHY WADE'S TECHNIQUE FOR TAPING EARS

My method of taping a Rottweiler puppy's ears is relatively simple. Does it work? I believe it does, but only if it is done between the third and sixth months. After that time, the ear carriage is probably set.

1. Use athletic tape (the type used to wrap baseball bats and hockey sticks).
2. Make sure the ear itself is clean both inside and out (tape won't stick to a waxy surface).
3. Cut a strip about five inches long. Secure it to the inside of the ear about halfway between the opening and the tip.
4. Cut another strip about five inches long. Secure it to the outside of the ear about halfway.
5. Secure both strips together.
6. Cut another piece of tape that is long enough to reach under the puppy's chin; then, making sure that the ear is correctly set against the head, secure both ear tape pieces under the chin.

"You can smell them, but please don't eat the flowers!"

As early as nine weeks, you can start training your puppy to be set-up and play "show dog" on a table.

Training your puppy to bait into show position takes practice.

Note: Make sure the taped pieces are tight enough to keep the ears from folding but loose enough to allow for some air circulation. You can leave it on for about three or four days if the pup doesn't pull it off first. If, when it comes off, the ear looks good, there is no need to do anything else. Usually the procedure has to be done several times over several weeks, but always allow up to three days in-between to allow the ear canals to dry and so avoid ear infection.

A second stressful period, usually for the dog and the owner, is between twelve and eighteen months, when the previously happy-go-lucky male puppy reaches puberty and, like all rebellious teenagers, decides it is a time to test the limits of what is going to be permitted. Usually this stage is mercifully short, and if the owner has established a good relationship with the puppy, firm and steady handling will see both owner and dog through the rough spots.

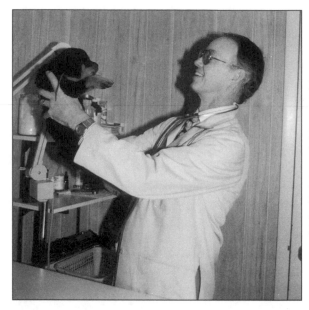

It's never too early to begin a good relationship between you, your Rottweiler and your veterinarian. If you have bought the puppy, take him or her to the veterinarian as soon as possible and bring the puppy's health record with you.

Put a choke collar on your puppy for training sessions, which should begin as soon as you bring the new addition to your family home.

"Henry learns to come."

Informal training begins the moment you bring the puppy home. Learning his name, recognizing simple commands like come or down, and housebreaking are all part of the puppy's routine. By now you know that Rottweilers are very intelligent, and one is surprised at how many spoken words the puppy learns in addition to those unspoken gestures we humans hardly ever notice. Formal training, however, usually has to wait for the puppy to mature emotionally and mentally to match his size. Rottweilers grow up faster physically than they do mentally, and one has to remember that a big, six-month old puppy is still a baby that tires easily and has an attention span much shorter than that of an adult. Most dog training clubs do not accept puppies younger than six months for formal training, but do have puppy kindergartens where younger puppies learn to relate to other puppies. These classes are fun for both puppy and owner but, because of the Rottweiler's susceptibility to parvovirus, we recommend that you discuss attending classes for a young puppy with both your breeder and your veterinarian before signing up.

Perhaps the best advice we can give on raising a puppy is that you get what you put into it. The amount of time, patience, effort and love you give to the puppy are mirrored in the relationship you have with the grown dog.

We are lucky indeed, when we find a stud who is outstanding—both phenotypically and genotypically. Ch. Falco v.h. Brabantpark, ARC Gold Producer with his young sons Rodsden's Axel v.h. Brabant and Rodsden's Ander v.h. Brabant. Both sons finished and all became MRC Hall of Fame members. *Ritter*

Chapter 11

Breeding . . . Theory and Experience

THEORY

Before embarking on a breeding program in Rottweilers, have a firm idea of which definition of breeder will best fit you. There are, in any breed, people who produce puppies . . . and then there are breeders. For the sake of the Rottweiler, breeding should remain with sincere, responsible breeders. The onus is on the new generation of breeders, because it is on them—their commitment, their involvement, and their developing knowledge—that the Rottweiler's future will depend.

Deciding to become a Rottweiler breeder is a little like taking marriage vows. It is not to be entered into lightly or ill-advisedly, but with full understanding . . . and you will find that "for better or worse, for richer or poorer, and in sickness and in health until death do us part" also applies. It is how one handles the worse, poorer, in sickness, and the responsibility for having engineered the existence of the puppies, which is a lifetime proposition until death do us part, that helps determine whether one has become a breeder. The term *breeder* is without gender—whether you manage the stud dog or the brood bitch, the commitment must always be complete.

In general, the theory of breeding purebred animals is that like, more often than not, produces like . . . *but not always!* First refining a breed and then refining individuals in the breed as closely as possible to a written and/or visible standard is the challenge.

Breeding a working dog is the greatest challenge; and breeding one of the finest of working dogs, the Rottweiler, is the ultimate challenge. With dogs, we must breed not only for one or two significant characteristics (such as milk production in dairy cattle or track records in race horses), but for a whole rainbow of characteristics. We must breed for rather specific standards of beauty, as well as for characteristics of temperament that allow the individual Rottweiler to function as a utility dog, companion and protector. We must breed for the soundness in structure that best allows the individual dog to perform as his basic character requires. We are trying to fashion a dog with a full complement of genetic colors, realizing that some of the characteristics will come in various hues of intensity in the individual animal, but all must be there.

The genes that each individual dog carries, which have been given by his parents—50 percent from the sire and 50 percent from the dam—and his genetic predisposition from his ancestry, are the colors the breeder is given to work with. Environment and nutrition will shade those colors as the dog develops. With luck, your puppies will express in themselves the best characteristics of the breed, if you have put the best into them. We will not go into genetics, because we are not geneticists. But remember, you deal with dominants and recessives; you work with complicated genetic structure and balance, especially in faults such as hip dysplasia; recessive, polygenic, incomplete penetrance, etc. To be sure, breeding is never a sure thing, but the uncertainty is what makes it endlessly fascinating.

Some Basic Definitions

Gene: A unit of inheritance. Genes are arranged in linear fashion along the chromosomes. Complementary genes act together to produce an effect different from that of either acting separately. Modifying genes alter the action of other (major) genes. Suppressive genes act solely to suppress the action of other genes.

Dominance: The power of one of a pair of genes to mask the effect of the other member pair. (The offspring of a first generation will inherit the dominant characteristics.)

Recessive: The opposite of dominant, a gene which is masked by the dominant member of a pair. Recessive characteristics lie dormant and may appear in the second or third or later generations. Should it happen that two individuals are bred together having the same recessive characteristic, then the recessive character becomes dominant in their progeny. This applies to genetic faults and is why, in Rottweilers, two perfectly marked parents can produce puppies with white markings. As you can see, it takes two to tango!

Genotype: Refers to the total gene complex, or what is derived from the individual's parents . . . the hereditary pattern.

Phenotype: Refers to the characteristics that can be seen in the dog itself or the visual manifestation due to the action of environment on the hereditary pattern.

We are very lucky, indeed, when we find the dog who is both phenotypically and genotypically great. We use the term luck because the way the genes line up in the individual puppies is up to chance. But the genes came from the parents, and their genes from their parents. Whatever emerges had to be there, or the predisposition—somewhere in the parentage—that characteristic was there waiting for the right combination of genes to get together in that one puppy. This can be for good or bad, of course. This is how a very great dog can come from a mediocre background . . . or a very faulty dog can have an excellent background.

Inbreeding: Inbreeding is the breeding of the closest possibly related individuals; mother to son, father to daughter; sister to brother. Sometimes the term is used to include slightly more distant relationships such as half-brother and half-sister.

Inbreeding has as many disadvantages as advantages. Its advantages can be that it fixes type more quickly than other methods; it tends to the formation of distinct families within a breed, and it is better to select families than just individuals: it is the severest test of breeding worth—hidden faults may be brought to light which can then, hopefully, be bred out. Inbreeding then fixes characteristics and increases the prepotency of individual animals.

Its disadvantages are that it affects all genes, not just the ones the breeder wants affected. Therefore, it fixes faults even more readily than virtues because faults are in the main due to recessive genes. Any animal showing the fault must have inherited the gene for it in duplicate and therefore from both parents. It can lead very quickly to the deterioration of the breed. It is no method for the novice because it requires much knowledge of both pedigree and the actual individual dogs, as well as their ancestors and progeny. It can break up and disperse favorable genetic combinations for the desired characteristics, which will then suffer accordingly. To succeed, inbreeding needs outstanding animals of which there may be but few available. It can perpetuate a line of mediocrities that is harder to overcome than the occurrence of isolated faults, because it is due to a general lack of merit. And, then, the breeder must be willing to cull severely. In short, it is a powerful but dangerous tool. (You would think that the ADRK system would use this tool, but they very seldom do so. Occasionally a breeding involving a slightly more distant relationship is done, but remember, Germany is a small country, geographically, under strict breeding rules guided by people with more complete documentation and knowledge available than most Americans have.)

Linebreeding: Linebreeding is bringing together individuals within a particular line of descent in the attempt to relate the progeny as closely as possible to a particular ancestor of outstanding merit.

Much of what has been said about inbreeding also applies to linebreeding, but it is a less powerful and also a less dangerous tool. The outstanding male ancestor's influence can be greatly extended if that individual is

The Stud Dog Class is offered at Specialties as a non-regular class. It is judged on two of the dog's "get." Ch. Rodsden's Kane v. Forstwald, CD, ARC Gold Producer was Best of Breed and Best Stud Dog at the 1981 Colonial Specialty under Mrs. Bernard Freeman. His "get" shown here, Rodsden's Tristan v. Forstwald and Rodsden's Toni v. Forstwald, both became champions, obedience titlists and MRC Hall of Famers. *Chuck Goodman*

recognized while he is still living and matings direct to him are possible. If he appears only once on each side of a pedigree, his influence is diluted, depending on how far back he appears. Excellence in the animal being linebred to is essential because linebreeding to mediocrity will not produce excellence. The breeder's knowledge of the genotype is just as necessary for linebreeding as for inbreeding, and exactly the same qualities in the dogs being bred are needed. The outstanding individual is the requirement of both approaches. (It is painful to observe a novice breeder linebreeding to a dog whose outstanding faults are glaringly obvious in many of his progeny.)

Outcrossing: Outcrossing is the mating of individuals less closely related than the average. It is the only way in which new genes can be introduced to an established family.

By outcrossing, a breeder can combine in his own line's genes from other lines. If the parents have been carefully selected, the resulting genotype will be good. It will more often be a combination of good and bad, but you can then select the good and continue the breeding program using the good. So, neither in inbreeding nor outcrossing can you produce any gene not existing in the individuals being used, and undesirable genes are as likely to be inherited as desirable ones. To provide new genes or to prevent the fixing of some defect in the linebred or inbred family, you outcross. But the outcross must also be genotypically superior, or you are simply introducing more undesirable genes.

In choosing any of these programs, you still select for similarity in desirable points in phenotype. However, if you do not study the pedigree and the genotype, and continue only to breed like to like as individuals, you can tend to produce a population of extremes.

In theory then, you are trying to bring together a dog and a bitch whose combined genetic colors are very good for the characteristics you are trying to reproduce, and whose predisposition for good qualities is similar. At the same time, you do not want to bring together a dog and bitch whose genetic colors for faults are similar, and whose predisposition for unwanted characteristics is the same. Since every dog has some features that could be better, the breeder never gets the opportunity to mate two perfect animals together. Even if we agreed that the two were perfect in phenotype, there is still the genotype to worry about. We are trying to find the prepotent nick for all the goodies we want in the resulting puppies. Prepotency is the power of passing on good (or bad, but most often refers to good) qualities because they are genetically possessed in duplicate and must therefore be inherited by all offspring. If the sire and dam are both prepotent for a certain characteristic, it therefore predisposes the puppies in the litter toward this characteristic and the line coming from this breeding toward this characteristic.

So the wise breeder will choose individuals to breed together with a view to the dogs complementing each other, to improve each other's weak points and to strengthening and fixing good points. Because this must be done not only on phenotype but also on genotype, the breeder will have to become a student of pedigrees . . . but pedigrees are only of value if the breeder knows something of the animals listed in them, can see or learn about littermates and progeny, and has a pedigree with some documentation in it. In the U.S., this documentation can only include beauty titles, working titles and OFA numbers (CERF and Elbow certification numbers). This is where the European breeder has such an advantage. You can read about the wonders of the German *Ahnentafel* (pedigree) as developed under the ADRK system elsewhere in this book.

The breeder will show wisdom if he knows that a championship title proves only that someone thought the dog had merit under our system of judging, but this is better than only taking the word of the owner, who might be somewhat prejudiced. A champion, whose pedigree documented here or in

Europe shows evidence of careful selective breeding for appearance and performance is what our breeder is seeking.

Again, remember that it takes two good dogs to pass on all the characteristics needed to produce puppies whose potential to contribute to the breed is there. One great breed partner cannot do it all. The sum total of one great genetic portrait is not enough to make up for mediocrity in the other. If you breed two mediocre dogs, you will get mediocre dogs more often than not. You may get lucky once in a while and breed an outstanding one, but that is not good breeding—just good luck. And good luck often runs out!

EXPERIENCE

Of course, achieving breeding success is very much easier in theory than in practice. Good breeding is based on selection. Selection is based on the individual, the pedigree and the progeny. Just how does our breeder warp the odds in his favor?

In Rottweilers in the U.S., the breeder enjoys several distinct advantages; but one of the advantages is no longer applicable to the American gene pool. The Rottweiler Fancy was once a rather small community of breeders who knew each other, their dogs and their pedigrees. The knowledge they may have lacked they could learn from each other and from Europe with a minimum of effort. This is no longer true. The dearth of fanciers having in-depth familiarity with the gene pool must be terribly confusing for today's newcomer seeking information and guidance and wishing to become a breeder.

But we still have some advantages to bequeath. There is still a strong nucleus of concerned people and responsible breeders in the Rottweiler clubs of America, and our communication with each other has increased along with the number of clubs. A new breeder has somewhere to go to ask the questions and get the answers he needs if he will only do it. A new breeder has documentation available for learning about progeny and littermates through fine AKC publications and the excellent newsletters in the breed clubs. The breeder has the national OFA hip dysplasia registry, plus eye and elbow registries now linked with AKC. Although we have no systematic testing and documentation on character here as in Europe, we do have many new performance titles that can be documented and many new opportunities for participation in sanctioned or unsanctioned events to test our dogs' instincts and character. And he can expect this to be documented in pedigrees and periodicals.

The best way to warp the odds for any and all aspects of breeding expertise is still depth of pedigree. And in the Rottweiler, this means depth of pedigree for all things, not just beauty. In Germany, we have seen the head breed warden of the ADRK work out potential breedings on paper by assigning number values to the individuals in the line. He would say again and again, It is the *line* that is important! But he had much, much information on the

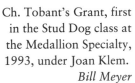

Ch. Tobant's Grant, first
in the Stud Dog class at
the Medallion Specialty,
1993, under Joan Klem.
Bill Meyer

lines and had seen most of the dogs in them. It was still somewhat subjective but more scientific than our system. If our breeder cannot do this, he can at least watch what others do who are successful, investigate and ask.

In our experience, to be successful you must breed two good dogs with more good littermates and good dogs behind them than bad. And it helps if some of them are outstanding! Even so, you cannot expect to completely eliminate faults, but you do want to dilute them. You hope to breed some outstanding individuals along with the good ones, of course. But in multiple births, do not be too discouraged if sometimes the unwanted genes can get together instead of all the wanted genes in an individual puppy.

Some Suggestions from Our Experience

1. Do not inbreed with Rottweilers; It can produce everything from unmanageable temperaments, to infertility, to problems that we had never before seen in the breed, and the dogs produced may not be any more handsome or trainable than those from linebreeding or outcrossing. (We could not possibly show you photos of all the really fine Rottweilers in this country, but those published in this book and those that have contributed to the breed in some way were the results of linebreeding or outcrossing.)

2. If you want your breeding to develop a certain characteristic—for example, the preferred, rich rust markings—the fastest way is to double up on this characteristic in the parents, and hope, if you have not seen the grandparents, that they also had this characteristic or could produce it. You may still get some puppies with light markings, but you should expect more with the rich rust color. You then double up on this characteristic again in the next generation to try to fix it in the

line. If the dog you are breeding from lacks the rich rust color, then breed to a dog proven to be prepotent for excellent color. You will still get some of each, which you breed back again to dogs with the wanted characteristic. You know that the trait for lighter color is probably still in the genetic pot you are drawing from, but you are reinforcing the pool for the good color genes with each breeding.

3. Improving on the head model can be accomplished in one generation; the breeding partner should have the head type you are looking for, and his/her pedigree should have produced a line of correct-headed models.

4. Test breeding a bitch with one missing tooth (not a disqualification but a serious fault of structure—remember that in judging and breeding, faults of structure are to be given more weight than faults of beauty) may well end up with one of the best puppies from the litter having two missing teeth (a disqualification). Never test-breed a stud dog with any serious faults of structure because you have the option of putting that fault into so many more test breedings than with a bitch and the temptations to continue testing are ever-present.

5. In the Rottweiler Standard, complete lack of pigmentation in the mouth is listed as a serious fault, but it is a beauty fault. In breeding, there are several questions one must consider about pink mouths.

   A. The heritability of the problem has not been determined.

   B. The influence of diet, supplements and stress have not been determined.

   C. The mouth turns pink at unpredictable times as the dog ages. In the same litter a dog may retain the dark mouth until he dies and another may lose the pigmentation any time from puppyhood into advanced years. The dark mouth suddenly turns pink at age three or six or seven after the dog has been used in a breeding program.

   D. We have never been able to predict with statistical reliability which puppy at seven to eight weeks, when they usually go to their new homes (or you decide to keep one), will end up with a pink mouth. All we can do is go back to the original theory and realize that it is better to breed a dog with a beauty fault from a litter and parents that have not developed that fault in significant numbers, than to breed a dog with a fault whose parents or littermates have the same fault in common in significant numbers.

6. Remember that the Standard calls for a *medium-large* Rottweiler. To keep this size in more of the progeny, the easiest way is for the breeding partners to be similar in size. However, if one of the breeding partners is toward the tall or the short end of the Standard, choose a breeding partner toward the middle or opposite end of the Standard.

7. Repeat a good nick. If you are fortunate to breed a litter that has proven to produce what the Standard calls for in most of the puppies, with a number of outstanding individuals, repeat that breeding. Your brood bitch has one litter a year and perhaps five or six in her lifetime; wasting her seasons trying to improve on a great breeding is non-productive of establishing your line or kennel name.

8. With a first mating to prove your young stud dog, try him with a proven brood bitch, one who has already been bred successfully (and easily, you hope) and has produced a litter.

9. Trying to breed for temperament is probably one of the most difficult assignments because it is the least well defined. We must have a Rottweiler that can live in today's world in our frequently litigious society. Yet we must try to retain those traits of temperament that made us choose the Rottweiler in the first place (and ensured its survival through the years). The best advice we can give is a simple formula: If the breeding partners do not have the aforementioned criteria, simply don't breed them.

10. The stud dog gets all the credit and also, usually, all the blame for what the litter produces for the breed. Remember that, in multiple births and with the larger number of offspring a stud dog produces, it would be very unusual, if he is used very often, *not* to produce some unwanted characteristics. An incorrect bite and an occasional white spot happens in Rottweiler litters. (If it happens in more than one or two pups in the litter, we would not repeat that breeding, although the white spot can disappear and the bite can self-correct.) Some of the puppies sired by your dog are likely to develop hip dysplasia. This is a fact of life in Rottweilers. No matter how great a depth of pedigree your dog has for good hips, he may produce CHD, occasionally, because

    A. CHD has a very complicated genetic transmission.

    B. Since some of the dogs back in the pedigree were certified at twelve months or under two years and OFA now insists upon a minimum age of two years for certification in order to get statistical reliability, we will never know for sure which dogs in the pedigree were really HD-free, and/or which might have developed HD later, and

    C. An OFA excellent, good or fair in the parents doesn't always produce a like rating in every puppy. If it did, HD would be under control by now. Each rating can produce all others, including severely dysplastic, but OFA statistics have proven we must stick to the theory of purebred dogs in that, as we have pointed out, like more often than not produces like. It is, therefore, most important that your stud dog come from a great line and that he is prepotent for all the good things in his line while still keeping in mind he may not succeed every time with every puppy.

Probably by now our new breeder has decided to become a non-breeder. But by way of encouragement, may we say that in becoming a real breeder, your enjoyment of the Rottweiler is greatly increased. It is no longer necessary to personally own those great Rottweilers—having participated in their planned breeding should be ego trip enough. The enjoyment and pleasure you have given other Rottweiler enthusiasts by doing everything possible to preserve and enhance the breed's character is a longer-lasting and more deeply satisfying reward than any trophy sitting on your mantle.

Chapter 12

Managing the Stud Dog . . . Theory and Experience

THEORY

Managing the stud dog is perhaps the most challenging aspect in the breeding of purebred dogs. It carries the first responsibility, and the decisions made concerning the use of your dog as a stud influence the future of the breed in many ways. Let's discuss the responsibilities first.

Although only 50 percent of the genetic make-up of the puppy comes from its sire, a stud dog's influence on the breed as a whole is far greater than that of the dam for the simple reason that he can service many bitches and sire many puppies during the course of his lifetime, while the dam's influence is expressed only in each litter she whelps. Since the manager of a stud dog should also consider himself a breeder, he should feel responsibility toward the puppies his stud dog has produced. His interest in them, although not as profound as the owner of the brood bitch, will continue for their lifetime, too. The stud dog has the advantage of considerably more progeny testing so that his value to the breed can be determined earlier than that of the brood bitch.

Since it is the bitch that comes to the dog, it is the stud dog manager's responsibility to set high standards so that the phrase "at stud to approved bitches" has some meaning. One should also be sure the bitch's owners are approved. No matter how great an individual stud dog is, his worth is diminished by allowing him to be used with bitches of marginal breed quality. And even if the bitch to be bred has recommendations, if the owners do not meet the requirements of ethics, discipline and concern for the breed, in the end the stud dog's worth will also be diminished if he is allowed to be used in such questionable incidences.

Is it safe to assume that all owners of Rottweiler stud dogs belong to breed clubs with Codes of Ethics? No, probably not (most serious purebred dog breeders do belong to at least one breed club). But if you don't belong to a breed club with a Code of Ethics, set your requirements and then do not make exceptions. If you lessen your requirements, even out of friendship or because the bitch comes in season a month before she is due, very soon you and your stud will have the reputation for breeding for convenience and for money, and the responsible breeders—the ones with the better bitches—will shun you. Some of the finest studs in the United States at the present time are managed by people of discipline. Concerned owners of brood bitches do not have to take the chance that their puppies' half-brothers and sisters will be from undisciplined breedings. There is a very broad breeding base in contemporary American Rottweilers. One has a choice.

So it is a true test of discipline and character to manage the stud dog. Granted, your opportunities to make exceptions can come up very frequently if you have a good dog. If you cannot afford, both financially and emotionally, to support the discipline it takes to manage a stud dog, then we can only suggest that the standard for breeding quality and ethics that you set for yourself in managing a stud will determine what you and he will be remembered for as Rottweiler history continues to be written. Consider carefully and put the best interests of the breed first!

It is assumed that your stud dog has the basics outlined in the many Codes of Ethics observed by Rottweiler clubs and the Standard for the breed. But a stud dog must have more than the basics. Since none of us agree on the perfect Rottweiler, he must at least be very good in many aspects, excellent in some and, hopefully, superior in others as an individual, in his pedigree, and in prepotency. The champion in the U.S., or in Europe, who shows evidence of careful and selective breeding in his pedigree, appearance and performance is the ideal.

EXPERIENCE

Your stud dog should be kept in peak condition, rather lean than heavy, free of internal parasites, and not a carrier of brucellosis. A suitable environment and mode of life are important. Mating is a natural instinct and much suffering may be caused to stud dogs if bitches in season are not kept strictly isolated. The instinct to mate is excited primarily by scent, not only the scent of the bitch's vaginal discharge but also the scent of her urine. It is not advisable to keep dogs and un-spayed bitches in a home unless facilities are available for isolation of the bitch in season. Not only are unwanted pregnancies a probability, but dogs are creatures of habit, and when a dog has been frequently scolded for showing interest in a companion bitch, it is quite likely he will be inhibited when a bitch is brought to him for breeding.

More Suggestions from Our Experience

1. Make arrangements in advance—When at all possible, arrangements should be made before the bitch comes in season. The bitch and her owner should be approved and an agreement on the stud fee and related conditions should already be reached.

2. Provide a stud contract—*Dog World Magazine* has a printed contract for sale, or you can write your own. It should include, at a minimum, names, titles, OFA numbers (or other certifications) of the breeding partners plus dates of mating and due dates for the litter. Terms of the payment of the stud fee and what constitutes a litter should be clearly stated. If paid in cash, the stud fee is usually due at the time of service—the owner of the bitch is paying for the service, not the litter. (One live puppy usually constitutes a litter.) If the bitch fails to conceive, a repeat breeding to the same stud (if available) or one of like quality with appropriate credentials should be guaranteed. If your stud dog is not available for a repeat breeding and no suitable substitute can be offered, the stud fee should be returned. Generally, you ask that the bitch be returned at her next season, but this can be negotiated.

   Stud dog owners should be able to provide a safe, clean and comfortable environment for the bitch if she must be sent instead of brought in by the owners for breeding. No charge should be made to keep the bitch for the three or four days necessary for actual breeding. Of course, if she has to be kept for a week or longer to suit the convenience of the owner, board can be charged.

3. Stud fee—In theory, a stud fee should be the same as, or close to, the average selling price of a puppy. It is possible to make any arrangements agreeable to both parties, such as accepting a puppy, or puppies, in lieu of a cash stud fee, or leasing the bitch to breed to your stud. The stud dog owner should be willing to help place the puppies by recommending the litter and the owner to inquirers.

4. Litter registration application—Never sign a litter registration application in blank. It's also a good idea never to sign the litter registration application until stud fee terms have been satisfactorily met. After the puppies are whelped, the owner of the litter should forward to the stud dog owner an AKC litter registration application properly completed except for the section requiring signature of the stud dog owner. If the litter owner also sends along a check made payable to the AKC, the application can then be forwarded directly by the stud dog owner to the AKC for processing.

5. Pedigree—The stud dog owner must provide the owner of the litter with a four-generation pedigree, with the names spelled correctly and including all titles and certification numbers, AKC registration

numbers or foreign numbers and certifications. (It is a pet peeve of ours that sometimes people who claim to be breeding working Rottweilers do not know or care enough to put the appropriate working titles on the pedigree.) If you have photographs or reprints from publications of your dog, it is nice to provide the owner of the litter with enough to answer inquiries and/or give to new puppy owners, To sum it up, you should definitely take an active interest in this litter even if you aren't the "lucky one" who gets to do the clean-ups!

6. Best time to breed—The best time to breed the bitch is when she will stand for the dog, but if she is to be brought or sent for breeding, you generally ask for her to arrive on the ninth or tenth day after the first signs of her red discharge. She then has a day to settle in before trying for a breeding on the tenth or eleventh day which is, for 90 percent of the bitches, the first time when they will accept the dog. Some vets will do smears to determine if a bitch is about ready to ovulate and some do progesterone counts. Be prepared to breed the bitch twice, 24 to 48 hours apart and have two people in attendance during the actual mating (preferably one being the bitch's owner). One helper holds and steadies the bitch, and one assists and steadies the dog so that when the "tie" is made, no damage is done to either dog or bitch. It is a good practice to have a muzzle handy to keep the bitch from discouraging your stud or biting him (or the handler). A tie is achieved when, after mounting the bitch, the dog inserts his penis, using strong thrusting movements, into her vulva. This action brings about a vigorous erection, and two bulbs, which form the base of the penis, enlarge to about the size of golf balls (with a Rottweiler). The dog pumps seminal fluid containing the spermatozoa with each tail twitch and the bitch usually moans or cries as a signal that the mating has been successfully completed. If a bitch objects too much, it could be that you are trying too early, or even possibly too late. Mating is a natural process; it should present no difficulties with a normal dog and bitch ready for service.

7. Food and footing—It is best not to feed either dog or bitch within a short time of service, and both should have a good opportunity to relieve themselves before mating. Try to have a room or run (from which they cannot escape) where there is enough space for the preliminary play and courtship, but not so large as to allow for too much chasing about by the stud. The footing for the stud is important—carpeting or rubber matting over concrete, gravel or grass is best. The dogs should be introduced while on lead. Remember that some form of playful snapping is a sort of token resistance and is understood by both animals. Try to use the same location for each service; habit and conditioned reflex come into play here. (Our Elko would start whining

and drooling the minute the station wagon turned onto Fair Oaks Road in anticipation of what was waiting for him at the end of the driveway at Rodsden Oaks!)

8. Courting—Stud dogs vary in their behavior. The first time the dog is used, he may show some initial confusion. The ideal stud is keen, but not so keen as to eliminate all of the courtship ritual. If the stud omits some of the preliminary courtship, he can bewilder and panic a maiden bitch. On the other hand, if the courtship continues for longer than a half hour, you are only tiring both partners and it is wise to separate them temporarily. However, do not get discouraged. Have patience; courtship is a part of the physiological process of mating. It is nice when your stud dog develops a balance in his courtship which keeps the bitches happy, as well as those having to wait in attendance.

(When we wrote that stud dogs may vary in their behavior, we remembered one that tied the bitch in thirty seconds and turned himself around, because tail-to-tail with the bitch is the most comfortable position for the two to wait until the tie ends; the one that seldom ever tied, but had to be held clamped together with the bitch for at least five minutes, usually fifteen, which explains the present condition of our knees; and the one who upon tying, fainted and was completely out for thirty to sixty seconds. The first time it happened, we thought he had died! Ah, some memories are fonder than others.)

9. Training a new stud—When training a new stud, do hold the bitch and train him to allow the bitches to be handled as well as himself. A bitch will quite often evidence some discomfort during the actual mating, and while tied will moan or scream, wiggle or try to sit down. Gentle but firm handling and reassurance is in order. A tie is the best assurance of a successful breeding, but in the case of an outside tie, as long as the dogs have been held together for at least five minutes, you can be fairly assured that you did get a breeding. One drop of semen can contain many millions of sperm, so the length of the tie is not to be considered indicative of the number of puppies to be expected. A five-minute tie is as good as a forty-five-minute tie, but you can generally expect a tie to last about fifteen to twenty minutes. You never go off and leave the dogs together—tied or untied! Sometime you may have to turn the two dogs loose together in the enclosed area and stand quietly by until the dog has tied the bitch, but you must be there to steady them until the tie breaks. After the mating has taken place, return the bitch to her quarters and put her somewhere she is not likely to urinate for an hour or so. Your stud may think he is ready to perform again immediately, but do take him to his room for a drink and a rest away from the immediate vicinity of the bitch.

The first time a litter sired by your stud is registered with the AKC, his name will be published in the *AKC Stud Book*. Subsequent litters sired by him will be registered in the *Stud Book* but will not be published. However, the results of how well you have managed your stud dog are not written in the *Stud Book*. If your stud writes his own chapter in Rottweiler history, it is because you have made the extra effort. You have held your discipline. You have been lucky in those who have owned your dog's progeny. And, then, too, it might be that you have really experienced the greatest good fortune of all . . . to have managed that truly superior stud dog.

Chapter 13

Recognizing the Great Brood Bitch

It is no secret that the sport of purebred dogs can be very sexist. In actual competition, the males (dogs) are first in the ring and usually have a better chance at Best of Winners or Best of Breed; they naturally radiate a masculine grandeur that draws the judges' admiration. In Rottweilers, more dogs are specialed (shown as champions in Best of Breed competition) than bitches; the dogs get all the credit for the quality of a litter (the puppies are aways recognized and labeled with the name of the sire—"Yes, for sure, that's a Dux puppy!" You never hear, "yes, for sure, that's a Frolich puppy!") and all the publicity (the stud dog issue is always larger than the brood bitch issue in any publication). *But . . .* it is the brood bitch that will be the foundation of your breeding program. Anna Tilghman, of Andan Rottweilers, describes the Rottweiler brood bitch as more precious than diamonds and rubies, worth her weight in gold, silver and/or platinum, not to menton frankincense and myrrh. The brood bitch's optimum breeding age is from two to six years, after which litter size drops precipitously. Her ovaries at birth contain 300,000 ova; at breeding age, 50,000; at nine years, 500.

To acquire such a paragon is not a simple matter. Think of the heavy, long-term investment the brood bitch represents in time, money and effort! Whether you buy her as a puppy or young adult, or whether you breed her yourself, you are in for a long wait with considerable suspense because the qualities she must possess to be a worthy producer demand your devoted, patient nurturing.

" . . . it is the brood bitch that will be the foundation of your kennel . . . " Best Brood Bitch at the Colonial Specialty, judged on two of her "get," Ch. Disco v.h. Brabantpark, MRC Hall of Fame member, with her young daughter, Ironwood's Canid who was also Winner's Bitch, and son Ironwood's Cade.

"What she is as an individual . . . " Ch. Windrock's Fanni von Richter with her "get": Ch. Windrock's Rolex and Ch. Windrock's Sophie v. Richter.
John Ashbey

The ABCs of recognizing a great brood bitch would include:

A. *What she is as an individual* is the first thing you recognize. She will be of correct breed type and correct character, and will show willingness to please while working and socializing. She will have no serious faults and will come from a pedigree that shows depth in all respects. She must be sound, of course, in mind and body. She may have demonstrated these attributes with documented titles. Strictly speaking, conformation and performance titles will not make her puppies any better, but such achievements put a nice gloss on the bitch's genetic credentials—if the breeder wishes to pursue them.

B. *How she handles the breeding, pregnancy, whelping and raising of the litter* will add to your recognition of her as a promising brood bitch. During the breeding, she should not show any extremes in fear,

"... by how she
handles ...

... raising of the
litter ... "

shyness or aggression toward the stud, and she should demonstrate steadiness and acceptance. In fact, we want her to actively enter into the courtship.

During the first month of her pregnancy she should act just as she always has. (Bitches don't often have morning sickness, but we had one who would spend a day refuting this about two weeks into each pregnancy.) But as the whelping date approaches, we hope she starts acting "nesty." It is a very cooperative brood bitch who shows some sign of being in whelp *before* her due date and then whelps her litter *on* her due date. (With a bitch we have bred at least twice, we give her some leeway in this respect. We often wonder why a simple pregnancy test for bitches has not yet been developed!)

During the whelping, we want her to be concerned but not hysterical. She should remember her obedience and lie down when told so that we can monitor her contractions and position ourselves to help her if necessary. If her initial reaction to her first whelp is one of awe, we want her soon to take over the opening of the sac, the cleaning and stimulating of the pup, and severing of the umbilical cord. We want her to love them the minute she has them! We want her to whelp easily with no problems a live, strong litter and then have enough milk to feed them all. (These maternal instincts and physical concerns in a brood bitch are somewhat hereditary. A good brood bitch—a good mother—often produces good mothers.)

During the five weeks the brood bitch is raising her litter, she should continue to nurse without any problems, to keep the pups spotlessly clean, and to play with them gently, at the same time she is training them to submit to her. You want her not to be a "klutz," but to enter and leave the whelping area with some finesse and lie down slowly and carefully. (During those first days when the pups are so small, sometimes even the most careful bitches will roll on or step on a pup. Immediate CPR can sometimes revive the traumatized puppy, but do forgive your bitch in any case.)

C. *The final recognition will come to her by what she produces.* All breeders hope their bitches will produce champions, Specialty, Group and Best in Show winners, and *all* Rottweiler breeders hope that in those handsome heads their bitches have produced will also be true Rottweiler minds. In this day and age, many more requests for puppies come from people who want Rottweilers primarily as family pets, companions and for protection. To them, what is inside the dog's head is more important than the dog's outward appearance. We also measure success in breeding by the numbers of families that ask for another Rottweiler or a second or a third to replace their old ones that have died; or the sons and daughters of Rottweiler families who want *their* sons and daughters to experience the wonderful feeling of growing up with a Rottweiler in their own families.

Ch. Fine's Sooner Magic v. Forstwald, CD with her young daughters Fine's Ciara v. Covenant and Fine's Seka v. Whelan Covenant. *Bill Meyer*

Ch. Gamegard's Femme Fat'al with her daughters, Ch. Gamegards Image De Femme, a BIS winner and Winner's Bitch, Gamegards Izadorable. *Chuck Tatham*

Rottweiler fancier Tony Stockanes can explain it to you better than we can; and, anyway, no book about the experience of owning a Rottweiler would be complete without introducing you to the wit, charm and sensitivity of Tony and his stories about the breed. They were first published as a series in the *Medallion Rottweiler Club Newsletter* and made the *Newsletter* so much fun to read that we do believe people joined the MRC at that time just to get the *Newsletter* featuring Tony's stories. The MRC has published these stories in a little booklet called *The Helping Paw,* illustrated by Sue Rademacher, whose dry humor, expressed in her line drawings, is a perfect complement to Tony's delightful stories.

"Does I want a Show Biz Baby?" Ch. Rodsden's Ander, CD (Ch. Trollegens Frodo CD ex Ch. Rodsden's Red Pepper), owned by Harriet and Tony Stockanes.

DOES I WANT A SHOW BIZ BABY?

by Tony Stockanes

Coming close to the big day, faithful reader. You dress like a dog person, your speech is a chant of idiomatic *dog personology*, and you're ready to buzz down to the breeder's to pick out your dog, right? Not . . . quite.

You have to decide whether, first crack out of the box, you're going for show or pet quality. Sweet mercy, you whimper, does it make a difference? Compadre, it could make as much as three or four hundred little crisp ones' difference.

But having said that, I'm going to let you in on a really terrific secret of dog personing. I have to whisper this: Since you ask, no, it *doesn't* make any difference. Not essentially. Keep this under your fedora because it's practically heresy. And now that you know that secret, I'm going to let you in on *why* it makes no difference.

For one thing, if you opt for show quality, no reputable breeder can or will guarantee that's what you'll get. Open an oyster's shell and you may pluck out a pearl—but the Big Tote Board of Life says it's 10-1 you'll find a dead, gray oyster. Your show-quality lunker may grow up to have a gait like a '38 pick-up with two flats and a fanny spread like dear Aunt Lily's. Or, just maybe, that pet-quality rascal will collect points like a blue serge suit picks up lint. It can happen. Believe me.

That's not the important thing, though. It's a goofy fact about a Rottweiler. When you get it home and it has snuffled around for a day or two and it cocks its head when it hears its name, you're going to look at it and suddenly discover it's no longer a dog, it's YOUR dog, and gol-dingy, it's the greatest dog in the world. Happens every time. After two weeks nothing and no one will convince you it isn't Bo Derek, a lifetime pass to Disneyland, and a barrel of Chivas Regal in a black and brown package.

Oh, a dyspeptic judge may not agree, some nit-picking expert might cite a couple hundred flaws, but, smugly, you'll know that's all

"We think she's hanging around the wrong show biz crowd."

"Now tell me. What is it you
don't like about his front?"

nonsense. To its owner, each and every Rottweiler is a four-alarm, 24-carat Westminster BIS winner. An owner may mumble, "Well, he's just pet quality"; but deep down he doesn't believe it for a minute. And he's right.

"Pet quality" has a deprecating sound. Let me describe a pet-quality dog.

You may have heard about Ander and Fred. But before them there was Saxon. The only noble thing about him was his name. Entered as the only dog in conformation, he'd have placed a solid 11th.

Saxon was born middle-aged. Some dogs have dry heads (another of those terms: non-dog persons just say unwrinkled); Saxon's face made prunes look like cue balls. He had more chins than the whole Osmond family put together. His jowls stopped three inches short of his last rib.

He developed dysplasia.

Generally his expression was, "I've just been cut out of dad's will without a pfennig." His ears sagged a bit, his trunk was too short and he made up for that by having a nose too long. The best that could be said for his coat was it kept his bones from spilling all over the floor. When he was happy he slumped against the nearest human leg and grumbled deep in his throat; unhappy, he squatted with his nose wedged in a corner, his back turned to the world, and grumbled. Sitting, he was a dead ringer for an old-fashioned cuspidor and walking—alas, walking he was a graceless disaster. His run, a shambling, lurching effort, would make a judge giggle or weep. Occasionally he sat next to a toad outside the back door, both of them silently watching the sunset. You could identify Saxon because he was bigger.

He was a beautiful dog.

When we first saw the inimitable Bruin, we thought HE looked peculiar because he didn't resemble Saxon.

He knew men should be, at best, tolerated, but he adored all women. For a lady burglar, he'd help load the silverware.

Did I say his expression was habitually morose? It seemed so—but old Lon Chaney would have envied him. He could arrange those myriad wrinkles into hundreds of expressions, each subtly different.

Saxon honored us with his company for almost ten years and grew lovelier every day.

He plodded through obedience classes as though he'd written the manual, but some things he never learned. Until he left us, he firmly believed that if he did it verr-rry slowly, he could creep up into your lap and you'd not notice.

He knew that going outside when it was excessively hot was stupid, and snow was a personal insult.

He was just—pet quality: He never got within a mile of a show ring, never won a point, and his only medal was a rabies tag. He drooled a bit when he was young and as he got older, his mouth was a leaky mess. Memories of his most recent meal were always tucked in the fold of his lip. In his last years, his coat looked as though he'd picked it up at a fire sale, and he huffed going up stairs. During the last six months he wheezed going *down* stairs.

He never did anything memorably heroic, never charged into a burning building to save a baby, never plunged into an icy stream to drag me to safety. He just trudged through his days being Saxon.

Televised basketball fascinated him; he hated it when his rug was moved a centimeter from its accustomed place, and he would spend twenty minutes putting it back just right. He was such an awesome terror, doves in the back yard didn't even flutter away when he paced his stolid, stately rounds.

When there was laughter in the house, his furrowed muzzle arranged itself in a contented grin; if there was tension, he was a solemn mediator. Voices raised in anger? As diversion, the loudest was gifted with a bone or a bedraggled toy.

And when the whole world believed I was some kind of fungus, it was damned hard to tell whether that nudgingly affectionate nose in my palm was pet or show quality.

He was convinced doors would open and people awaken if he simply sat close to them and stared. They would and they did.

He was nothing exceptional, just Saxon. Of course when he died, we wept. The neighbors cried. The VET cried.

He's been gone for almost three years now and few days go by that I don't look out to see him between Fred and Ander, trudging along the back fence carefully keeping to the path he'd worn, pausing now and then to inspect a caterpillar, looking for just that perfect spot to water. And few days go by that I don't wish that pet-quality hunk was curled in a square of sunlight on the carpet, grizzled nose tucked under a paw, dreaming whatever old dogs dream.

The secret you should know is, show quality and pet quality are really meaningless terms, something strangers who don't know any better decide. Like all Rottweiler owners, we've been very lucky. We've never had anything but show quality.

Chapter 14

Whelping—Before, During and After

Before a bitch is bred she should be checked for internal and external parasites, brought up to date on all her shots (the puppies get their first immunity from the dam), and tested for cervicitis, vaginitis and brucellosis. When she does come in season, mark the date on the calendar and the dates she was bred. Count forward sixty-three days from each breeding and those are her due dates. The dates are not, however, a positive indication of exactly when she will whelp, as it can be anywhere from fifty-eight to seventy days after the breeding. A record of when she came in season, what days she was bred and the date when she actually whelped will give you some idea of when to breed her the next time you plan to do so.

She should be fed and treated just as she was before breeding for the first month into gestation. An overweight bitch has problems getting in whelp and can have serious birthing and lactation problems. But between her fourth and sixth weeks of gestation, she should have her caloric intake increased by 20 to 40 percent over her maintenance diet. Protein should be in the form of a quality, high-protein canned dog food, cottage cheese and cooked eggs. One of the best supplements for the pregnant bitch is fresh beef liver (preferably raw, if she will eat it, but if not, then cooked). She should be fed several ounces three or four times a week. Her protein intake, however, should not be increased more than 40%, since too much protein can damage the kidneys. At about the fifth week, her total daily intake should be divided into three meals a day from the two you would normally feed. Her condition may make it difficult for her to digest large amounts at one time.

It is a good idea to X-ray sometime between days fifty-two and fifty-four to get an idea of the number of puppies, their position and size. This is a noninvasive procedure at this point in the pregnancy. When the X ray shows your bitch to be definitely in whelp, it is time to start gathering supplies, which

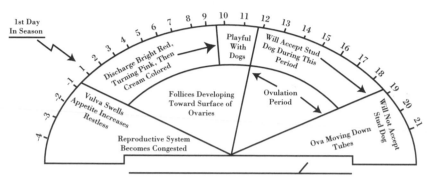

BITCH'S NAME – MONTH IN SEASON / YEAR

The Bitch's Normal Ovulation Cycle
Fill in actual dates and keep as a reference for future cycles.

should include terry towels or washcloths, a digital thermometer and a room thermometer, bulb syringe, Betadine, surgical gloves, Dopram, petroleum jelly, scissors, a scale that measures in grams and ounces (not a baby scale or bathroom scale) and, of course, a whelping box with potty box and an overhead heat lamp.

Begin taking your bitch's temperature using the digital thermometer a week before the due date, preferably at the same time each day, before she becomes active. Normal temperature for dogs is 101° to 102° Fahrenheit, but before whelping, the bitch's temperature drops to 98.5° to 99° Fahrenheit, indicating that she should go into labor within several hours after her temperature returns to normal. (Another indication that she may become the great brood bitch is her acceptance of this procedure!) As whelping time approaches, she may show a vaginal discharge which should be clear to yellow. This is normal, but a black, red or green vaginal discharge *before* any pups are delivered indicates placental separation and is a sign of an impending problem.

She should be allowed to get used to the whelping box in advance for short stretches. By putting newspaper in the box, you allow her to use her instinctive nesting behavior, scratching and digging to her heart's content. Rug remnants just the size of the whelping box floor, which can be discarded when they become dirty, make her more of a happy camper in the whelping box and provide good footing for the puppies. Be sure the rug has a stiff backing so that all the nesting does not disturb it. When she starts to whelp, take the nesting newspapers out, because a puppy could get lost under them. After she is definitely finished whelping, or the next day, put down a fresh rug. Never put newspapers down on a floor that has been scrubbed with bleach in any amount until the floor is completely dry. The newsprint and the bleach form a toxin that can damage the puppies.

THE WHELPING BEGINS

The whelping experience begins when the bitch starts to shiver and show signs of extreme restlessness. Any woman who has experienced labor in the birth of her own children will recognize contractions that precede the actual birth ... and empathize with the bitch. If HARD labor continues with no puppy delivered in an hour, it may be a sign of dystocia and indicate a problem. But after she delivers a puppy or several with the accompanying placentas, she may seem to be resting (the uterus *is* resting), which allows subsequent puppies to be moved to the cervix and for the resumption of labor. More than three hours of rest between puppies with no sign of moving back into labor also indicates a problem.

There are several things that can be done to help solve the problem before it is necessary to call the vet. If the labor goes on too long with no puppies being whelped, contractions can be stimulated by feathering the roof of the vaginal tract with your hand in a lubricated glove. This stimulation may move a puppy into a position where it can be grasped and delivered. If you

A healthy litter will nurse vigorously and sleep soundly even while their tails are being docked by the rubber band method. Provided that the puppies appear to be thriving and gaining weight, the authors have puppies' tails docked by the veterinarian at three or four days.

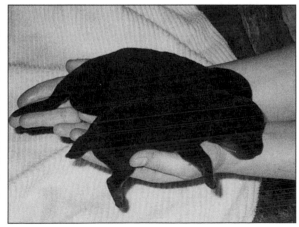

Occasionally, though rarely, a puppy is born with a naturally short tail. Such a rarity, familiarly called a "stumper," is shown in the foreground of this photo. This tail, however, is still too long and this puppy will have to be docked with its littermates.

If, for any reason, the brood bitch cannot nurse her puppies, a surrogate will have to be found. The best is a foster mother, but that is not always possible. Tube feeding and bottle feeding can also be successful. This homemade nursing rack is an ingenious timesaver for a harried puppy raiser.

are experienced in giving shots and your veterinarian has confidence in you, it is time to give the Oxytocin shot, which he has given to you to use in case of emergencies or at the end of the whelping. Familiarly known as the "pit" shot, it causes contractions which helps clean out the uterus of any remaining afterbirth, placenta and residue. Pit is never used until at least one puppy has been whelped. There is nothing you can do to induce labor in bitches. If there is no response within twenty minutes, a second shot can be given. More injections are not likely to enhance labor and a Caesarian section may be the only solution. Rottweiler bitches are usually hardy whelpers who produce large litters, and from our own experience, we have had to do only two Caesarians in forty-five years. Your brood bitch may very well end up with eleven lively pups that she may have delivered rapidly and safely in the course of only three hours. Finally, the last pit shot is given; or she can wait until morning for the vet to check her.

Most of the pups will just sort of squirt out, but if one gets stuck so that you can see it all or partially out and there appears to be no progress with the delivery, you can help by pulling the puppy in a downward direction in synch with the bitch's contractions. Once the head and shoulders—or tail and hips in the event of a backward or breech presentation—emerge, pull gently with a steady continous motion regardless of the contractions—DO NOT jerk the puppy out! In the multiple birth of puppies some may be presented breech, which usually causes no problem. (The little tail comes out first, wagging, instead of the little head and the pink tongue, licking.)

Once the puppy is out, the sac should be removed immediately, either by the bitch or by you, and the mouth should be cleared of mucous. Tilting the head down at a 45° angle will help drain the fluids, or you can use the bulb syringe as an aspirator. One or two drops of Dopram under the tongue will help a puppy who is gasping for breath to elicit deep breathing. When the puppy cries, you know he has arrived safely. Rub him with the towel to dry him and to get him to cry and offer him to his mother; her warm tongue is the best stimulator. If the bitch has not separated the placenta from the newborn, allow it to drain for a minute or two—actually there is no hurry—and cut it with scissors about one or two inches from the puppy's abdomen. If permitted to do so, many bitches will eat the placentas at this point. Eating placentas brings in the milk but it is not necessary for a bitch to eat them all! Dab a disinfectant, such as Betadine, on the cut end of the cord. The cord will dry up and fall off within two or three days.

The puppies are examined and weighed as they are whelped and returned to their mother. We do not take the puppies away from her even when she is delivering another puppy, but instead roll them out of the way. A newborn puppy will start nursing immediately, which indicates that its sucking response is correct, and it should be allowed to continue to have the opportunity during the whole whelping session. At this same time or during the hours immediately following the delivery, the puppy should pass a brownish plug. This is the first stool, or *meconium,* and its passing tells you that the puppy's anus is open. If the rectum appears to be obstructed, or if no stool is produced within the first day, gently insert the lubricated end of a thermometer to make sure the anus is open. There have been cases where the anus was not open, in which case, even if surgically opened, survival was limited.

We have never seen a Rottweiler puppy with a cleft palate but if it should happen, such a puppy should be culled as it will not survive.

The room thermometer should be placed periodically on the floor of the whelping box where the puppies are to make sure that the heating lamp over the whelping box is keeping the ambient temperature at the puppies' level to between 85 and 90° Fahrenheit during whelping. A wise saying to which every breeder must pay heed is that *a chilled puppy is a dead puppy!* A newborn puppy's temperature is from 95 to 97° Fahrenheit. So if a puppy appears chilled, weak or anorectic, its temperature should be checked with a rectal thermometer. No milk or oral supplements should be given if its temperature is below 95° Fahrenheit until its temperature returns to normal. And how do you warm the puppy up gradually? Incubators (seldom is there an incubator handy), towels warmed in the dryer or jugs filled with hot water next to them in the whelping box will do it, but the easiest way is to pop that little one in your shirt pocket or next to your body (and here's where we women have a natural advantage). The temperature should not be raised too rapidly, so do not use a heating pad. But remember after the litter is whelped that a healthy litter of puppies that stays with the dam normally requires little or no extra heat, so turn down the heat lamp until it is comfortably warm in the area but stay and watch the litter to make sure that no puppy gets separated too far from the dam. We sleep next to the whelping pen for several nights until we can be certain that we do have that paragon of paragons, a great brood bitch who stays with her puppies and takes care of them.

After she has whelped, she will be as exhausted as you are from attending and, after a rest, just as ravenous. Feed her all that she will eat in two or three feedings a day. Continue with the calcium supplement that she has been getting starting the week before whelping. Lactation ushers in a second period of great stress for your brood bitch. During the heavy lactation period, your bitch's diet should contain 28 to 30 percent protein and 20 percent fat.

Check the bitch's milk and her breasts twice a day to be sure she is not developing mastitis. The bitch should be checked over by your veterinarian at the same time the puppies' tails are docked—at about three to four days old if all are healthy and gaining weight. Weigh the puppies daily for the first two to three weeks, because weight gain is a good indicator of health and it gives you the opportunity to cuddle them and get the pups used to the feel and smell of a human being. Rottweiler puppies usually weigh between twelve to sixteen ounces at birth. Puppies that weigh below ten ounces at birth have difficulty surviving and must be put up to the bitch for nursing and a head start over the larger puppies at least four times a day. You can rotate the litter, but this must be done day *and* night. Or you can supplement by bottle or tube feeding with a good formula or commercial bitch's milk supplement until the little ones catch up. These little puppies in the litter will get this extra socialization at an early age; remember that early social experience has a tremendous influence on the development of a dog's behavior.

It is not just how the brood bitch responds to her puppies that helps form their character. A puppy needs lots of smell, body, visual, and acoustic contact with human beings during this initial socialization period, which lasts

Weigh healthy newborns every day for the first week and once a week thereafter.

roughly from the fourth to the seventh week of life, if it is going to accept man as a fellow species. It is much better if it has this kind of contact with several people, men and women; otherwise it may be extremely fixed on one person or one sex. It is your responsibility, as the breeder, to see that the puppy gets plenty of human contact and social experience during this period. We, personally, are more than happy to share this responsibility with our families and friends. During the first few days after whelping, your brood bitch may not be willing to share this responsibility, but the good-natured brood bitch will shortly see the advantage and by five or six weeks will seem to be saying to herself, "*motherhood-shmotherhood*—whoever wants them can have them, teeth and all!"

Our lives as breeders were enhanced greatly by recognizing and keeping the great brood bitches, and by such a simple improvement in the whelping box as adding the potty box. The little darling puppies will, when their eyes are opened and they can toddle about at two to three weeks, actually stop nursing to toddle into the box to relieve themselves. Sometimes they miss by a little but the intent is there! If you have designed this potty box just the

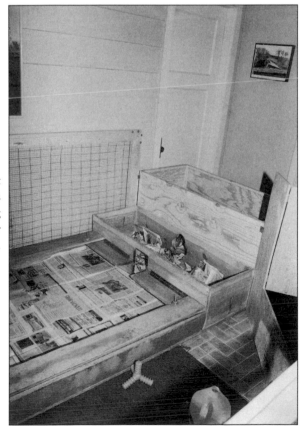

A spacious, three-part whelping box provides for play space, sleeping area and toilet for a litter of Rottweiler puppies.

width of a newspaper (the trim size of the *Wall Street Journal* is best and it lies flat), you can roll up the paper from one end with ease. Shredded newspaper on top of the thick layer on the floor allows the droppings to filter through and keeps the puppies from walking in their "output."

The lives of the puppies will be extended if the whelping box is built about five feet by four feet with six-inch by one-inch sides with a six- by one-inch board extending over the box on all four sides, providing a guard rail so that the dam will not accidentally crush a puppy against the side. We prefer the six-inch board to the dowel arrangement many breeders use because as the pups get older, it provides a cavern-like space where they love to sleep and a board to walk around, which helps us to determine which will be the gymnast in the group. The potty box is attached to one side with an opening from the whelping box into it and a sliding door of thin presswood or strong cardboard which can close it off until it is needed or when separating the pups for clean-up. The bitch should be able to get out of the box and away from her puppies for R and R, so build a pen out of hardware wire around the whelping

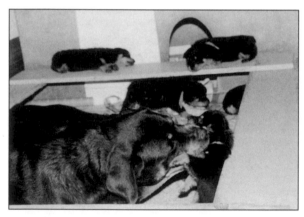

The six-inch-wide board around the whelping box acts as a safety zone for newborns to prevent their being crushed by their mother. Later, the shelf becomes a boardwalk to play and snooze on and the top of a cave to play games in.

Weaning can begin when puppies are between three and four weeks old, using a premium-quality puppy formulation. The pan shown here has a raised center and keeps weanlings from walking through their food. Such a pan can be ordered from any good kennel supply company.

box of a size to accommodate her and a litter of eleven when they are weaned. Use hardware wire, which is tightly woven, so that a puppy cannot get its paw through but the puppies can see through it when they are old enough to climb out of the whelping box. We don't want them to spend their early life looking at the ceiling or standing on their hind legs to look out at the world beyond their pen.

A large litter takes a lot out of the brood bitch and so you will start weaning the puppies early. We start at about three and a half weeks by offering them a mixture of a high-grade commercial puppy food and warm water mixed in a blender to the consistency of a thick malted milk. Dip your finger into it and let them have a taste, then put their little mouths in the bowl. At five weeks put down a dish of the dry food with water alongside and leave it with them. They will find that the crunchiness of the dry food feels pleasant on those emerging teeth. By the time they are ready to go to their new homes they are on dry food and water. A high-grade puppy food provides all the nutrients, minerals and vitamins a normal puppy will need to thrive.

People frequently ask us if we aren't sad to see the puppies leave. The answer is "no," because we have already been through the hardest part of having a litter—finding and having good people waiting to take the puppies home to become a part of their new families. Age seven weeks is the best time for a puppy to leave the litter for future trainability, according to the dog behaviorists. By this age the puppies would rather be with people than eat. When the new family comes to pick up their puppy, we live all over again the excitement and delight we experienced, so many years ago, when we brought home our first puppy.

Staying with their mother after weaning has a very beneficial effect on puppies and will result in better-adjusted adults.

Chapter 15

The German Rottweiler Club

Bad Oeynhausen, West Germany isn't as bad as it sounds. In fact, in October 1982, it was rather festive because it was the site of the ADRK's 75th anniversary jubilee (dating from the 1907 founding of the German Rottweiler Club in Heidelberg). The authors joined ADRK members from around West Germany to celebrate a club that had not only endured, but given the world such a remarkable breed. We doubt the club founders could have imagined that such a jubilee would be attended not only by their countrymen, but by admirers of the breed from around the world. But then, the ADRK has never taken anything about the Rottweiler lightly.

When the ADRK accepted responsibility for the breed in 1921, the members faced the awesome tasks of organizing the club's affairs, establishing breeding rules to preserve and improve breed type, promoting performance events and maintaining accurate, detailed records for both breeding activities and performance results. One of the ADRK's first duties was producing a revised Standard, which the club did in 1924. This Standard stated that:

> The Rottweiler is an excellent guard, companion and working dog. The kind of dog most sought after is powerful and square built, with beautiful red or yellow markings, robust in appearance but not lacking in nobility, and particularly well-endowed as a guard, companion and working dog.

What is interesting in this Standard is its description of what the Rottweiler is not:

> The plain red Rottweiler which used to occur, though not very often, with a black or light mask or a black line down the back, as well as Rottweilers of other colors, blue or brown, are not recognized because of suspected cross-breeding, and the same applies to long-coated Rottweilers. All timid and nervous animals, and those with a stupid expression, are completely rejected.

This Standard was an amalgam of those Standards before it, combining the characteristics from each which were deemed most desirable.

The task of producing a studbook (or breeding register) wasn't quite as clear-cut, since at least three different studbooks existed simultaneously, and one can imagine that duplication, even triplication of entries, occurred. There could also have been dogs which met the Standards of a particular studbook but not the Standards of another. To add to the confusion, the same dog, in addition to having different registration numbers in differing studbooks, could also have had different names! The paperwork involved in producing the first ADRK studbook in 1923 must truly have been monumental, and maintaining the studbook remains an ongoing concern. A new problem appeared when the Berlin Wall came down and Germany was reunited, forcing the ADRK to develop a policy to incorporate the appropriate East German Rottweilers into the ADRK studbook.

With a new studbook, in 1924, 1,039 litters were registered, with 2,723 individual dogs and 2,882 bitches going on the rolls.

In the introduction to this first studbook, the Founders expressed the following wish, "may this book be useful as an encyclopedia for all Rottweilers, and may it add to the advancement of excellent breeding while maintaining the famous character of the breed." This is why a studbook maintained by a breed club like the ADRK, as opposed to a kennel club covering many breeds, is so much more useful to the breeder. The ADRK studbook contains a wealth of information; it is not simply limited to dogs' registration information or detailed information on individual litters. It also includes results and critiques from breeding evaluations, scores from working trials, lists of dogs unsuitable for breeding (and the reason they are unsuitable!), and a listing of X-ray results for those dogs X-rayed during the period covered by the studbook. In addition, the early studbooks were sprinkled with wonderful photographs of early dogs and pioneer breeders, so that they also serve as a written history of the club.

The ADRK is the breed club for the Rottweiler in Germany, and belongs to the *Verein Deutsche Hundwessen* (VDH), which is an organized body for all German dog clubs, but does not keep studbooks. It does publish a newsletter, *Unser Rassehund*, which included a Rottweiler section that the ADRK considered its newsletter until the ADRK began its own newsletter, eventually called *Der Rottweiler*, in 1978. The VDH is a member of the *Federation Cynologique Internationale* (FCI) headquartered in Brussels, Belgium. There is considerable interest in the FCI today, as the AKC and FCI, along with The Kennel Club (England), have begun meeting with the goal of establishing universal breed Standards.

THE FCI

The FCI is made up of the national canine organizations of each member country; only one kennel club from each country or territory may belong. Both the VDH and the DVG are members of the FCI.

The national kennel clubs of more than forty countries are FCI members. The FCI ruled that, in member countries where breed clubs keep their own studbooks (such as in Germany), the governing national organization must certify the export pedigrees issued by the breed club. In the case of a German-bred Rottweiler, the VDH will certify an export pedigree issued ONLY by the ADRK. We have often had to tell the uninformed American owner of a German dog not possessing ADRK papers that the dog is not registerable with the AKC since the AKC cooperates with the FCI. On the subject of breed Standards, FCI rules state that all member countries must use approved FCI Standards, and that these Standards are considered to be the Standards of the breed from its country of origin. Thus, the FCI breed Standard for the Rottweiler is the ADRK Standard, and it serves over forty countries. The FCI also supports national dog shows and working trials with international title competition. They offer titles for International Beauty Champions, International Working Titles, Agility and Obedience Titles. These international titles require wins in different countries to be valid.

Nothing is more highly desired by the global Rottweiler enthusiast than the right to advertise an International championship on a dog's pedigree although few, if any, titles are less understood. An International championship does not mean simply that a dog is a champion in two countries (i.e., the U.S. and Canada). The FCI International championship means that a dog has been awarded a CACIB (a conformation championship) under three different FCI judges in three different countries; one country must be either the country of the breed's origin or the owner's residence. Winning first place does not guarantee a CACIB since the judge can withhold the award while still conferring a first placement. An International championship is awarded after the fourth CACIB is awarded, provided it was awarded at least a year after the first. In addition, the Rottweiler, being one of the German utility breeds, is also required to have earned CACITs (international working awards) to be considered an International champion.

The FCI does not license judges. It accepts the judges licensed by the national clubs in the judges' own countries.

Through the FCI, one can appreciate the influence the ADRK has had on all the member countries in which Rottweilers are recognized.

PINK PAPERS

Since the ADRK maintains the studbook, it also issues the pedigree, or *Ahnentafel,* which is about as far a cry from the AKC certified pedigree as the ADRK studbook is from the AKC's (the AKC studbook simply lists the name of the dog and AKC registration number the first time a dog is used for breeding). The ahnentafels of thirty years ago were detailed histories of the individual dog and traveled with the dog with each change of ownership. The form included a five-generation pedigree with the titles earned by the dogs, and in later years the X-ray hip status, as well as information on the number of siblings, breeding tests completed, scores earned at trials, show results, and recordings of sales.

The ahnentafel has been revised, although not necessarily improved, over the decades. Twenty years ago, it included, within the five-generation pedigree, critiques on the parents and grandparents. There was also a place to record the date and results of X rays for hip dysplasia for the individual dog. Ten years ago, the ahnentafel was down to four generations, and there was no space for show or trial results. While today's computerized ahnentafel presents a four-generation pedigree and essentially the same information as those pedigrees of ten years ago, the digitized form lacks the individuality that those old ahnentafels had. One change which is proudly advertised is the issuance of "pink papers," so called because they are on a pink-tinged stock and denote select breeding stock. To have pink papers, both of the dog's parents and all of the grandparents must have working titles.

BREED WARDENS

During the 1970s, the American Rottweiler Club asked of its members "Do you wish to see an organized system of breed wardens instituted on a regional basis?" The majority voted a resounding "NO." However, the value of breed wardens has been a topic of vigorous argument ever since.

Between 1924 and 1925, the ADRK introduced the breed warden whose responsibility it was to counsel the breeder, supervise the breeding and rearing of dogs, and protect the integrity of the studbook by having the power to decide which litters could and could not enter the studbook. Breed wardens are chosen at a local level, and report to breed wardens covering a larger area, who in turn report to sectional breed wardens, who then report to the head breed warden. This august person is a member of the Board of Governors of the ADRK, and arguably the most influential individual in guiding the development of the Rottweiler in Germany.

The breed warden system ensures that breeders will follow the rules of the club, and that the dogs bred meet the criteria established in the Standard. It is interesting to note that in 1925 following the introduction of a breed warden system, the registrations for litters was cut almost in half from the previous year.

The breed warden whom we thought did the most for the American Rottweiler was Friedrich Berger. Blessed with an incredible memory for dogs and pedigrees, he served as Germany's head breed warden for seventeen years. We will always recall Friedrich in his apartment surrounded by stacks and stacks of information on the Rottweiler, smoking a cigarette, and scribbling notes on pedigrees. This was in the 1960s and 1970s, before the ADRK and most other dog clubs used computers. Friedrich was the ADRK's human computer. He judged several times in the United States and had a fatherly interest in the breed here. He saw the potential in the United States and was keenly aware of the impact of German imports on our breeding programs. We can't fathom what he would think of the breed today, but we are sure it wouldn't be the same had he lived longer. His funeral was attended by Rottweiler fanciers from around the world, and the ADRK honors him each year by holding the Friedrich Berger show.

ZTP

Since the breed wardens, and particularly the head breed warden, are responsible for guiding the breeding program, it makes sense that they must preside at breeding suitability tests. ZTP is the most common abbreviation in the Rottweiler world because few breeders want to write out the word *zuchttauglichkeitsprufung* after every dog that has passed this test!

Prior to being bred, all German dogs must pass a ZTP. In the past, a dog was allowed to try to pass only twice, then dogs were allowed to try as often as was needed to pass, and now a dog can only go to a ZTP three times. The ZTP first evaluates the dog's conformation, and then its character. While both considerations are subjective and require experts for evaluation, it is the character test that causes the most controversy.

Breeding selectivity tests for character began in 1942, when the Rottweiler was in demand as a military dog. Today, most Rottweilers never serve in the army, so a substitute yardstick was needed which would test those characteristics needed for a guard or military dog. The Schutzhund sport served that purpose. A major criticism of the German character test alleges that it simply tests the suitability of a dog to be trained in Schutzhund, and is not a true character test. This argument is debated throughout Europe, but one must return to the fact that the ADRK has a system in which all dogs are evaluated prior to being allowed to breed. This serves the breed infinitely better than the American system, where the AKC only requires breeding stock to be purebred.

Dogs which pass the ZTP and have met additional conditions can then go to a *Körung* (test for highest breeding suitability). It's a bit like earning a BA degree, then getting a doctorate, and finally becoming a fully tenured professor.

The Körung requires that all breeding stock possess non-dysplastic hips, that males have a SchH III degree and bitches at least a SchH I, and that the dogs have earned either very good or excellent ratings in conformation at dog shows. Progeny are tested from a prescribed number of litters to determine that they do not possess inherited faults. The dog must also pass evaluations similar to the ZTP, but which are graded more severely.

If the dog passes the Körung, it is considered "endorsed" for breeding—or as it appears on the pedigree, *gekort*. Körung dogs are usually in high demand for breeding and, consequently, have the greatest influence on the breed. Because of this, the requirements for the Körung change periodically to reflect changing directions in the ADRK breeding program. After two years, the dog must go to a second Körung to keep the endorsement. Dogs that pass a second time are listed as *gekort bis EzA,* which means that they have been accorded highest breeding suitability designation to the end of their breeding days.

KLUBSIEGER SHOW

In Germany, dogs rated very good (*sehr gut* or *SG*) and excellent (*vorzuglicht* or *V*) at shows can go to a Körung. Most shows are comprised of the following classes for each sex: 12–18 months, 18–24 months, two years and over without a working degree (open class), and two years and over with a working degree (*gebrauchshund* class). Most *siegers* or *siegerins* (Grand champion dogs and bitches) are chosen from the latter class. The judges who usually preside are ADRK judges—men and women who have come up through the ranks, first as owner/handlers, then as breeders, later as breed wardens, to apprentice judges, and finally as full-fledged specialists. There is also a Head Judge who sits in the ADRK Presidium with the President, Vice-President, Head Breed Warden and Head Training Warden.

A significant difference between Klubsieger shows and AKC shows, as we have already mentioned, is that each exhibitor is presented at the end of the show day with a written evaluation from the judge on his or her dog. Also, each dog in a class is rated anywhere from *V* (excellent), to *SG* (very good), *G* (good), *Ggd* (satisfactory), to *Nggd* (not satisfactory). The judge may also withhold a rating on a dog, but this is seldom done.

Prior to 1971, the ADRK considered its "Specialty show" to be the Bundessieger show, which is an all-breed event. The dog and bitch that win that show, if they have the qualifications of a working title, having passed a ZTP, and having hips free of hip dysplasia, are given the title *Bundessieger*

ADRK 1994 Klubsieger Falco v.d. Teufelsbrucke, SchH III on his way to a 1995 repeat of his great triumph. This is *the* original German-style show.

or *Bundessiegerin*. This means champion of the *bund* (or of all of Germany). It is a prestigious title because the qualifications of the dogs entered are very impressive even though the number of dogs entered may not be very large (especially when compared to entries in American shows, where prestige is often equated with the number of dogs defeated—quantity doesn't necessarily bring quality with it).

When the ADRK held its first real Specialty show in 1971, called the *Klubsieger* show, everyone trotted off to Rottweil for the occasion. Over the years, the Klubsieger show has grown and eclipsed the Bundessieger show in prestige, although to be awarded Klubsieger or Klubsiegerin, the dog does not need to have a working title. Regarded as strictly a beauty event, the judges have been careful to award the Klubsieger and Klubseigerin titles to dogs with Schutzhund degrees, with the exception of only three dogs in the last twenty-four years.

Like our Specialties, the Klubsieger show offers more than the usual classes. There are puppy classes, the youngest aptly called the "baby class," a kennel class and a sieger class, which is similar to our Best of Breed competition (although it is separated by sexes). Some of the Klubsiegers have actually competed in our Best of Breed competition, as a surprising number have been imported to the USA (including Karol vom Wellesweiler, Condor zur Klamm, Bronco vom Rauberfeld, Mirko vom Steinkopf, Gary vom Gruntenblick, and Danjo vom Schwaiger Wappen).

The predominance of Klubsiegers with working titles is an indication of the current value the ADRK puts on working Rottweilers. Today, titles replace doing the actual work of a police or military dog, since few owners work dogs in those services.

The 1925 ADRK studbook announced the first edition of the *Leistungsbuch* (book of achievements in training). Today's ADRK studbook includes a section listing dogs and their scores at Schutzhund trials.

YEAR	KLUBSIEGER	KLUBSIEGERIN
1971	Bulli v. Hungerbuhl, SchH II	Dolli v. d. Meierei, SchH I
1972	Bulli v. Hungerbuhl, SchH II	Edda v. Schloss Ickern, SchH I
1973	Grief v. Fleischer, SchH II	Afra v. Haus Schottroy, SchH I
1974	Karol v. Wellesweiler, SchH III	Anka v. Lohauserholz, SchH III
1975	Axel v. Fusse der Eifel, SchH III, FH	Biene v. Geiselstein, SchH I
1976	Ari v. Waldhuck, SchH III, FH	Asta v. Lohauserholz, SchH III
1977	Carlo v. Fusse der Eifel	Asta v. Lohauserholz, SchH III
1978	Aias	Assy v. Haugenfeld, SchH I

continues

YEAR	KLUBSIEGER	KLUBSIEGERIN
1979	Condor zur Klamm, SchH II	Assy v. Haugenfeld, SchH I
1980	Dingo v. Schwaiger Wappen, SchH III	Babette v. Magdeberg, SchH I
1981	Nero v. Schloss Rietheim, SchH III	Carmen v. Old Germany, SchH I
1982	Bronco v. Rauberfeld, SchH III	Itta v. Zimmerplatz, SchH III
1983	Mirko v. Steinkopf, SchH III	Hulda v. Konigsgarten, SchH I
1984	Falko v. d. Tente, SchH III	Hulda v. Konigsgarten, SchH I
1985	Hassan v. Konigsgarten, SchH III	Yvonne v. Markgraflerland, SchH III
1986	Iwan v. Fusse der Eifel, SchH III	Anka v. d. Nonnenhohle, SchH I
1987	Ilco v. Fusse der Eifel, SchH III	Golda v. Sonnenberg, SchH I, FH
1988	Gary v. Gruntenblick, SchH III	Cita v. d. Nonnenhohle, SchH I
1989	Danjo v. Schwaiger Wappen, SchH III	Ina v. d. Silberdistel, SchH I
1990	Ingo v. Fusse der Eifel, SchH III	Dina v. Kannenbackerland
1991	Noris v. Gruntenblick, SchH III	Edola v. Hertener Wappen, SchH I, FH
1992	Noris v. Gruntenblick, SchH III	Dorle v. d. Teufelsbrucke, SchH II
1993	Ken v. Schwaiger Wappen, SchH III, FH	no title awarded
1994	Falco v. d. Teufelsbrucke, SchH III	Xama v. Rauchfang, SchH I
1995	Falco v. d. Teufelsbrucke, SchH III	Brenda v. d. Zirbelnuss, SchH I

DEUTSCHE MEISTERSCHAFT SHOW

Schutzhund means "protection dog" in German and is a sport designed to test those mental and physical requirements for working dogs—military, police and guard dogs (see Chapter 8). Schutzhund training in Germany is a true sport, and is conducted accordingly. There are training clubs throughout the country where members meet, eat, drink beer and train, train, train their dogs. The combination of the social aspects with the awareness that, especially for a male Rottweiler, a career as a show dog or active stud requires advanced working titles, encourages a great many owners to train their Rottweilers. Having visited the gatherings of several of these clubs, we can attest to a congenial atmosphere that encourages owner-trainers to attend several times a week to train—for Schutzhund training requires discipline and total dedication to a final goal of a well-trained dog. Three problems in the United States with the sport are a lack of discipline among dogs and trainers, a lack of competent trainers, and the fact that, unfortunately, the lack of a working degree is not a deterrent to a dog's future as a show dog or a producer.

The *Hauptausbildungswart,* or head training warden in the ADRK, is responsible for all training aspects of the Rottweiler, including training assistants, evaluating judges, and scheduling trials. What the Klubsieger show is for beauty, the Deutsche Meisterschaft show is for working ability. This show reminds us of the Gaines Regional Invitational Obedience Trials in the U.S. because only the best are there; no training degrees can be earned and, to the inexperienced eye, the dogs and handlers are putting on flawless presentations. All dogs participating in the Meisterschaft show are at the most advanced level, SchH III. The winner is the *Leistungsieger* for that year.

LIST OF LEISTUNGSIEGERS

YEAR	DOG
1949	Pluto vom Jackobsbrunnen
1950	No trial
1951	Blanca vom Cilabrunnen
1952	Marko vom Filstalstrand
1953	Barry vom Rheintor
1954	Leistungssieger title not awarded
1955	Barry vom Rheintor
1956	No trial
1957	Castor von der Bokermuhle
1958	Arko v. Hipplerhof
1959	Axel vom Spiekerhof
1960	Bob vom Hause Hader
1961	Arko vom Fichtenschlag
1962	No trial
1963	Dolf von der Schmechting

continues

LIST OF LEISTUNGSIEGERS (CONTINUED)

YEAR	DOG
1964	Arras vom Moritzberg
1965	Droll vom Baumbusch
1966	Quick von der Solitude
1967	Ajax vom Asenberg
1968	Casar von der Luneburger Heide
1969	Alc Zerberus
1970	Armin v. Konigshardt
1971	Armin v. Konigshardt
1972	Axel v. d. Wegscheide
1973	Cralo vom Mischa
1974	Felix v. Sonnenberg
1975	Astor v. Hause Pfarr
1976	Barry v. Waldhuck
1977	Barry v. Waldhuck
1978	Etzel v. Amselhof
1979	Osko v. Klosterchen
1980	Axel v. Rhein-Elbe-Park
1981	Bengo v. Klosterchen
1982	Axel v. Rhein-Elbe-Park
1983	Axel v. Rhein-Elbe-Park
1984	Enzor v. Saufang
1985	Erasmus v. Magdeberg
1986	Casar v. d. Wester Lohe
1987	Rocco v. Horster Dreieck

YEAR	DOG
1988	Max v. Konigsgarten
1989	Rocco v. Horster Dreieck
1990	Fjordbakkens Andy
1991	Boris vom Schloss Borbeck
1992	Barbarossa v.d. Rauberhohle
1993	Castor v. Hause Swiatecki
1994	Chris v. Fusse d. Bergstrasse
1995	Briska v. Dornblick

Very few leistungsiegers have been imported to the United States, although we have imported offspring from some of these great workers. The first American champion UDT dog was Ch. Axel v.d. Taverne, UDT, a son of Leistungsieger Bob vom Hause Hader. We imported Axel for James and Erna Woodard. Obviously, in this case outstanding working ability was passed on. But, as ADRK's breeding program is based on the premise that the breeding of Rottweilers is the breeding of working dogs, we tend to assume that all Rottweilers possess the ability to excel at working if given the opportunity. Qualities of beautiful conformation seem to be more selective, and so the beauty-titled sires are in more demand, especially by the U.S. where regrettably little importance is placed on working ability.

While there is no doubt that the ADRK is the master at understanding what a Rottweiler should look like and how it should think as a protection dog, there is one area where the ADRK actually lagged behind the American Rottweiler fancy!

We remember trips to Germany in the 1960s when we asked the breed wardens, judges and experienced breeders, "What about hip dysplasia?"

"Ah," they said, "we can tell by looking at the dog."

"No," we said, "you can't."

We may have asked the question, but it was the Netherlands Rottweiler Club, which is the second largest Rottweiler club in Europe, that forced the issue. A program set up at the University of Utrecht under the late Dr. N. A. van der Velden to study hip dysplasia was being supported by the Netherlands Rottweiler Club. Encouraged to X-ray some of their dogs at Utrecht, the ADRK was stunned to find that there was indeed a serious inherited health concern. Finding that the breed did have a problem, the ADRK immediately set up a long-range program to try to eradicate the disease. Having complete control over registration, the ADRK could monitor all the breedings and slowly eliminate those lines which contributed more significantly to the disease than others. It seems a slow remedy, but as the Germans pointed out, the Rottweiler is not only hips, one must be aware of the total dog. Today, most of the dogs bred with the blessing of the ADRK are free of hip dysplasia as determined by X-raying at a minimum of fifteen months. Dogs with slight to moderate dysplasia can only be bred to dogs that are certified by the ADRK as free of the disease.

INTERNATIONAL FEDERATION OF ROTTWEILER FREUNDE (IFR)

The awareness that other clubs in other countries were involved in medical research with their Rottweilers may have been a motivating factor in the ADRK's proposal in 1968 to initiate a federation of Rottweiler clubs from around the world to address such issues as unifying the Standard, establishing a temperament test useful for all countries and comparing studies on common health concerns.

Representatives from Austria, Denmark, Finland, Great Britain, Holland, Norway, Sweden, Switzerland and the United States all met in Essen, West Germany in May 1969. The authors were among the delegates from the United States, and we approached this conference with an optimism similar perhaps to that of the delegates who attended the first meeting of the League of Nations. Through subsequent conferences, we have found that the International Federation of Rottweiler Freunde (IFR) had at least two more qualities similar to the League—great expectations and irreconcilable differences between countries.

At this first conference, the purpose of the IFR was stated as follows: to bring Rottweiler clubs throughout the world closer together, to work for the common good of the breed and to preserve this outstanding dog for future generations. Resolutions passed at this conference included the organization of the Federation, with the president of the ADRK being the first president and the second president being nominated from the country where the next

The awards presentation to the highest scoring team in competition at the International Federation of Rottweiler Friends (IFR) Festival, 1993. And the winner is . . . the United States. Pride is written all over the faces of the American team as the strains of the Star Spangled Banner are heard.

The Austrian Army Rottweiler Drill Team celebrated its 30th anniversary with a presentation at the 1995 IFR Congress and Festival outside Vienna.

conference would be held. The following responsibilities were assigned to the IFR: a) Standardize the judging of the breed; b) maintain, stabilize and intensify the characteristics of the Rottweiler as a working and protection dog; and c) help and teach the members in questions of breeding, raising and maintaining Rottweilers, advising members in all cynological questions and assisting in the buying and placing of Rottweilers. The IFR further hopes to Standardize breeding rules for all the member countries. Lofty ideals, ambitious plans, but are they feasible?

The second IFR conference was held in Scheveningen, Holland in May 1972, and the member countries from the first conference returned. It was a splendid conference with enlightening reports, particularly on hip dysplasia by second president Dr. van der Velden. The third conference, in May 1975, was in Vaasky, Finland.

The fourth conference was in beautiful Vienna, Austria, in October 1978. The authors had, by this time, attended the first, second and now the fourth conference. At each we listened to lectures on hip dysplasia, character, and teeth—although we had no proposal for a universal X-ray program, no temperament test which was feasible for all the members, and we understood that we fault Rottweilers with missing teeth but have no idea what we do about extra teeth. We had, of course, met some remarkable people in the breed from all around the world.

The fifth conference was convened in October 1982, at Bad Oeynhausen, West Germany to coincide with the 75th anniversary of the ADRK. Delegates arrived from Sweden, Denmark, England, Belgium, Finland, Switzerland, the U.S. and Norway. Two events at this conference were significant. First, the United States was represented by the American Rottweiler Club (previously, all U.S. clubs that wished to send delegates could do so). Secondly, the only club on the continent rivaling the ADRK in size and influence, the Netherlands Rottweiler Club, had dropped out of the IFR.

The sixth conference, surprisingly enough, was held in King of Prussia, Pennsylvania in May 1985 following the CRC Specialty. Delegates present included Horst Naumann—Germany, Olavi Pasanen—Finland, Sven Hyden—Sweden, Dorothea Gruenerwald—U.S., and Clara Hurley—Italy. A particular concern at this conference was the issue of docking tails, since the Council of European Countries endorsed a policy prohibiting tail docking. Not surprisingly, the IFR voted against the prohibition of tail docking.

The seventh conference was held outside Helsinki, Finland in June 1988. Austria, England, Finland, Norway, South Africa, West Germany, Switzerland and Australia (a new member) were represented. The American Rottweiler Club had failed to pay its dues to the IFR, so it had only an unofficial representative present. (In early 1989, the ARC voted to pay the required dues in order to be reinstated as an IFR member). Again, there were discussions on character and teeth, plus lectures on osteochondrosis, cruciate ligament damage and eye diseases.

The eighth conference was held in September 1991, outside Oslo, Norway. The poor attendance was particularly notable for this conference. Only twenty-two people attended to hear lectures on wolves, elbow lameness and a study on hereditary cataracts in Norwegian Rottweilers. Perhaps sensing that activities where more dogs were involved would boost attendance, the IFR conference or "Congress" decided on a name change.

The authors attended the 9th conference, now officially called an IFR Festival, in Notwil, Switzerland in September 1993. Germany, France, England, Denmark, Finland, Italy, Austria, Norway, Sweden, the Czech Republic, South Africa, Australia and the U.S. joined Switzerland for the discussions. The subject of the conference was a question hanging over all our heads: "Are we breeding a Rottweiler suitable for today's society?" To quote the chairman of the conference, Hans-Jurgen Eberbach of the ADRK, "This future (of the Rottweiler) means that we have to survive in the society of today and tomorrow. We have to face the problems. But it cannot be our task to change our Rottweiler with all its excellent features. We can only face the future by accepting the responsibility we have as Rottweiler owners and by avoiding any situation in public leading to a complaint."

The tenth conference was held in Bruckneudorf, Austria in August, 1995. Belgium, Germany, Finland, France, Israel, Italy, Norway, Portugal, Sweden,

Switzerland, Slovakia, the Czech Republic, Hungary, Austria and the United States either sent delegates or appointed proxies for voting. The centerpiece of this festival was the celebration of the 30th anniversary of the Austrian Army's Canine Corps, which had been using and breeding Rottweilers for the past three decades.

As far as the United States was concerned, the most significant vote to come out of this festival was the acceptance of a proposal from the American Rottweiler Club to hold the next festival October 2-9, 1997, in Wheaton, Illinois, the week preceding the 1997 MRC Specialty. The most significant vote to the authors was Joan Klem being chosen the fourth IFR president. At this writing, we look at 1997 as an opportunity to show the world what we have accomplished with the Rottweiler in the New World—from recognized AKC events such as tracking, dog shows, agility and herding to those events seeking AKC sanctioning like draft dog trials.

Have these conferences been worth the effort (and financial strain) on the countries hosting them? What has been accomplished?

1. They have fostered a healthy competition between countries. Beginning with the Finland conference, the IFR has hosted an international IPO (*Internationale Prufungsordnung der FCI* or International Trial Regulations for FCI—exercises required for titles essentially identical to Schutzhund exercises) competition met with great enthusiasm by the participants. It is the closest thing in Rottweilers to matching the ambience of an Olympic event. What tremendous national pride we felt when, in 1993 in Notwil, our American team consisting of Captain Peter Piusz, Janet Noble, Mitzi Robinson, Dean Calderon and Cheryl Miller stood on the top podium and held up the World Championship Trophy as our national anthem rang out through the horns of a local Swiss band that had, fortunately, included it in their repertoire. Our 1993 American team was the first non-German team to have won first place!

2. They have given those attending the conferences a look at the quality of Rottweilers being bred in the hosting countries as each conference has been scheduled around a large dog show in the immediate area.

3. Although few official resolutions have been met, the exchange between delegates, outside the confines of the official programs, have provided us with insights into the Rottweiler Fancy in countries different from our own, a realization that we share so many triumphs and problems within the breed and wonderful friendships extending now almost thirty years. Perhaps Herr Eberbach said it best in 1993, "We all belong to the same community because we all love the Rottweiler and we stand up for it."

One thing is certain about the IFR—without the leadership and support of the ADRK, this noble experiment would never have come into being, and surely would not have continued.

TYPE

His image—his silhouette—distinguishes the Rottweiler from every other breed . . . balance and proportion, 9 as to 10 in body length (slightly longer than tall); depth of chest 50 percent of the height, almost square . . . compact . . . neither coarse nor shelly . . . his bone and muscle must be sufficient to balance his frame—his appearance must reflect his function—TYPE is the essence of a breed . . .

Chapter 16

On the Experience and
Privilege of Judging Rottweilers

"**H**ow do you judge?" That question is most frequently asked of us as judges. An inner voice wants to answer, "Why, superbly, of course!" But what people really want to know could be better phrased as, "What criteria do you use to make your evaluations of each individual dog?" Perhaps it would be simpler to go back to the original question, "How do you judge?" for the clearest answer.

You begin with the Standard, the written description of the ideal Rottweiler, which includes a statement about the breed's character and function, and the movement or gait that the dog must have to perform those functions. The Rottweiler Standard also lists serious faults and disqualifications. Memorizing the Standard is not enough. If you are seriously considering judging, you must understand every part of the Standard. You must become so familiar with what you have studied that applying the Standard to living dogs becomes second nature.

Reading books and studying videos are worthwhile, but not enough. You must make opportunities to familiarize yourself with as many very good living Rottweilers as possible. Go over these dogs and discuss them with as many knowledgeable Rottweiler fanciers as you can; by studying dogs, not only at shows or seminars or in a breeder's home, but at as many performance events as possible, you will broaden your knowledge. Remember, learning to judge must be a positive experience; you cannot learn to recognize virtue by studying faults. You must fill your eye and mind with the image of the ideal. We have grown up with the Rottweiler and lived with the breed for most of our lives. You might not have been as lucky, so you must make or take every opportunity to burnish your knowledge and judging expertise.

You will have learned from all this that the most important criterion in judging is our Standard's definition of type. You must learn to recognize type, because type is the essence of a breed. It is that image, that silhouette, which distinguishes each breed from every other. In the Rottweiler, type has its origins in the breed's purpose and function and is comprised of those characteristics which have been bred into the Rottweiler long enough for them to have become stable and reproducible with some uniformity. When you think of the typical Rottweiler, you not only picture body structure and head, markings and coat, but movement and character. So as our Standard tells us, we are looking for a dog that is medium-large, robust and powerful, and black with clearly defined rust markings. His compact and substantial build denotes great strength, agility and endurance. Dogs are characteristically more massive throughout with larger frame and heavier bone than bitches. Bitches are distinctly feminine, but without weakness of substance or structure. Unfortunately, our 1990 Standard does not describe the Rottweiler's function but the preceding chapters in this book have. Summing it up briefly, we would say the judge in the ring is looking for an athlete.

Putting yourself in the position of judge, when a class enters the ring, the first thing you are looking for is type. As you send the class around the ring gaiting at a trot to start your evaluation, you are, of course, looking to see whether any are noticeably limping. However, you are also looking for that silhouette, that balance and proportion that define type in body structure. You are looking for a silhouette that is almost square, nine tall to ten long, and a depth of chest that is almost fifty-fifty, depth of chest to length of leg. Let us call that *the forest*, the overall body type, balance and proportion. A Rottweiler must have the build of a trotter for sustained running at a trot, and he must look like an athlete that could perform any task required.

In the individual examination you are looking at *the trees* that make up *the forest*. Many exhibitors wonder why a judge makes certain decisions in the ring on a given day. Well, the judge judges *inside* the ring, up close and personal, which gives him or her the advantage of being able to evaluate the trees better than could be done from outside the ring. The judge can see the eye color (which you hope is dark), the eye shape (which you hope is almond), the bite (which you hope is scissors), the dentition (which you hope will be full, 42 teeth, or at the very least 41) and the mouth pigmentation (which you hope will be dark). The judge can best see expression, ear carriage, dryness and head proportions up close. The judge can feel for the hardness of the muscle tone, the harshness of the coat, the undercoat, and in a dog, both testicles. The judge can take a good look at the feet: Are they round and compact with well-arched toes? Does the dog stand straight and true without toeing in or out, front and rear? Is the angulation front and rear correct with well-laid-back shoulder blades and stifle joints well turned? Does the neckline curve smoothly down over the shoulders into the back? What about the topline? Is it straight, firm and level? How about color and extent and definition of markings? Is it rust, orange, light tan, clearly defined in the right amount or smudgy or too large and bright?

"Does the dog stand straight and true without toeing in or out, front and rear?"
" . . . Does the neckline curve smoothly down over the shoulders into the back, lending a touch of elegance and refinement to the dog . . . a dog with refinement is also one that is beautiful, noble and proud-looking with beautiful, clear outlines and a harmoniously proportioned body . . ."

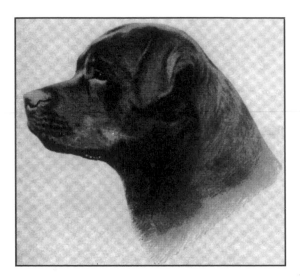

A beautiful German head—the 1950's

Ch. Rodsden's Berte v. Zederwald, CDX—the 1980s.

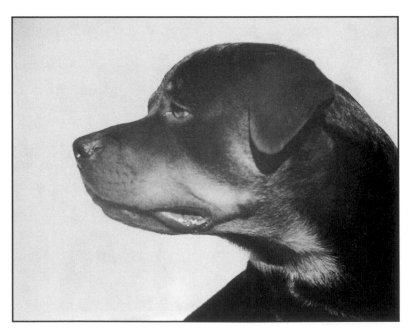

Ch. Northwind's Donar of Rodsden—the 1970s.

Ch. Vom Sonnenhaus Krugerrand, CD—the 1980s.

Ch. Ironwood's Cade, CD—the 1990s.

Ch. Powderhorn's Mile of Wencrest—the 1990s.

Ch. Afra v. Hasenacker, SchH I, CD—the 1960s.

Am. & Can. Ch. Birch Hill's Juno, CD, TD—
the 1970s.

Ch. Lindenwood's Anaconda, CD —the 1980s.

Ch. Foothill's Fiesta vom Boss, owned by Mark and Tammie Lewis, in a pose of typical Rottweiler watchfulness.

Therapy Dog International Raja vom Rauberfeld, CD, SchH I, CGC is shown here with a group of interested seniors in a nursing home visit with owner Bill Buehrer.

Ch. Rodsden's O. Henry of Cadan, as a puppy, showed himself to be a natural when he passed his Herding Instinct Certification test.

James J. O'Connell, Jr. takes Lowenhart's Cronus, CDX over the teeter-totter during course familiarization before an Agility Trial.

Parade dog carting California style.

Weight pull in the snow.

Starting the track
on a crisp fall day.

The realization of the breeder's best efforts is a litter of obvious quality and overall
uniformity. Anyone with an eye for a dog can appreciate these puppies.
Hayes

Am. & Can. Ch. Von Boylan's Boldly Bridgette, CD, BH—the 1990s.

Ch. Seren's Nightwood Bit of Magic, CD—the 1980s.

Ch. Lyvngwerth's Devotion v. Ponca, CD— the 1990s.

" . . . he must have a free, far-reaching, ground-covering, easy, efficient gait . . . ."

When you have made mental notes of all this while the dog is standing, you have the handler move him so that you can assess his gait. You want to see whether what you have observed in the standing dog is translated into proper Rottweiler gait. In assessing movement it is especially important to remember the function of the breed. In order to have the endurance, agility and strength to perform his tasks, a Rottweiler must have a free, ground-covering and efficient gait. Extraneous movement such as paddling, flipping, hackneying in front, kicking out and toeing out in the rear reduces efficiency and wastes energy, all of which reduce endurance. His function requires that a Rottweiler must be a trotter. There is little sideways, swinging movement of the trunk in trotting. At a trot, if he is efficiently covering the ground with long strides, his back will remain firm and relatively still. The course of motion will be harmonious—as the Germans put it.

During the whole time he is in the ring, you have been observing his attitude, which gives you hints to his character. Does he show confidence? Is he comfortable in the situation? Is he interested in and aware of his surroundings, alert without overreacting? During the individual examination, you get

These dogs are both very square in their proportions and the photos catch them at about the same instant in their gait sequence, but the dog at the left does not have the reach and drive of the dog at the right. He lacks the "ground-covering" length of stride, and so must take more and shorter steps to cover the same distance as the other dog.

to see how he reacts to his handler and to you as a stranger performing up close and very personal examinations.

Then you put it all together and go back to type which is the sum of all the components. You will never find a forest with all perfect trees. Do not, therefore, miss the beauty of the forest for the details of the trees. You will never find a perfect dog (and if you thought you did we wouldn't all agree with you anyway), so in the final analysis, you judge the *total* dog; you do not fault-judge.

Since we have admitted that we will never find the perfect dog, we must develop priorities. Judging is never black and white; it has a lot of grays and you must decide what you can forgive in each individual dog balanced with the total impression he has given you on that day. The Standard helps us set our priorities and our limitations as it lists serious faults and disqualifications.

We like to think of serious faults as divided into serious faults of structure and serious faults of beauty/cosmetics. You give more weight and are less forgiving to serious faults of structure than to serious faults of beauty. Your priority is to find the dog with the best structure and the fewest beauty faults, of course.

Serious faults of structure: Lack of proportion, undersized, oversized, reversal of sex characteristics (bitchy dogs, doggy bitches). Level bite; any missing teeth.

Serious faults of beauty: Yellow (bird of prey) eyes, eyes of different color or size, a hairless eye rim. Improper ear carriage (creased, folded or held away from cheek/head). Total lack of mouth pigment (pink mouth). Open, excessively short, wavy or curly coat, total lack of undercoat, any trimming that alters natural coat. Straw-colored, excessive, insufficient or sooty markings; white markings anyplace on dog.

Another way of defining priorities in the breed is to look at official critiques done by breed experts and/or breed wardens in the ADRK where they are trained to critique and must do it routinely. If it is mentioned in a critique, it is a breed priority in the Rottweiler, and must be given consideration and weight when assessing the total dog. As an example, we present here the critique of Fetz Oelberg, SchH II, along with his photo. The critique's value is clear.

> **Critique:** Of medium size, excellent in type, well built, substantial, strong boned, dry, hard, very good fore and aft, strong straight back, correct angulation, pronounced muscularity and male, dry constitution. Good head, stretched slightly, small ears carried high, dark eyes, scissors bite, 42 teeth healthy and strong, very good tightness of elbows, good tightness of pasterns and hocks. In movement, he is a trotter with far-reaching stride, active drive from rear . . . very good reach in front. Character is full of life, alert, fearless, steady . . . typical Rottweiler expression . . . CLASSY!

Learning to judge in the ADRK includes apprenticing in the ring and writing your own critique on each entry as the official judge is writing his. You are training yourself and being trained to see what the priorities are and to express it in writing or dictation. You then have the advantage of comparing what you saw with what the judge or breed warden saw. (You had better be pretty close in your evaluations or you will be apprenticing for a long time or, perhaps, never again.)

The closest training you will get for approval as an AKC judge to compare with the ADRK system is, of course, the hands-on examination and discussion at Judges' Institutes and seminars. Writing critiques and thinking as you judge in terms of a critique takes practice. But it is, after all, how we evaluate or view our own dogs; we just never had to express it or write it down. That is the hard part. Another reason the AKC format does not require critiques is that it is time-consuming. An ADRK judge never wants to judge more than 70 dogs a day. AKC judges are expected to judge 20 to 25 dogs an hour with a maximum of 175 at an all-breed show or 200 at a Specialty in any one day.

Originally, the AKC had an apprentice system for judging approval. It proved too time-consuming and unwieldy in a country as vast as the U.S. With such a large dog show population and shows almost every day of the year, the need for judges had become acute. As a consequence, AKC judges have had little experience in giving or writing critiques. It is only when you are invited to judge under FCI rules or in foreign countries where critiques are required that you get your chance to try your hand at it. You are even slower when you do not do it routinely, but you do develop your own system or code or get hopelessly lost (and desperately relieved when you notice that the field has lights which can be turned on as your judging day continues into evening).

Fetz v. Oelberg, SchH II, bred in Germany by
Herman Reiling and owned by Paul Harris.

Our Rottweiler Standard has limitations or gives us parameters in judging because it has disqualifications. If on examination you find that a bite is overshot or undershot, or that the dog has a wry mouth or two or more missing teeth, you must disqualify him. A long coat, any base color other than black, and absence of all markings are also disqualifications. Since a breed Standard is not only for judging but also the guideline for breeding, we list ectropion and entropion* as disqualifications. Entropion and ectropion can be diagnosed only by a veterinary ophthalmologist and not by a judge in a ring.

---

*Ectropion: *The scientific term for exceedingly loose lower eyelids or haw-eyedness such as is common in Bloodhounds, for instance. We are sure surgical correction can be done on a Rottweiler but such surgical correction is, as with entropion, an AKC disqualification. Ectropion is also genetic in origin.*
Harold R. Spira, Canine Terminology, *(New York, Howell Book House, 1985).*

*Entropion: *An anatomical abnormality due to spasm and contraction of the muscles controlling the eye rims. This, in consequence, causes the affected eyelids to turn and roll in toward the eyeball. The resultant contact of an eyelash to eyeball produces a state of semi-permanent irritation, indicated by squinting, excessive tear flow and other symptoms. Both upper and lower eyelids may be affected, the lower more frequently. The problem may occur on one or both sides.*
Surgical correction affords the only permanent cure. A skillful surgery doesn't leave scars but surgical correction of entropion is an AKC disqualification. Still, it must be left to a veterinarian to diagnose entropion. In Rottweilers, entropion appears to be genetic in origin.

You have now studied the Rottweiler Standard and if you understand all of what you have been reading, it is now time for you to be the judge! Many thanks to Robert Cole and *Dog News* for permission to reprint the article, which appears in Appendix A.

So you still want to be a dog show judge? Okay, now consider that **AKC judging approval regulations begin with the following Introduction** and consider it carefully:

The AKC Constitution explicitly grants to the Board of Directors the authority to issue and revoke approvals to judge dogs.

In summary:

- The approval to judge is a privilege granted by the Board, *not* a right available on demand to anyone who believes he or she is qualified to judge.

- It is important to understand the difference between equality of opportunity to judge and identical treatment of applicants, given the reality that abilities and experiences are decidedly unequal.

- The greater the emphasis on the unique abilities of each applicant to judge new breeds, the better the approval process will work.

A footnote on judging: The judge can judge only what is presented in his ring on a given day. What the judge sees and puts up can have an influence on the breed for sure, and is a big responsibility, but the primary responsibility and influence begins with the breeder. The breeder is the first judge. Now, it stands to reason that with over 100,000 puppies being registered by the AKC in a year, there are a number that are not very good first judges. So that puts an added burden on you, the AKC judge, not only to decide which entry deserves the first, second, third or fourth ribbon, but to decide whether an entry deserves a ribbon at all.

When your original approval is granted, you will be asked if you wish to judge Junior Showmanship.

JUNIOR SHOWMANSHIP WITH THE ROTTWEILER

As the *AKC Guidelines for Junior Showmanship* remind us, a principle of Junior Showmanship is to afford the opportunity to learn the spirit of competition. Winning is important, but is secondary to development of sportsmanship in competition. Junior Showmanship provides the young people with the opportunity to learn how to lose as well as win. It really bonds them with their dogs and their breed and is often the beginning of a lifetime of enriched involvement in the sport of purebred dogs. So we could say that our Juniors are the future of the Rottweiler. Junior Showmanship in Obedience adds

Kala Brown, age
ten, with Ch. Wright's
Joint Venture, CGC.
John Ashbey

Lindsay Balder, age ten,
with Der Hagen's All
That Matters. *Bill Meyer*

another dimension of discipline and sportsmanship and is promoted with trophies for highest scoring Junior in Obedience at several of our major Specialties.

Junior Showmanship classes are non-regular classes that are judged solely on the ability and skill of juniors in handling their dogs as in the breed ring. It provides them with a meaningful competition in which they can learn, practice and improve in all areas of handling skill and sportsmanship.

Juniors usually show the breed that lives with the family, so in that respect if your youngster is interested in competing in Junior Showmanship, he or she is luckier to live in other than a Rottweiler family. Many judges and fanciers feel that there is always a danger that a Junior handling a Rottweiler may not be able to control such a big, strong working dog. (And in all-breed Junior Showmanship the flashier breeds that appear easier for a Junior to control often have an advantage.) But there have been a good number of successful Juniors showing Rottweilers in all-breed Junior competition. These young people usually began by having success at our Rottweiler Club matches or Specialties.

It is especially important in Rottweiler families with children interested in Junior Showmanship to match up the right Rottweiler with the right child. A small, twelve-year-old girl who enters the ring with a large male will give the judge (and the other Juniors in the ring) a few anxious moments. As mild and mellow and well-trained as the large male may be and as cute as you may think a little girl looks with a big dog, remember that unpredictable things can happen in a ring full of dogs. What if another dog gets loose and attacks the Rottweiler? Even the mild-mannered dog may try to defend himself. One of the things a Junior judge looks for is how smoothly, with economy of motion, the child sets up the dog. A small child with a big dog makes for lots of movement.

Not so many years ago the Juniors judge could ask the child questions about the breed or anatomy or dog management, but now under no circumstances should the judge use questions as a means of testing a Junior's knowledge. The judge will examine and evaluate the class of Juniors in four basic areas: proper breed presentation, skill in the individual dog's presentation, knowledge of ring procedures and appearance and conduct. Actually, the judge should hardly be aware of the handler's presence while completing the examination, so unobtrusive should be the handling.

In presenting a Rottweiler to the judge, the junior should be prepared to show the bite and dentition himself and should show the whole mouth so that the judge can check for missing teeth just as in the breed ring. The judge is not judging the dog or disqualifying for missing teeth. In Junior Showmanship the judge is only concerned that the Junior should demonstrate the ability to handle the dog as it is handled in the breed ring, showing the dog to its best advantage in pose and in motion, thus demonstrating knowledge of how to handle their specific breed.

Kalley Krickeberg, age twelve, with Ch. Birch Hill's Abandon, CD. *Booth/Ritter*

Brett Worsham with Ch. Von Der Lors Anastashia Cade. *Mitchell*

THEN—Chandra Klem, age twelve, with Ch. Rodsden's Porsche Forstwald, CD.

NOW—Chandra Klem Plencner with Rodsden's Lexi of Parrok, CD. *Kim Booth*

THEN—Correy Krickeberg, age fifteen, with Ch. Weissenburg's Legend. *Booth/Ritter*

NOW—Correy Krickeberg, professional handler, with Ch. Rodsden's O. Henry of Cadan, CD. *Meyer/Ray*

The judge wants to know how well the junior follows directions, uses space and executes the requested gaiting patterns. And the judge is not really evaluating either the dress of the handler nor the grooming of the dog, but rather that an effort has been made.

Nothing can compare with the nervous anticipation that a mother (or aunt) or grandmother experiences during the judging of her get in Junior Showmanship. Junior handling can be a very positive experience for children growing up if the good sportsmanship carries over from inside the ring to those on the outside of the ring. Many Juniors have turned out to be great assets to the sport as adults with a continuing interest in the breed and much to contribute. Junior Showmanship provides a solid foundation for a young fancier's future success in the sport of purebred dogs.

Chapter 17

The Experience of Judging in Foreign Lands

Judging in foreign lands is one of the most gratifying and complimentary experiences a Rottweiler authority can ever have. Having been honored with judging invitations by Rottweiler clubs in many parts of the world, the authors wish to use this chapter to share our experiences with you, as a present or prospective judge, and give you a deeper perspective on this side of doing your part for the long-term good of the Rottweiler worldwide.

Foreign assignments mean that the invited judge has been cast in the position of a recognized expert, and makes that judge's opinion on the dogs of the region valuable to the inviting club and the region's fanciers. It is also a great responsibility for the individual judge. The inviting countries are usually emerging in the Rottweiler breed, and the help they get from our opinions is invaluable. It is therefore every judge's responsibility to teach as well as to evaluate dogs in the ring. The visiting foreign judge will often be asked to write critiques on all or part of the entry and, even if one is not asked, the wise judge will keep notes so that the right comment can be proffered when individual exhibitors approach with questions.

When you are invited to judge outside AKC jurisdiction, you should judge under the rules and regulations of the kennel club sanctioning the show. Most often, the classes are different from those of the AKC, and their Standard is not the same. The decisions you make on the individual dogs, of course, come from your discipline and experience in the breed, but if their Standard has no disqualifications, then you cannot disqualify. The one universal rule for disqualification, however, is a dog that bites any human in the ring.

A seminar on the breed is usually scheduled, giving you further opportunity to teach and explain the terminology in your critiques, and to summarize the strong points you have noted as well as those needing improvement. At the same time, you get to know the people and their problems in the breed as well as the country and its problems. Dog shows are a good weathervane for economic and social stability in a country. When a country starts or continues giving dog shows, it implies that at least part of the economy is healthy, because the sport of purebred dogs is expensive. When a country starts having dog shows, you know it is not at war. When a country starts inviting foreign judges to judge its shows, you know that the Cold War is really over!

JUDGING IN:

Great Britain

The Kennel Club (so called because it was the first kennel club) rules with authority over the British and the British Commonwealth and ex-Commonwealth purebred dog Fancy. Its rules and class regulations differ significantly from those of the AKC in a number of important points.

No matter where you judge, you start with the puppies and go through the scheduled classes in the same methodical way until you reach the winners. One, two, three and four, and sometimes five and six, are the same placements in every country. The difference lies in how the winners are determined, and what awards the winners are given. Under The Kennel Club rules, the winners of the classes in dogs and bitches at championship shows run off for the Challenge and Reserve Challenge Certificates, C.C. and R.C.C., for each sex. From the C.C. winners at Specialty shows, you will select Best in Show and Reserve Best in Show, which can be of the same sex, and Best of Opposite Sex. There is no champion class, so finished champions compete in the regular classes alongside dogs being "made up." If there is an outstanding champion being shown, it makes it difficult for new dogs or young dogs to finish. As a result, under KC rules, there are fewer champions finished than under AKC rules, which may be an argument in Britain's favor. As the judge, you do not have to award a C.C. anymore than you have to award Winners unless the individuals are worthy of becoming champions in your opinion.

The English Standard does not list any disqualifying faults, so a judge cannot disqualify any dog unless he bites a person in the ring. If you consider the dog to be vicious, you can dismiss it from the ring. A judge will feel more comfortable with the AKC rule that if the dog attacks you, it is disqualified. It doesn't have to be successful in biting you to get disqualified. Under the AKC rule, the unsuccessful first attempt disqualification also keeps the next judge out of harm's way. A number of the countries whose kennel clubs and breed Standards were modeled after The Kennel Club are now in the process of switching to the FCI system and the FCI Rottweiler Standard, possibly because of the inadequacies of the British Standard.

When judging in Great Britain, you are asked to critique only your first two placements in each class; at Championship Specialty shows, there are eight classes, one of which has such a complicated determination of eligibility that it makes you glad to be the judge and not the exhibitor. (Exhibitors

The dogs you will judge are quite typical. Winner of the bitch CC and Reserve Best in Show at Australia's third National Specialty.

in Britain sometimes exercise their right to enter the same dog in more than one class, leaving the ring steward to sort it out and the judge glad to be the judge, not the ring steward.) The English are very keen on competition, and the entry is usually large enough to find worthy dogs for all the placements. The early English Rottweiler somewhat resembled a Bullmastiff in head, wet mouth, and wrinkles, so it is nice to see an improvement in this respect in the dogs. The type has also improved greatly in that fewer tall, long-bodied dogs are being shown.

The entry at Specialty shows is normally large enough to require two judges who, after judging their classes, get together to assess and determine the Best in Show and Reserve Best in Show, which may be of the same sex, and Best of Opposite Sex. If they cannot agree on the placements, an appointed referee, who is usually a breeder, will make the final decision. Good manners occupy a high priority among the English, and the dog Fancy is no exception. Everyone defers to the senior judge if there is a difference of opinion. You don't want to have your hosts call on the referee at your first English judging assignment, even if the Reserve Dog C.C. is the one that remains in your memory as the one you wish you had bred.

The shows overseas do not normally provide professional photographers. In fact, a camera may not even be in evidence, so you will rarely have any photos of the winners or the goings on at the show. And if a camera does appear, it is usually in the hands of an amateur whose photos of the winning dog make you wonder if it is the same dog you judged.

There are many things to love about the British other than their good manners, good sportsmanship, and well-behaved Rottweilers, starting with the names of their Rottweilers. Some that stand out to us include Potterspride Poison Pedlar, Amicus Perhaps Love At Yorlander, and my special favorite, Warrimead Heaven Knows Its Bellecose. Then there are the addresses— Woodlock, Holt Lane, Hook near Basingstoke, Hampshire, Gamegards Cottage, Warwick Road, Little Canfield, near Great Dunmow, Essex. And who but the British would have a display entitled *Four Centuries of Dog Collars* in a museum room? We found them at Leeds Castle, the grounds of which would make a perfect venue for a Rottweiler Specialty.

Australia

Australia is a continent with a quarantine. Rabies does not exist there, and great precaution is exercised to see that it does not gain a foothold. Therefore, the Rottweilers you will be judging are, for the most part, from English breeding because English dogs are also generally rabies-free. The first Rottweilers arrived in Australia in 1962 when Captain Roy-Smith arrived, bringing some dogs with him from England. There have been a few German, Finnish, American and even Italian dogs imported, which has broadened the breeding base. The approval of the use of frozen semen has also helped by introducing some different, fresh bloodlines. When the breeding base is limited, one cannot hope to establish correct type; and when the type that is available does not match the breed Standard in some respects, it is time to upgrade or, in some cases, start over. From our own experience, when my brother, Pat Rademacher, and I first traveled to Germany in 1963 to buy Harras and Afra and meet the German Rottweiler at the Bundessieger show in Hanover, it was like meeting a whole new breed. Starting over seemed to be the only sensible decision.

In spite of limitations in the Australians' breeding selections, the dogs you will judge are quite typical. The depth of quality in the ring does not approach what you will find in the U.S., Germany or the Netherlands, but it still allows you, as a judge, a choice. You do not have to forgive much to come up with a winner. Once, you would have had to forgive a lighter eye and a heavier more Bullmastiff-type head, with loose skin and heavier flews. But those problems are now being addressed in the breeding programs. From the ninth Championship show of the Rottweiler Club of South Australia in 1986, to the third National Rottweiler Specialty hosted by the Rottweiler Club of Queensland in 1991, there was a noticeable improvement, and many earlier problems were not evident in the ring.

Australia was once a member of the British Commonwealth of Nations, so the Kennel Control Council modeled its rules, classes and Standards after those of The Kennel Club in England. Each state in Australia has its own Kennel Club and Rottweiler Club, and each gives its own shows (The Royal National show of Queensland—an all-breed event, for example). Judging at a Royal sounds so much more impressive than saying you are judging at your hometown show. The South Australia Rottweiler Club Championship show is a local or state club Specialty. The Rottweiler Clubs have joined together to form the National Rottweiler Council of Australia. The third National Rottweiler Specialty was held in 1991, but the National is not held every year, primarily because of finances.

As with British shows, judges must rely heavily on the ring steward to advise them of the double entries, and to keep them sorted out. An entry of the same dog can be made in any number of classes for which it is eligible in any country, but it is done only in countries with Kennel Club rules. Under those rules, you award a Best in Show and a Reserve Best in Show, which does not have to be of the opposite sex. The Australian-bred class will also have Best and Best of Opposite Sex awards. As a judge, you will probably not have a problem keeping track of what is happening, because the ring steward keeps you informed of the classes, marks the judge's book and can even hand out the awards, although it's best to keep that privilege for yourself. As a result, you can work through up to 250 dogs a day because all you are required to do is judge the dogs. You select a first, second, third, fourth, fifth and sixth place dog; as the dogs go to their placement markers, you turn around and the next class is in the ring. (Imagine the problems if Australia had professional handlers as we do.)

At a Specialty, judging proceeds more slowly because the club will usually have asked you to give critiques on all the entries. As in every part of the world, the Rottweiler has been growing in registrations and entries in Australia, so you will have at least two days of judging at a Specialty.

In Australia, the classes and Standards may change because Australia recently voted to join the FCI, but the warm, generous hospitality of the Australian Fancy will never change.

Canada

Canada doesn't seem at all foreign. Dogs cross the border between the U.S. and Canada with no problems at all. The only thing that is needed is a valid health certificate for your dog with rabies inoculation noted. The Rottweilers you will judge in Canada come primarily from U.S., German and English pedigrees because Canada has no quarantine. The dogs can and do compare well with the dogs in American shows. Actually, many dogs from the U.S. also compete actively in the Canadian shows.

The Canadian Kennel Club (CKC) classes are the same as the AKC, but it takes only ten points instead of fifteen to finish a Championship. The

Judging in Canada is a joy. Sylvie Fafard handling her future Can. Ch. Von Galingen's Satin Sheets, having a good day at the Quebec Specialty under Joan Klem. *Stonham*

Rottweiler Standard is the same and handling is comparable. If you are judging in Quebec, it helps to know a little French, as everything is printed in French as well as English, and sometimes the natives do not understand, or profess not to understand, everything that you express in English.

There are several well-established clubs in Canada that hold Specialties, and the Rottweiler Club of Canada holds a National Specialty, which moves around the country just as our American Rottweiler Club National does. All-breed shows and Specialties are sometimes scheduled for the same day, with the Specialty being judged in the evening. The Sovereign Rottweiler Club of Ontario, the Rottweiler Club of Quebec and the National hold very well-run Specialties which are a joy to judge. Whether you go as a judge or as an exhibitor, you will find attending a Canadian all-breed show or Specialty great fun.

Caribbean Islands

DOMINICAN REPUBLIC

In the Dominican Republic, which shares the same island of Hispaniola with Haiti, there are all-breed shows and Specialties sponsored by the local breed clubs and, once a year, a Specialty sponsored by the Agriculture Department during the Agricultural Exposition held in the capital of Santo Domingo. (Santo Domingo was where Christopher Columbus landed, and there is a handsome lighthouse and statue to remind the visitor of this.)

Rottweiler registrations are still quite small, and membership in the Rottweiler Club reflects this. For a small club, the members work very hard. Since there is no quarantine, they have the occasional import, or entry that comes from the U.S. to show at their shows, to use as a breed model.

JAMAICA

Jamaica has an established Rottweiler club which gives its own Specialty show, usually outdoors under a huge fig tree on the rugby grounds or on the Jamaica College Grounds, with a tent set-up similar to that of American outdoor shows. Jamaica became a British colony when the British took the island away from Spain, and it became a member of the British Commonwealth in 1962, so the Jamaica Kennel Club rules and classes are similar to those of The Kennel Club. It offers the *Mid-Limit* class for dogs that have won only one C.C. or Reserve C.C. or three or more first prizes, except in the puppy class. However, you will be asked to judge by the AKC Standard.

Jamaicans can buy dogs only from the British because the Jamaican government believes rabies to be hereditary and, of course, British dogs are rabies-free. When the only dogs one can import come from a country that already has a very strict quarantine and limited importing, there is a problem. Unless restrictions are lifted and/or the use of frozen semen is allowed, a judge may continue to have to use the prerogative of withholding ribbons. You cannot be a good teacher unless you exercise your own discipline in the breed. Unfortunately, sometimes even the Rottweiler of the best quality either has a faulty bite or other disqualifying faults by the AKC Standard and/ or does not move well. Again, especially when judging overseas for these young, developing clubs, you must try to teach type because that is the first and most important criteria anyone must learn about their breed. Fortunately, you usually do find several entries that you can award the Challenge Certificates to and still uphold your discipline in the breed. If you are invited back several years later, you may find it easier to make your awards. (Jamaican imports and their breeding practices have improved.)

Judging Best in Show in Jamaica
under the fig tree.

TRINIDAD AND TOBAGO

Although very much under British influence, since most of the Rottweilers come from England and their shows and classes are the same as in the other Islands, Trinidadians can import dogs directly from Germany or the U.S. The quarantine kennels seemed adequate for an older dog who is already socialized and trained, but would be very hard on a puppy. It is also quite expensive, so the opportunity to import directly has at least two barriers, the expense and the unwillingness of good breeders to send their best dogs into the quarantine.

As on the other Islands, the Rottweiler fanciers are very earnest in their desire to establish the best of the breed, in spite of very formidable handicaps. They feel that inviting breed experts to judge is one way of doing this. Of course, if it is a breeder-judge, they are particularly eager to establish a good rapport and contacts which might lead to the availability of importing good dogs.

Scotland

Your good manners require that you write a thank-you note and a summation of your experiences of the shows you judge overseas to the club that gives the show. Joan Klem's experience of judging the Scottish Rottweiler Club sixth Championship Show in March, 1991 was summed up in this letter to the club:

> When I looked out of my window at the Burns Monument Hotel and saw Brig-a-doon, the bridge over the river Doon, I knew it was going to be a special weekend. The venue for the show was ideal, with a large enough ring for even Mrs. Klem to move them out as she is wont to do. . . . I do not enter into foreign judging assignments with a preconceived notion of what to expect, usually. But I was aware of the terrific problems of vicious dog publicity our breed has been suffering in Great Britain, so I was pleasantly surprised to see that it had not impacted the older dog classes, only the puppy classes. Your dogs, overall, are of good type, correct size, and I saw more consistency in correct head models than I see in some areas of the U.S. There were still a few of the old Bullmastiffy type with heavy flews and pronounced dewlap, but not many.
>
> Although the small entry of puppies did not present a large enough sample to say for sure from this one show that the future quality of the breed may suffer, I predict that it will. When the responsible breeders in our clubs are asked to limit breeding, it means the depletion of the gene pool for quality dogs and fewer responsible breedings.
>
> The media hysteria has done irreparable damage to a great Working breed in Britain. It should be ashamed of itself! It is a small world, and what hurts one person in the breed hurts us all. We want you to know our concern and only wish we could help in some way. Perhaps the best we can do is to make sure it doesn't happen in the United States.

There is no judge in these photos from the Scottish Rottweiler Club's sixth Championship show because the judge was taking the pictures as there was no professional photographer. The C.C. winner and Best in Show winner were from the Post-Graduate class. The C.C. and Reserve Best in Show at the Scottish Specialty came from the Open Bitch class. Judge Klem served as the photographer.

If all things were as they should be, I would suggest that you could now start to work on correcting some of the beauty faults that were there in a significant number, such as light eyes and light markings (*canaries* as Friedrich Berger, head breed warden in Germany, used to call them). Also, as a club, could you work on the Standard? When a Standard has no disqualifications, you are sending out mixed signals to the judge and the breeder, "this is the way you should do it but you don't have to." And since I am making suggestions, here is another one. Please do not ask the judge to leave in dogs who are limping and just put them at the end of the line. A dog limps because he hurts, so you are doing neither the dog nor the handler any favor by keeping him in the ring with a dog who isn't in consideration; nor are you really doing any favor for the owner, who must watch a very nice dog have to be moved to the end of the line behind some not as nice dogs because he happened to be limping that day.

You have many good things going for the breed in Scotland, not the least of which is a club which seems to enjoy putting on a large Championship show as well as partying together. From the excellent ring stewarding, the good sportsmanship, to the great conversations at the Disco and everything in-between, I want to thank you, everyone, and say how very much I enjoyed my lovely visit to Scotland. Every time I use my Edinburgh crystal glasses which you sent home with me, I shall remember it! I will also pray that this terrible time in our breed will pass and that reason will return.

Mexico

The Mexican Kennel Club operates under the rules of the FCI, and holds all-breed shows and international shows, with judges from various FCI countries officiating, at which the dogs could become international champions if they passed all the requirements. The *Club De Mexico Rottweiler, A.C.* has held a National Rottweiler Specialty Show each year, beginning in 1989. The Mexican Rottweiler fancier has been busy trying to bring into the scene the best or, at least, some of the most prominent bloodlines from the U.S. and from Germany. As a result, the classes provide fairly typical representatives of the breed. You are asked to rate the dogs, V = excellent, SG = very good, G = good (which is not so good), but you are not asked to give written critiques. You do address the crowd in the ring on completion of judging, explaining the decisions you have made on the winners. Since Mexican shows are held under FCI rules, the classes include a Working Dog class.

New Zealand

New Zealand is another island country with a quarantine, so the dogs you will judge have, for the most part, descended from Australian dogs, which in turn descended from English pedigrees. Their classes and Standard are also from The Kennel Club rules.

The first Rottweiler was registered in New Zealand in 1970, and the breed soon found a nucleus of devoted fanciers. In a relatively small area, fanciers still support three Rottweiler Clubs that give Championship shows and promote Obedience and Agility competition. There is a limited breeding base so we did not find too many that could be awarded a V rating, but you can find winners in each class and award the C.C.s. You will be asked to write critiques and give ratings. When we were there, the sun did come out after a storm for the judging of Best Head and Best Mover, obviously non-regular classes, but regularly judged at Specialties. Unfortunately, the best head you may have seen in the classes is not necessarily entered for Best Head class, and the best mover may not show in the Best Mover class.

Although it may rain on their show, it never rains on the New Zealanders' hospitality. We learned to understand the Maori (the New Zealand aborigine) culture from the Maori family that worked on every committee in the show and hosted our visit, and to accept the gracious and warm friendship immediately offered to us.

Best Bitch in Show and Best in Show at the New Zealand Specialty. It stopped raining and the sun came out.

Night shows under basketball court lights have certain handicaps.

The Philippines

The Philippines Rottweiler Club is a young club, but the members are very determined to have their influence felt in the Rottweiler breed in their country. The Specialty we were at was held in the evening following an all-breed show held at the same location. The Philippine rules and Standard are from The Kennel Club, but the Rottweiler Club had asked us to judge according to the AKC Standard. This, as has already been explained, brings the exhibitors into the real world. The Filipino Rottweiler fanciers are determined to import as many of the good and/or winning bloodlines from the U.S. and elsewhere as possible. Their research comes primarily from *The Rottweiler Quarterly* in the U.S., and they can quote the systems results verse and rhyme.

South Africa

The first Rottweilers were brought to South Africa by German settlers in the 1900s, but the first Rottweilers to be registered with the Kennel Union of South Africa, KUSA, had to wait until 1934, just a few years after the first were registered with the AKC. The South African Rottweiler will come from Dutch,

English, and German pedigrees, but the British influence became the dominant one and the Kennel Club rules, classes and Standard were the ones adopted. In 1987, things changed for the Rottweiler breed, and the German influence took over as they adopted the FCI rules and Standard.

The Rottweiler's popularity increased in South Africa until it became the second highest in registrations in KUSA (second highest in registrations sounds familiar). There are seven Rottweiler clubs in South Africa, and they all support shows and hold Specialties with all-breed shows or independently. The popularity of the Rottweiler, and increased interest in competition, was advanced when Dudley Bennet's Ch. Tankerville Bastian caught the attention of the judges and became the top winning dog of all breeds for several years. The momentum continued when Sophie Langen's Ch. Von Sophias Bulli was named KUSA National Dog for 1989–91. The dogs you will be judging in South Africa come from an established breeding base.

The 20th Anniversary Show of The Rottweiler Working and Breeding Association of Transvaal was held at the Epol Show Arena Grounds. It has a large enough area to hold your ring and an obedience ring with sufficient distance separating them. (Your host club and the oldest of the Rottweiler Clubs in South Africa, The Rottweiler Working and Breeding Association of Transvaal, holds an all-breed obedience trial in conjunction with its Specialty.) The grounds have a small clubhouse, and the ring has a holding tent for the dogs and an officials' tent so that your transcriber and her typewriter are protected from the elements (the elements at that time of year being the African sun and the winds of the African veldt). She types your critiques as you dictate so that each entry may have their copy before they leave the grounds (a German-style show, for sure).

We have found that judging good dogs is a lot more fun than judging mediocre or poor ones. The entries are, for the most part, in competition, especially the champions, so we had a very good time and made hard decisions. Seven years earlier when we had judged, we found a very good male to put up, Ch. Tankerville Digby, bred, owned, and handled by Dudley Bennet; this time it was a bitch (we always look for a good bitch as the bitches are so important to the breed and often get overlooked). We had been looking for and found the excellent type, the balance, the fabulous movement of a natural trotter and the temperament we like to see in the ring, which could be described as pleasantly full of spirit, and that extra something every judge looks for on the day, pizazz! Best in Show went to Ch. St. Tuttston Pazazz, owned and beautifully handled by 18-year-old Leanne Tutt.

By the time Best in Show was awarded, the light was beginning to disappear. We were having such a good time moving the dogs in the big ring, critiquing, and making those hard decisions, that we misjudged our time and had forgotten that we had all those non-regular classes still to judge. The Best Head could be judged up close by the setting sun, but the Best Gait had to be judged by the best dark silhouette passing in front of the one floodlight

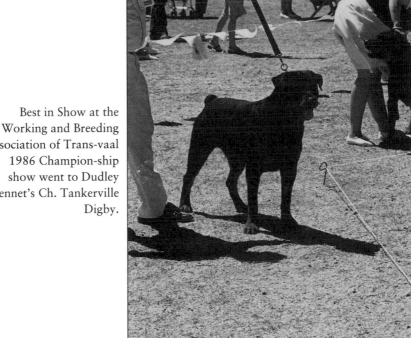

Best in Show at the Working and Breeding Association of Trans-vaal 1986 Champion-ship show went to Dudley Bennet's Ch. Tankerville Digby.

Best in Show at the 1993 RWBAT show to the bitch with the extra "pizazz," St. Tuttson's Pazazz, owned and handled by Leanne Tutt.

shining from the clubhouse. Actually, the young man whose dog won the event had been training the dog for a year especially for it. That young man and his dog were in great condition and were both built as marathon trotters should be.

A giant step forward for the breed in South Africa was the formation of The Rottweiler Council of the Kennel Union of Southern Africa. It was formed by delegates from the major clubs who sat down to work together for the breed's benefit and, as a result, has had a great influence on KUSA. KUSA listens and acts on the Council recommendations. For instance, the Council recommended that no dog may receive the title of champion unless its hips have been X-rayed and found to be within the parameters agreed upon and KUSA did it. The Council has made available to the Rottweiler clubs microchip scanners as the preferred method of identification (South Africa seems further ahead on this than the U.S.). Another proposal that has great merit is the Special Pedigree, which will be awarded to dogs that have met certain criteria. KUSA also listens to and acts on proposals from the Council while in the U.S., we can only get the AKC to promise to let the ARC know if any red Rottweilers apply to be registered.

Although the end of apartheid has been marked by fewer registrations in purebred dogs and a decrease in entries at dog shows in South Africa, the sport and our breed are in good hands with those strong, dedicated clubs and they will bounce back.

As judges, we have never been treated with more warmth, friendship, and consideration than we were by the wonderful friends we have made in the Rottweiler Clubs in South Africa. They take you into their homes, their hearts and their minds.

Taiwan

With so much trade between the U.S. and Taiwan (and as many Rottweilers being purchased for Taiwan), you would think that more of the young people would speak English, but our interpreter was not young, and knew nothing about dogs and dog shows. This was problem number one! The judge's book and catalog were printed in Chinese, as was the Rottweiler Standard, which was sent to us after the judging visit. As it is illustrated with an AKC Champion and our sketches, it would seem to be the AKC Standard. Now, anybody can figure out that *strasse* means street in German, but Chinese? In addition, the language is printed from right to left and from top to the bottom of the page in columns (not that it made any difference to us, since we can't read a word of it).

Problem number two: On our first visit, the show was an all-breed show and we were to judge Rottweilers and the Working group. The other breeds, Groups, and BIS were to be judged by a Japanese judge who spoke no Chinese or English. We felt we were better off than he was, except that he had judged in Taiwan before, and had already gone through the cultural shock of a toilet that consists of a hole in the ground, no ring dividers, no placement numbers, trophies the size of the Taj Mahal in the middle of the ring during judging, no judge's table or chair (a one-legged stool that fit his

Judging in Taiwan in 1988 with ring dividers and numbers and, the same two- to four-month-old class to start the assignment.

posterior but not ours was in the center of our ring), and of a first class that consists of six eight- to twelve-week-old puppies!

Problem number three: Rottweilers in Taiwan are not as friendly as Rottweilers in America! This is what we had been told and we were glad we had been warned. Not so friendly Rottweilers, some of whom have collars on instead of choke chains (and needing pinch collars), are handled by absolute novices (grinning happily, although obviously not understanding any one of your directions, including pointing them to the *end* of the line in last place and *not* to the front of the line in first place), and have every fault ever mentioned in any Standard. We had been listening to our Chinese Berlitz tape on our many trips to the grocery store in the station wagon so that we learned to say 1, 2, 3, 4, in Chinese, but five, six, and seven we felt we would never need. Wrong! The number of awards was decided in the ring right before judging the class. We were horrified when told we must give out five trophies in a class where we had difficulty finding an entry worthy of first place. In pantomime, we were able to communicate the problem with the overbite and underbite and limping, but the missing testicle gave us problem number four.

Problem number five: How do you judge the Group? This is settled by those in charge, who instructed us and the Japanese judge to put up the Rottweiler and the Pomeranian, since those two breeds had the largest entry. Sounded logical to us; problem solved! Our first judging experience in Taiwan ended with the children from the local school running through the playground where the ring had been with the most imaginative kites flying at the end of the string in their hands. All that was needed were fireworks!

Judging in foreign countries is more than a ticket to world travel. It is as much about teaching and learning as it is about giving and taking. Exhibiting in foreign lands, like judging, offers you the same opportunity to become both a student and a teacher. In the Rottweiler breed, it is very important for us all to be good ambassadors for our country and our breed; at the same time, you'll have a great time doing it.

So, do you still want to be a dog show judge? *You bet!*

Chapter 18

Predictions for the Rottweiler in the 21st Century

What predictions would the Romans, who originally brought the Rottweiler's ancestors to Germany, have made for the future of those dogs? That the need for such dogs would last as long as the Roman Empire?

The dogs lasted longer.

What prediction would the German butchers have made for the future of their *metzgerhund*? That these Rottweiler-prototypes would last as long as cows were driven to market and butchered meat was brought home in carts?

The dogs lasted longer.

What prediction would those early German Rottweiler Club members have made for the future of their breed? That the Rottweiler would survive World War I?

The dogs survived World War I, World War II, the global chaos between the wars and beyond.

So we begin our predictions for the 21st century with "the Rottweiler will still be with us." But will it be the same Rottweiler that we know today?

Yes and no.

Physically, there should be little change for the Rottweiler. As we have pointed out throughout this book, the "look" of the Rottweiler has altered very little in the last 100 years. There has been constant refining to that look, but it hasn't been tinkered with too much. As long as our goals are to have a medium-large dog that exhibits agility, a dog that we consider an athlete, we will keep the Rottweiler within the size-range it is now. The question of whether or not to dock the tail will still be up for a vote—but the "stumpers" will prevail.

The character of the Rottweiler will essentially be the same, but the way we test that character, or the means for the dog to express those desired character traits, will have changed. For example, steadfastness may be measured by the Rottweiler's willingness to patiently navigate a draft-dog course, while the ability to forget unpleasant experiences will be tested in the farm yard, where the dog continues to herd after being kicked by unruly livestock.

The Germans have said that in the future we must have a kinder, gentler breed. We believe they refer not to a modification in the Rottweiler's basic character, but to the temperament presented to the public. Legislation will have forced owners, breeders, and judges to see to it that the breed is perceived not as a danger to the community, but as a companion and helpmate. It is not that the Rottweiler must evolve into an animal with a softer nature in the 21st century, it is that we must promote different roles for our breed which accentuate that softer side.

We will no longer view the Rottweiler, or advertise the breed, as the premier guard dog—the alternative to a smoking gun. We dare not, lest the breed be banned from municipalities across our country, or for that matter, across the world.

PREDICTIONS ON A LIGHTER NOTE

In the 21st century, the Rottweiler's versatility will be stressed above everything else. We will see the breed competing in such a wide variety of events that the AKC's computer will be habitually out of memory, and it will take even longer than it does now to receive an AKC certificate in acknowledgment of a title. ARC member Cathy Thompson will be directing a staff of ARCites to tabulate the data for the 100 pages needed in the ARC newsletter to record production and working awards. The ARC pictorial will be available only on disks because the size, if printed, would make it impossible to mail.

The IFR will alternate locations between Germany and the United States— the two countries with the largest memberships, the most dogs, and the most money. Besides, after the success of the 1997 IFR Festival in the United States, only the German Fancy would have the audacity to believe that it can top that festival. There will be more countries, especially those in South America, that will join the IFR. Ursel Hoffmann, who did an outstanding job as secretary/treasurer during the end of the 20th century, will continue in that position while mastering e-mail in multiple languages.

The AKC, having faced several lawsuits regarding the integrity of the Standards, will refuse to allow the registration of any Rottweiler color not specified in the breed Standard. To make up for lost revenue from registrations in breeds with well-defined Standards, the AKC will accept the registrations of a multitude of breeds whose Standards have been written on the wind but not necessarily written down on paper.

Rottweiler Specialties will be so large that the clubs will be forced to hold their shows in large cities' football stadiums which have been vacated by teams moving to the suburbs. The MRC Specialty will be at Soldier Field in Chicago.

And what will these authors be doing in the 21st century? Hopefully, we'll be hanging around to update *The Rottweiler Experience* while enjoying the companionship of a lovely, old Rottweiler. And we'll confidently be handing over the breed to a public with a better knowledge of the breed's history and function, a public that understands the moral responsibilities of owning a Rottweiler, and that shares a love for a breed which has endured, prospered, and ultimately survived because of its great affection for, and loyalty to, its human masters.

Appendix A

You Be The Judge

by Robert Cole

THE ROTTWEILER

You are judging two classes of Rottweilers, Bred By Exhibitor and Open, four dogs in each class i.e., A, B, C and D and E, F, G and H. You will award ten ribbons, four to the first class, four to the second class, Winners to the best of the two classes, and Reserve Winners to the second best of the two classes. You may make your ten decisions now and then read the following descriptive information, or read the information first. My order and the reasons for my order are given near the end of this article.

TYPICAL—The ideal Rottweiler is a medium-large, robust and powerful dog. His compact and substantial build denotes great strength, agility and endurance. Dogs are 24–27 inches in height; Bitches 22 inches to 25 inches. Dogs are characteristically more massive throughout with larger frame and heavier bone than bitches. Bitches are distinctly feminine, but without weakness of substance or structure.

Proportion should always be considered rather than height alone.

The length of body from forechest to rearmost projection of the rump is slightly longer than the height of the dog. The most desirable proportion of height to length being 9 to 10. Depth of chest (level with elbow) is approximately fifty percent the height of the dog.

The head is medium length, broad between the ears; forehead seen in profile is moderately arched. Cheeks are well-boned and muscled but not prominent. Skin on head is not loose; it may form a moderate wrinkle when alert. Level muzzle is fairly deep and has a ratio to back skull of 2 to 3. Nose and lips are black, mouth pigment is dark. Bite is a complete scissors bite.

Eyes are medium sized, almond shaped, dark brown in color with close fitting eyelids. Ears are small in proportion, pendant, triangular in shape; when alert the ears are level with skull and appear to broaden it. Ears are set well apart, hanging forward with the inner edge lying tightly against the head.

The powerful, well-muscled neck is without loose skin. The back is firm and level, extending in a straight line from behind the withers to croup. Loin is short, deep and well-muscled. Croup is broad, of medium length and only slightly sloping. Short, docked tail gives the impression of elongation of topline. Tuck-up is slight. Good angulation of forequarters balances with hindquarters. Compact feet have well arched toes and thick pads. Front pasterns slope slightly forward and rear pasterns are perpendicular to the ground.

A, B, C, D—The best (height to length) balanced dog, but not the best Rottweiler in this Bred by Exhibitor class, is Dog A. Dogs B and C are better Rottweilers, although they depart from typical balance.

Dog D serves to illustrate twelve head and structural faults. Identify them.

First place is between Dog B and Dog C. Both are competitive, and I have not taken their separate departures from typical balance to an unacceptable degree. If I did, their departures would be immediately obvious. Dog B's legs are short, they should be the same length as the body is deep. Dog C's body is longer than the ideal height to length ratio of 9 to 10. Dog B's tail could have been docked shorter, however correct tail-set is more important than length.

Best height to length balanced is Dog A but he is lighter boned than desired. Like Dog B and C, he is sound but lacks the full compactness and substance required in guarding home, family, property and in police work. But again, not to an unacceptable degree. His large rather than small, round

rather than triangular, and low rather than high ears detract from an otherwise good head. In the rear, his croup slopes more than desired, and his hocks could be lower.

Dog D departs from typical in twelve visible ways: (1) his forehead is too pronounced; (2) muzzle is long; (3) ears are set too low; (4) neck lacks fullness, strength and arch; (5) skin is loose at junction of neck and withers; (6) shoulders are steep; (7) upper arm is equally steep and (8) hides forechest, and; (9) in conjunction with steep pasterns, forces body to rise above the elbow; (10) his rear is raised up higher than withers; (11) steep hind leg lacking required angulation at stifle and hock; (12) tail is incorrectly set on high (it should only be carried slightly above the horizontal when the dog is excited or moving).

1, 2, 3, 4—Dog C is long in body but not long in loin. He is my choice for first place. He is alert but calm and has a high degree of the self confidence necessary in dogs bred for working, guarding and tracking.

Looking at the whole dog, my choice for second place is short-legged Dog B. I award third to Dog A and fourth place to Dog D.

E, F, G, H—Finding the best Rottweiler in this class is not too difficult. Dog G represents my description of a typical specimen. Second and third place is between long-legged Dog E and heavy but sound Dog F. The intent, by contrasting these two types, reinforces appreciation for required Rottweiler balance. Fourth place Dog H's six visible faults are interesting.

Dog E's body and legs are incorrectly long, yet he presents an impressive picture. He also lacks stop (step up from muzzle to skull), has a high tail-set and poor feet. Sound but heavy Dog F's deeper than normal body drops below the elbow, creating an interesting departure from typical balance (different again from the balance created by the short legs of Dog B). Dog F's legs are the correct length, he is just very heavy. The Rottweiler should exemplify sturdiness, stoutness and substance without being fat or overpowering. The seven faults possessed by Dog H are: (1) shallow stop; (2) flat skull; (3) round eyes; (4) short rib cage/long loin; (5) roached topline; (6) low-set tail; (7) pronounced tuck-up.

1, 2, 3, 4—First place is awarded to Dog G, Second place to heavy Dog F, third place to long-legged Dog E, fourth place to interesting Dog H.

WINNERS AND RESERVE—Winners is between first place Dog C and first place Dog G. My choice for Winners is Dog G. Reserve is between Bred by Exhibitor first place Dog C and Second place Dog F (who has only been defeated by Winners Dog G). My Reserve choice is Dog C.

WHAT IF—JUDGES' STUDY GROUPS PLAYING "WHAT IF" MAY ASK:

What if at the Open class level Dog G (competing with Dog F for first) was saddled with one of the following faults: (1) yellow eyes; (2) eyes of a different size; (3) hairless eye rim; (4) total lack of mouth pigment (pink mouth); or (5) a level bite? (All five are serious faults.) Would you forgive Dog G this one serious fault (which one?) and award him first place over sound but heavy Dog F?

Judges' Study Groups will also create a second judging scenario using the same eight dogs by combining them into one class, placing the best four in order of merit, and then taking a longer time, go on to place the remaining four.

American Rottweiler Club Production Award Requirements

These awards are open to all Rottweilers, living or dead, that have distinguished themselves by their American-titled offspring. As production points accumulate, the individual sire or dam may receive the next higher award.

To be eligible for any award, a Rottweiler must meet the following four (4) requirements:

1. Must have produced at least one (1) AKC Champion of Record.
2. Must have produced at least one (1) advanced Obedience titled dog (CDX, TDX or SchH I).
3. Must have produced at least three (3) titled offspring.
4. Must have met the point requirements.

Bronze Production Award

Males	25 points
Females	15 points

Silver Production Award

Males	50 points
Females	30 points

Gold Production Award

Males   75 points

Females   45 points

Production points are calculated as follows:

AKC Champion	3 points
AKC CD	1 point
AKC CDX	2 points (3 points total: CD + CDX)
AKC UD	3 points (6 points total: CD + CDX + UD)
AKC OTCH	3 points (9 points total: CD + CDX + UD + OTCH)
AKC TD	1 point
AKC TDX	2 points (3 points total: TD + TDX)
SchH I	2 points
SchH II	2 points (4 points total: SchH I + SchH II)
SchH III	2 points (6 points total: SchH I + SchH II + SchH III)
FH	2 points

Application must be made for these awards. The application must contain the name of the dog or bitch, the names of the breeder and the owner and the owner's address and phone number. It must also contain the names and titles of the offspring. In order to verify the titles, the application must contain either the issue of the AKC AWARDS in which the titles were published, or a copy of the certificate. Schutzhund titles must be verified by a copy of the scorebook or page in USA or DVG magazine.

Appendix C

Medallion Rottweiler Club Code of Ethics

I. Purpose.

In Rottweiler breeding, the emphasis shall be placed upon working ability and the other outstanding qualities of character of this breed, as well as upon appearance.

Consistent with the aforementioned, I will agree to breed discriminatingly and only upon strong evidence of the possibility of finding suitable homes for the resultant puppies. I understand and agree that to breed unadvisedly may lead to overpopulation and contribute materially to the deterioration of the Rottweiler breed.

II. Records.

I agree, if I breed my bitch or use my stud in service, to keep accurate records of stock, matings, and pedigrees, and to register my breeding stock with the American Kennel Club.

III. Breeding.

I agree that only those Rottweilers will be used for breeding which have OFA (Orthopedic Foundation for Animals) certified hip X-rays (or certified by foreign counterparts of the OFA—imported Rottweilers must have OFA certification within six months after arrival in U.S.A. If frozen or chilled semen is used, the dog must be X-rayed and certified by the OFA or foreign counterpart at no younger than 24 months of age), no disqualifying faults as listed in the 1990 Official AKC revised Standard, and no radical departures from the official AKC Rottweiler Standard, such as the following:

Entropion, ectropion. Overshot, undershot (when incisors do not touch or mesh); wry mouth; two or more missing teeth. Unilateral cryptorchid or cryptorchid males. Long coat. Any base color other than black; absence of all markings. Excessive temperament exhibited as consistent.

I will further agree that, should I breed from lines in which I am knowledgeable that any of the above occur, I will disclose this to my buyers.

As the owner of a bitch: I will only breed normal healthy, mature bitches which have reached their 24th month. I will not permit my bitch to produce litters in three consecutive seasons. I further agree to cull deformed puppies.

As the owner of a stud dog: I will only breed healthy, mature dogs which have reached their 24th month, and I will refuse stud service to any bitch who has not reached her 24th month, or which I consider in poor health, or which has disqualifying faults or radical departures from the 1990 official AKC revised Standard. I will follow the custom to allow one repeat service (at the bitch's next season) where a bitch has failed to conceive after being bred to one of my studs, if the stud is still in good health and available, and at such time and place as mutually agreed to by the owner of the bitch and myself. I will encourage bitch owners to breed only if they have the facilities, time and resources to adequately care for a litter.

It is recommended that each member make a sincere effort to see that a reasonable portion of an anticipated litter by his bitch, or that resulted from the use of his stud dog, is suitably spoken for before a breeding takes place. A bitch may be bred to only one stud dog during any one estrous cycle.

IV. Health.

I agree to maintain good standards of health and care of my dogs including proper veterinary care. I further agree that proper mental health includes regular contact with people and exposure to the outside world.

V. Sales.

I will refuse to recommend breeders who do not conform to the obligations expressed in this Code, or to sell to dog wholesalers and retailers (such as pet shops), or to donate a Rottweiler for raffle purposes, or to sell or buy in litter-lots.

I will use a written agreement with any sales involving a dog.

I will pass on to the buyers of puppies or adult dogs accurate health, breeding and registration records and a four-generation pedigree. When appropriate, AKC limited registration procedures will be followed, and the buyer will be advised of the restrictions of this type of registration.

I will follow the general practice of breeders, that any puppy sold as a show prospect which subsequently develops a genetic disqualifying defect shall be: (1) replaced by the breeder with another show prospect puppy, or (2) the money refunded and the dog returned to the breeder or (3) the buyer's money will be refunded to the extent of the difference between the price of pet puppies sold from the same or similar litters with the buyer retaining the dog, or any other mutually agreeable alternative.

I will further recommend to my puppy purchasers that they render incapable of reproducing any dog which has developed disqualifying and serious faults, thereby rendering the dog unsuitable for breeding.

I will not release puppies before they are seven weeks of age, and then only with the full knowledge that they are healthy and have had the required medical inoculations and care.

I will urge my puppy purchasers to provide obedience training at the proper age. As a breeder, I will make a sincere effort to see that every dog will have an adequate home and be properly cared for.

VI. *Advertising.*

I agree that my advertising, oral or written, shall be factual and not worded so as to attract undesirable buyers, or to encourage the raising of purebred Rottweilers as an easy money scheme.

No price should be given in advertising Rottweilers.

VII. *Sportsmanship.*

I shall conduct myself at all times in a manner which will reflect credit upon me and the breed, regardless of the location or circumstances, but especially when attending dog shows, whether as an exhibitor or as a spectator. It is recommended that this conduct follow through at club meetings.

VIII. *Enforcement.*

I understand and agree that, upon receipt of sufficient written proof of violations of this Code of Ethics, the Board of Directors will proceed according to the Constitution of the Medallion Rottweiler Club, Article VII (Discipline).

A Grievance Committee of three members is to be appointed by the Board of Directors as required to report their findings to the Board for a vote by the Board.

IX. *Special Circumstances.*

I further understand and agree that should I, through no fault of my own, be in violation of any of the aforementioned provisions, I shall have recourse to the Grievance Committee appointed by the Board of Directors.

MRC Hall of Fame and Honor Roll Points Schedule

HALL OF FAME

Dogs   25 points

Bitches   15 points

The dog's owner must have been an MRC member for five continuous years.

Automatic Entry to Hall of Fame:

All American Obedience Trial Champions

Utility Dog Excellents

AKC Herding Champions

HONOR ROLL

Both sexes   7 points

Best In Show Wins:

First BIS   7 points

Additional BIS   5 points

Sanctioned AKC Specialties

MRC Specialty	BOB	entry + 1 point
	BOS	entry + 1 point

Other AKC or Canadian Sanctioned Specialties

Total entry 0–100	BOB	4 points
	BOS	3 points
Total entry 100–300	BOB	5 points
	BOS	4 points
Total entry 300+	BOB	6 points
	BOS	5 points

Entries will be determined by the number of eligible dogs competing in the regular classes of each sex.

Sieger Titles

Bundessieger (Germany)	3 points
Klubsieger (Germany)	5 points
Other sieger titles (Europe, etc.)	2 points

Conformation Points

AKC Championship	2 points
Champion in two countries	2 points
Champion in three countries	3 points
International Champion (title recognized by the FCI)	10 points

Obedience Points

AKC CD	1 point
AKC CDX	5 pts

AKC UD	8 points
AKC TD	4 points
AKC TDX	8 points
High In Trial	6 points
Score of 200	6 points

Completing obedience degrees in three consecutive trials with scores of 195 or more is 6 points. Canadian & Mexican points are the same for AKC points, except for High In Trial, which is 5 points.

AKC Herding Points

Herding Tested (HT)	1 point
Pre-Trial Tested (PT)	1 point
Herding Started (HS)	2 points
Herding Intermediate (HI)	5 points
Herding Excellent (HX)	8 points

Schutzhund

BH	2 points
FH	8 points
SchH I or IPO I (not both)	6 points
SchH II or IPO II (not both)	8 points
SchH III or IPO III (not both)	9 points

(DVG rules have changed so that SchH and IPO titles are earned with essentially the same exercise.)

Breeding

Offspring with one championship	1 point
Offspring with first obedience or tracking title	1 point

Offspring with an advanced obedience
or advanced tracking title (such as UD,
SchH III or IPO III, FH, or TDX)   1 point

   To clarify the above, the maximum number of points that a sire or dam can get from an offspring is three points.